MISSION-BASED MANAGEMENT

Leading Your Not-For-Profit Into the 21st Century

by
Peter C. Brinckerhoff

**A guidebook for the leadership of not-for-profit organizations
that want to serve more people, more ways,
and stay in business while doing it.**

MISSION-BASED MANAGEMENT

Leading Your Not-For-Profit Into the 21st Century

by
Peter C. Brinckerhoff

ALPINE GUILD, Inc.
Dillon, Colorado

An Alpine Guild Book

ISBN 0-931712-15-7

To obtain information about this book, contact Alpine Guild, P.O. Box 4846, Dillon, CO 80435

Library of Congress Cataloging-in-Publication Data

Brinckerhoff, Peter C., 1952—
    Mission-based management : leading your not-for-profit into the 21st century.

    1. Nonprofit organizations—Management.   2. Associations, institutions, etc.—Management.
I. Title.
HD62.6.B74   1994   658′.048-dc20   94-28766
ISBN 0-931712-15-7

This book is dedicated to my mother:
Inger Melchior Hansen Brinckerhoff,
1924-1994
by far the best writer in the family.

Acknowledgements

No book like this is the author's sole product. In my case, much of the theory, case studies, and applications presented here have been developed over my 15 years as a not-for-profit administrator, board member, and consultant. My consulting firm, Corporate Alternatives, has worked with thousands of not-for-profits since 1982, and the exceptional efforts of CAi's dedicated staff and clients show up here repeatedly. This book is therefore a compendium of consultation, research, applications, and experience, and like any observer in any field, I have incorporated ideas and experiences of others to apply to the field of not-for-profits. Where appropriate, and when not violating confidentiality, these people have been noted in the text. Where they are not acknowledged, they are still greatly appreciated.

Peter Brinckerhoff

About the Author

Peter Brinckerhoff is a nationally-known expert on improving the not-for-profit sector. He brings a vast collection of expertise and hands-on experiences from his time as a staff member, executive director, volunteer, and board member of local, statewide, and national not-for-profits. In 1982 he founded Corporate Alternatives, inc. a consulting firm dedicated to improving the business skills of not-for-profits across the United States. In the role of CAi's President, Peter has presented to, trained, and consulted with thousands of not-for-profits in every discipline and in nearly every state in the United States. He has also written extensively in *NonProfit World, Taft Non-Profit News, Board and Administrator,* and the *Whole Non-Profit Catalog*.

A former VISTA volunteer, Peter received his Bachelor's Degree from the University of Pennsylvania and his Master's Degree in Public Health from Tulane University. He lives in Springfield, Illinois, with his wife and three children.

Table of Contents

1. Introduction

OVERVIEW

Welcome. This book is intended for you, the leadership of our nation's not-for-profit charitable organizations. It is designed to give you a different insight into how top-quality not-for-profits *really* run, what works, what doesn't, and how to ensure that your organization is one of the ones that works, both this year and into the next century. It is intended to help you become a mission-based manager.

In this introductory chapter we'll review the core philosophies upon which I have based the book, examine the reasons that I feel the book is needed, and then take the first look at what the book holds, and the best ways for you as a reader and a management practitioner to use it. By the end of the chapter, you should have a better understanding of my philosophical perspective, and also be ready to get the most from the book as a whole.

The book is designed to be used as a guide, and as a reference for you to return to over and over. I know that your time is limited, and that you will be tempted to jump right to the parts that you are most interested in, perhaps *Financial Empowerment* or *A Bias For Marketing*. To the extent possible, I urge you to read the book from front to back. The chapters are in the order presented for a reason: they build upon one another; issues raised in the early chapters are discussed further in later ones, problems raised in one sometimes reappear in another. To get the most from the book, read it in order.

A. CORE PHILOSOPHIES

Before you continue, you need to know that the material in this book is based on three philosophies. These philosophies have been the core of my consulting, training, and writing since 1982, and they express better than anything I have seen my beliefs about what your organization is, and what it can become. Here they are:

1. NOT-FOR-PROFITS ARE *BUSINESSES*

Your organization is a *mission-based* business, not a charity. For-profits chase profits, not-for-profits pursue their mission. But just because you aren't primarily motivated by profit doesn't give you a license to be sloppy, or to ignore a good idea simply because it was initially developed by the for-profit sector. As a not-for-profit manager, you need to use all the resources at your command to do more mission, and the techniques of the for-profit world are, in many cases, very applicable. Actually, making the connection between for-profit business techniques and the not-for-profit world is what I have been doing since 1982, and many of those skills show up in this book: good marketing, keeping track of cash flow, good controls management, focusing on the things that you do best, and more.

How many times have you been told that you are a professional? Many, I'm sure. Well, perhaps for the first time, you are now being told that, as a mission-based manager, you are a business person as well. If you act like a business you can get more mission for your money, doing more with the limited resources at your disposal.

Using good business skills as a mission-based manager does not, I repeat, *not* mean dropping services simply because they lose money, nor does it mean turning people away because they cannot pay. But it does mean paying attention to the bottom line, having a strategic vision, negotiating in good faith and from a position of strength; in short, being business-like. Your organization is a business, and the more businesslike you are, the better it will be for your clientele.

2. NO ONE GIVES YOU A DIME

This may come as a surprise, but you do not really get gifts. You do not really receive donations, you do not really get grants. I know that is what all of us call them, but the problem with thinking of those transactions as gifts or donations is that the organization then acts like a charity. You become stuck in the mentality that you are so poor that the only way you can survive is by the beneficence of people or organizations richer than you.

Technically, that may all be true. But try looking at it this way, and see if you feel differently about yourself and your organization. Let's assume that you come to me for a donation, and you convince me that you really need the money for a service, or a building. I write you a check for $100.

Am I making the donation to you? Of course not. Am I giving a gift to your organization? You're getting closer. But what I am really doing, and what really happens in all of these transactions is that I am *purchasing services for someone who cannot pay*. No one sends you money and expects you to keep it in a vault somewhere. Whether you get a grant from the Feds, or a bequest from a local person, it is understood that you will provide services with the money you receive. In other words, and here is the key: *You **earn** all the money you get*. It is essential that you and your staff and board understand this and believe it if you are to adopt the characteristics of success that are presented in this book. Why? Because if you keep thinking of yourselves as a poor charity, you will continue to be treated that way, and not like the mission-based business that you are.

3. NOT-FOR-PROFIT DOES NOT MEAN NON-PROFIT

You have certainly noticed by now that I use the term not-for-profit, eschewing the commonly used non-profit. There is a good reason for this, and it is that there is a difference. *A non-profit is an organization that loses money*. Many savings and loans in the 1980's were non-profits, as were many of our domestic airlines and auto makers. Too many not-for-profits are also non-profits, a situation that we need to correct and soon. There is a reason that so many not-for-profits lose money, and it has to do with the perception that it is illegal and immoral for a not-for-profit to make money.

It is not. Nowhere in any state or federal law, and nowhere in any state or federal regulation dealing with taxation or corporate structures does it say that a not-for-profit cannot make money, cannot make a profit. In fact, in the IRS code dealing with 501(c)(3) organizations it says, "....the profits of the corporation shall not inure to the benefit of......". This clause precludes staff or board from inappropriately benefiting from the organization's profits, but the key to the phrase is that the IRS anticipates and accepts profits. Profits in a not-for-profit are *legal*.

Profits in your not-for-profit are also *essential*, a key element in financial empowerment, a subject that we will cover at length. Without profits you cannot grow, you cannot recruit and retain excellent staff, you cannot take prudent risks on behalf of your clientele. You will see in coming chapters that I will contend that you need to make money seven out of ten years. And to do less is not good mission-based management.

These philosophies form the foundation for everything that follows in this book. They are the core of mission-based management. If you agree with them, if you find yourself nodding and saying "That's great!", you are going to enjoy the book, and get a great deal out of it. If you are uncomfortable with the philosophies, I hope that the remainder of this chapter and the issues raised in Chapters 2 and 3 will convince you of the validity of these philosophies. If that doesn't work, then I think that the remainder of the book will convince you that there are many, many business applications that can improve your ability to do better mission more efficiently and effectively.

We will return to these philosophies at the end of the book, to look at how your funders can adopt them to give you more leeway to do your job. But for the majority of the book, we will concentrate on how you can make them a reality in your own management style, in your own mission-based organization.

B. WHY IS THIS BOOK NEEDED NOW?

The 80's were an extremely turbulent time for America's not-for-profits. During the Reagan Administration years of 1981 to 1989, most not-for-profits, those that depend on government funding for the majority of their incomes, had their perspective on life radically changed. No longer could these organizations depend on government (read: taxpayer) largess to cover their expenses, nor would regular cost of living adjustments (COLAs) solve their problems. No, not-for-profits would have to learn how to make do as more independent, more businesslike entities. Wouldn't they?

Those of us in the field thought so. In many organizations, things did change. New businesses sprang up, inside or outside the traditional organization's array of services. More educational opportunities for not-for-profit staff became available across the country and throughout the decade, not only at the continuing education and seminar level, but as graduate degrees in many top-notch educational institutions. More and more staffs sought and received the one type of course work that they had previously never had access to: basic, as well as advanced, management training.

Unfortunately, many organizations continued to do business as usual. After a brief foray into a new idea or service, they returned to their traditional sources of funding, squeezed more work out of their staffs, and tried to serve the avalanche of new people needing help. They continued to act like charities rather than not-for-profit businesses. Governments, foundations, and United Ways for the most part only exacerbated the problems by emphasizing cost controls over strategic planning and marketing, and fundraising over entrepreneurship. Planning, marketing, and entrepreneurship are essential components of an excellent organization–for-profit or not-for-profit.

This book is intended to put an end to the old way of doing things, to help you make the transition from an administrator of a charity into a mission-based manager. I know, from consulting and training thousands of not-for-profit staff and boards since 1982, that the organizations that *are* succeeding in meeting the needs of their clientele, the organizations that *are* stable financially, the organizations that *will* meet the challenges of the future have the characteristics discussed in later chapters. I also firmly believe that if your organization has those characteristics, or acquires them, *and consistently works to improve them*, you will succeed in serving the people that are depending on you. Unfortunately, too many not-for-profit managers, too many not-for-profit board members and too many not-for-profit funders are still stuck in the 1970's. And they are getting further behind every day.

Mission-based management is good management. It is more than stewardship, a term that has become widely used in the not-for-profit field in recent years. It is a philosophy that says "I will use all the best tools at my disposal to help my organization excel in the pursuit of its mission. The mission is the reason that we are here, but that is no excuse for sloppy or slipshod management. We would never tolerate poor quality services. We won't tolerate poor quality management either."

C. MISSION-BASED MANAGEMENT

This book is set up in a sequence and in a format that is intended to give you, the reader, the most benefit. By giving you an overview of both the format and sequence, as well as a brief peek at the benefits that you will get from each chapter, I hope that you will get more from our time together.

1. THE FORMAT

Each chapter starts with an **OVERVIEW**, intended to give you a brief summary of what the chapter will hold. The body of the text comes next, and I try, as much as possible, to give you illustrations and ideas for immediate use. These illustrations and ideas are highlighted by the terms ● **FOR EXAMPLE** and ☞ **HANDS-ON** respectively. Look for them in nearly every chapter. Near the end of the chapter is a **RECAP**, which is a brief review of the points that have been covered in the chapter, to allow you to draw all of the material together in your mind.

2. THE CONTENT

The book is broken down into what I call context-setting chapters, working chapters, and the final chapter which is a call to action for the funders of not-for-profits. Let's look at each chapter briefly.

6

Context-Setting Chapters

▶*Chapter 2: Where We Were, Where We Are, Where We're Going*
This chapter will give you an insight into how not-for-profits came
to the point where they are today, the way that your funders *really*
see your organization, how the ridiculous relationship between
funders and not-for-profits developed, and my predictions for the
world in which you will be managing for the next ten years.

▶*Chapter 3: What Works: The Characteristics of a Successful
Not-For-Profit*
In this chapter you will the nine characteristics that the successful
not-for-profit must have, characteristics that your organization must
embrace if it is to survive and pursue its mission well into the 21st
century. The working chapters then expand on each of these characteristics in detail.

Working Chapters

▶*Chapter 4: The Mission is the Reason*
The foundation of your not-for-profit is the mission. In this chapter
you will learn how to use your mission to the maximum: as a management tool, a marketing tool, a motivator, and a guide. You will
see how many organizations lose the edge that their mission provides. You will learn how to rewrite your mission to be the organization you want to be in the future.

▶*Chapter 5: A Businesslike Board of Directors*
Boards are so important that we will spend two chapters on them.
In this first chapter, we will start with a discussion of what makes
a board effective and what barriers there are to that effectiveness.
We will then review board responsibilities, staff responsibilities to
the board, and finally board liability and how to reduce it.

▶*Chapter 6: Building the Board You Need*
In this second chapter on boards, we will focus on showing you
how to recruit the board that you need, and how to keep the best
board members that you recruit. We'll analyze the different types
of board members, why they serve, and how you can meet their
needs and wants to keep them serving. We'll also review what
kind of committee structure you need to get the most from your
board members.

▶ *Chapter 7: Managing Your People*

In this chapter you will learn how to turn your organization literally upside down to get your priorities in order. You will learn the six key tenets of upside-down management, how to communicate better in person, in meetings, and in writing, how to listen to staff from all levels of the organization, how to do two-way evaluations, and how to set up recognition systems that reward rather than punish.

▶ *Chapter 8: The Controls That Set You Free*

Most not-for-profits either don't have controls in place, or they only have those that are mandated by their funders. This chapter will show you how well-written controls can set you free to manage rather than administer. We'll cover nine different kinds of controls and show you how to develop them, use them, and keep them up-to-date.

▶ *Chapter 9: Developing a Bias For Marketing*

This chapter will show you how to adopt a team marketing strategy, where everyone is involved in marketing to meet all of your varied markets' wants. You will learn who your markets really are, how to assess their wants, and how to evaluate your marketing efforts.

▶ *Chapter 10: A Vision to Make the Future*

This chapter will show you how to chart your future, how to develop a good, useful, meaningful strategic plan. You will learn in detail about the best process for planning, the reasons you need to plan, and the benefits of the planning process and the planning document. You will see how to use the plan as a tool for the benefit of your clientele. A suggested planning format is also included.

▶ *Chapter 11: Seeking Financial Empowerment*

This chapter will show you the five characteristics of the financially empowered organization, and how to get them in your not-for-profit. Then it will show you how to expand your universe of income streams and manage your financial information to better run the organization. You'll learn how to spend less through bottoms-up budgeting, and how to estimate capital needs far in advance.

▶ *Chapter 12: Maintaining Financial Empowerment*

Once you attain financial empowerment, how do you maintain it? How do you keep what you earn, so that you can apply it to your community? In this chapter we'll discuss the five ways that you can keep net income, review ways to seek and develop a long term relationship with a lender, how to create an endowment, and how to use your empowerment to the benefit of your clientele.

▶ *Chapter 13: Creating a Social Entrepreneur*
This chapter will show you how to take prudent risks on behalf of the people that you serve; how to think like an entrepreneur. We'll review how to set up a new venture, how to seek debt to leverage your success, how to decide what return on investment is enough, and how you can help your organization become a culture of new ideas and constant innovation.

▶ *Chapter 14: Changing Flexibly*
Flexibility in the face of an ever-accelerating pace of change is an important skill to learn. This chapter will show you how to become a change agent for your organization, how to recognize and overcome barriers to change. It will also give you some advice on how to hold on to your core organizational values as you accommodate to a changing world.

▶ *Chapter 15: A National Agenda: Empowering Our Not-For-Profits*
There is another side to the issue of making your organization a mission-based business: how can funders change to accommodate a more empowered not-for-profit sector? In this chapter you will see some specific things that I feel are critical to that empowerment, and you will come away with a list of things that you can discuss with your funders to help you move ahead.

3. GETTING THE MOST FROM *MISSION-BASED MANAGEMENT*

As much of what I talk about in the remainder of the book is based on teamwork, and bringing in lots of staff, board, and outside experts to help, I suggest that you work through this book as a team effort. Have a small group of senior managers, middle managers, and direct service staff read a few chapters and then get together to discuss their application in your organization. Ask the group; "Is what is presented appropriate for our organization? If so, what do we need to do to facilitate any needed changes? If it is not appropriate, why not? Are we doing the best we can in this area? How can we be better?"

By reading the book as a team you will get a more complete, a more organization-wide use of the book, and its benefits will be applied to your organization sooner.

RECAP

In this chapter, we've covered the key philosophies that are the basis for the book, and why the book is needed. We've also taken the first look at the contents of the book and how it is set up, so that you can make the most use of it to benefit your organization and the people that you serve.

I know that you have a tough and challenging job. As a leader of a not-for-profit, you have to concern yourself with many differing and conflicting needs and demands–those of your funders, your clientele, your board, staff, community, banker, and peers. You need to ensure that your organization is pursuing its mission with zeal, that it meets the changing needs of the community that you serve, and that you have enough money to make ends meet.

The tools to help you do those things are in the following pages. Good reading, and good luck!

2. Where We Were, Where We Are, Where We're Going

OVERVIEW

Before we start our journey together, it is important to understand how we got here, and what my vision for the coming decade is. Without those two pieces of context, it will be harder for you to grasp my ideas for what your organization can become and can accomplish.

In this chapter we will review how not-for-profits in this country came to where they are today, and examine the three rules that funders use when they think of you and your organization. We'll then turn to the future and review my seven predictions for trends that will profoundly impact you, your organization, and its ability to perform its mission into the 21st century.

A. HOW WE GOT HERE

The United States, more than any other nation in the world, is blessed with a volunteer spirit of helping others. In many developed countries, volunteering or charitable giving (other than to the church) is essentially unheard of. My personal experience with this difference in cultures was begun early on. My mother was Danish by birth and emigrated to the United States as an infant. There were (and remain) many relatives in Denmark and, during my childhood, many of those relatives came to visit us, often staying at our home.

Often in those years, my parents would need to leave to attend one of the board meetings of the many organizations that they served. When the reason for my parents' absence was explained, it was almost always greeted with puzzled expressions and questions from our Danish guests such as, "Why would you *give* your time away?" or "Doesn't the government take care of that for you?" To which my parents would reply, "Here, we have a tradition of trying to help each other."

Whether it sprang from a frontier necessity to help and be helped, from basic Judeo-Christian values, or just from our national economic abundance, Americans have developed a vast network of charitable not-for-profit organizations that assist the poor, rehabilitate the injured, educate the young and old, enrich our senses and sensibilities by providing access to the arts, and fulfill our spiritual needs.

From the beginning of this century until the onset of Lyndon Johnson's "War on Poverty," most of the funding for these organizations came from locally donated funds, raised in the community in which the organization provided services. A few large foundations of national scope, such as Ford and Rockefeller, provided special projects assistance, but mostly, the not-for-profit community made do with what its local community gave it.

Then, in the 60's, all that changed. Government, particularly at the federal level, began to provide funding, first in the form of grants, and later in the form of "purchase of service" contracts to thousands of locally-based, private not-for-profits. The Feds, and later the states, counties, and local governments, bought such diverse services as preventive health care, mental health screenings, residential community care for the developmentally disabled, breakfasts and lunches for school children, housing for the poor, art for the rich, economic development for minorities, books for libraries, research on a broad array of social, medical, and scientific issues, and specialized transportation throughout the nation.

With this cascade of funding—the good news—came an avalanche of red tape, bureaucracy, fast growth, reduced local control, and a seemingly endless series of priority changes and reversals—the bad news. This period (primarily 1964 to 1981) also saw the enormous growth in the sheer number of 501(c)(3)s (many created *specifically* to tap funds authorized in a particular piece of federal legislation), and the concomitant development of a huge cadre of vested interests embodied in the emergence of large professional staffs (within the not-for-profits), rapidly growing trade associations and, perhaps most importantly, a steep rise in the number of government employees whose sole job it was to fund, regulate, and audit these organizations.

This "rise of the staffs", at both the service provider level and within the governments that increasingly were the service provider's single biggest—and sometimes *only*—customer, led to the development of a set of philosophies of funding and oversight that were incredibly damaging to the not-for-profits at the time and are still hampering all of us today. The basic tenets of these philosophies are as follows:

1. WHAT WE SAY GOES

While being a logical assumption from the point of view of a major (often the only) customer, this tenet often degenerated into the feeling of "Whatever the staff at the Department of XYZ decides is needed in YourTown, is what we'll fund, and if you don't need it or if you need something else, well, tough." This attitude, of course, flew directly in the face of time-tested marketing theories of *asking* customers (in this case, the people that were ultimately receiving services) what they wanted. Additionally, this philosophy was in direct conflict with reality: no single broad national policy could possibly take into account all of the local variety and uniqueness that shows up in 50 states and 100,000 municipalities. By regularly not recognizing that different communities have different needs, policies and regulations that flowed from this philosophy were and are doomed from the start.

But the sheer momentum of dollars flowing from the state and federal capitals spoke louder than the voices of the service recipients. So, organizations acquiesced, services were often funded that people neither wanted or needed and, when the first budget of the Reagan years came along, these programs were tough to defend against cuts.

2. YOU CAN'T DO "WELL" DOING "GOOD"

This tenet is based on the terribly outdated but still overwhelmingly accepted philosophy that not-for-profits must virtually take a vow of poverty in order to not appear to be stealing from those to whom they are providing service.

This idea also, of course, nicely justifies minimal funding on the part of the main funders, an abundance of auditing and (in my view) unnecessary oversight, and a policy of "use it or lose it", probably the most shortsighted social policy of our generation.

▶ For those of you not familiar with "use it or lose it", it goes like this: if you negotiate a contract or grant amount for service with a funder—say a state—you get to use what is in the grant during the term of the grant period, usually a fiscal year. You may or may not be able to move funds from one budget line to the next depending on how nice your funder is but, by the end of the year, if you have saved funds (or spent less than expected, through excellent management, hunting for discounts on purchases, etc.), you lose the savings, because you can't keep what you didn't spend. Further, if you bring in additional income (from donations, earnings,etc.), it may reduce your income dollar for dollar.

What's the incentive here? To save money? Certainly not. Saving money is work, and if your organization can't keep what you save, why go through the effort? To earn more outside income? No, that's more work and, if the money is just going to be taken away, why take the risk? Does this encourage unnecessary spending at the service level? Certainly, and everyone knows it. Why does it continue? Because the Feds and the states are not willing to let not-for-profits keep too much money, keep what they earn, or have many, if any, net assets.

I call this inane policy "Poverty Chic" and it has been beaten into all of our heads for so long that most of us believe it. Funders do, the United Way does, staffs and boards do, and the public in general certainly does. How many times have you been questioned about the purchase of "nice" furniture, or tried to rationalize raising salaries, or not bought a piece of computer equipment because it *wouldn't look right*? I have, and I work with hundreds of not-for-profits who do regularly.

Has Poverty Chic saved money? In the short term, certainly. But it has also led in the long term to poorly-trained staffs, high staff turnover, a pitiful condition of the national not-for-profit physical plant (usually rented instead of owned), and essentially no non-fixed assets with which to address community problems without the funders' *further* assistance. The bottom line is that Poverty Chic has led to many not-for-profits becoming—and remaining—virtual indentured servants of their funders at the same time that the funders are urging the not-for-profits to become more independent and self-sufficient. "Use it or lose it" is one way. Underfunding—not paying for the full cost of service—is another. Encouraging monopolies is a third. By being encouraged and forced to be poor, agencies think poor, and stay poor. They are underfunded so they must scramble to stay alive today rather than plan ahead for the future: an action that can save money and provide better service. They make do with old, beat-up, inefficient equipment and buildings, losing money on repairs and the inefficiencies. They are never allowed to have "unseemly" fund balances (either by public pressure or regulation) so they can never grow. They have no working capital—without further assistance from the funders.

● **FOR EXAMPLE:** Most United Way agencies in this country still have a policy of only funding programs that are in deficit; if you don't have a deficit, you don't get funded. Does anyone seriously think that this encourages agencies to be self sufficient, or to generate enough funds to break even? *Of course it doesn't!* Why would an agency charge more to clients, raise rates elsewhere or do anything to risk its United Way "free" money? To the surprise of no one, they don't; they simply stay in a deficit condition so that the funding will continue. The United Way contends that it must assure that funds go to the most needy programs, but this policy just perpetuates the problem.

3. WHAT IS YOURS IS OURS

This is perhaps my favorite, because it underscores so much of what primary government funders really must feel: that not-for-profits that receive their funds are their property. In my work, I see this regularly with auditors of state funds (which may account for say 60% of an organization's budget) feeling that they must examine *every* transaction of the organization, evaluate *all* of the assets, look into *all* of the contracts, probe *all* the vendor relationships, even if some or most of those assets and contracts and vendors have nothing to do with the specific programs that the state auditor's department funds. The attitude seems to be that *"because we give you money, we have the right to strip you naked and judge you at our whim"*.

This attitude, while not only insulting, forgets the fact that the not-for-profit is actually *selling* the government agency or foundation a service, and that the payment for this service should not come attached to an unrestricted license to snoop and poke around at will. Remember this: as a for-profit, I contract with many state governments, and they don't audit *me*. Why should they then take your organization apart for inspection? Does being a not-for-profit make you automatically exempt from the Constitutional protection from unreasonable search and seizure? I think not.

The most incredible aspect of this attitude is that we all put up with it so willingly. It is a constant amazement to me that there has not been a general revolt against the level of scrutiny, oversight, and general arrogance of the funding sources. How can this have been allowed to evolve? How can the good, intelligent, and well-intentioned people at the local agency level have become so subservient, while the good, intelligent, well-intentioned people at the state and federal level developed policies that, in effect, contradict nearly all of their stated intentions, doing much more harm than good?

There are two answers, one psychological and one political.

First, the Psychological Answer. The more I think about the relationship between not-for-profits and their funders, the more curious it gets.

Look at it this way: how many for-profit companies regularly disparage their best customers? Very few, but how often do you and your peers gripe about the state/Feds/foundations at association meetings? Every time you are together, right? I thought so.

Moreover, when was the last time that you went to your state/federal/ foundation project officer and asked, "How can we make your job easier and do what you want done better and faster?" Never? Again, I thought so. But understand that in the for-profit world, market-driven companies ask those questions of *all* of their customers, especially the big ones, *all* of the time. They are constantly looking for ways to do things better, faster, easier, cheaper for their customers. (If you don't think that your funders are your customers, think again. We'll cover this in great detail in the chapter entitled *A Bias for Marketing.*)

Over the years, I have developed an analogy of the relationship between not-for-profits and their primary funders that I think (unfortunately) is very apt. It goes like this:

> In their relationships with each other, not-for-profits and their primary funders (government or foundations) take on the roles and attitudes of eternal adolescents and parents. Now, this is not to disparage either group, as both have contributed to the situation, but imagine how you would feel as either a teenager or the parent of a teenager if you were going to be stuck in that often frustrating and antagonistic relationship forever?
>
> In this relationship, the not-for-profits (filling the role of the teens) audibly seek more independence, question the wisdom of the funders (who act the parents' part), ask to be left alone (to do their own thing), and generally resent the house rules, but when the car breaks down or when something else goes wrong, they always come to the parent for help/money.
>
> For their part, the funders/"parents" audibly encourage the independence, tolerate the dissension and independence with irritation but benevolence (knowing that they know better) and urge the not-for-profit/"teens" to try new things ("but nothing too new"), experiment ("but not too far out")—but ultimately to always be home by midnight, submit all friends for inspection, and be prepared for a search of your room at any time. House rules.

I'm sure you have seen this relationship and probably been a part of it. Once you recognize the relationship for what it is, it is fairly simple to see how it evolved: People who are giving away the money (particularly those who work for the public) want to control how it is spent. Most not-for-profits and their staff and board really only want to be left alone to do what they do best: service. Neither group can envision true independence from the other. And no tradition, law, or social norm makes a not-for-profit independent on its 21st birthday. Thus it is easier to grudgingly accept the status quo than to really break away.

This is *crazy,* and I've been part of it at both board and staff level. No wonder both sides are so frustrated! And yet, I see it continue over and over and over, even when both sides are aware and acknowledge the problems inherent in not allowing the not-for-profits to grow up and leave home. After all, many not-for-profits *are* over 21.

Now for the Political Answer. With the media excited about any and all "scandals" that they can find, government is reduced to spending millions of dollars to provide oversight to prevent hundreds or thousands of dollars from being misspent. And this is the fault of all of us. We don't demand that the media print the whole story. We don't demand a cost-benefit analysis of the fraud prevention section of an agency. We just listen to the story that says "Welfare Mom Cheats Agency of $40,000" and get all worked up about how poorly the agency is run and what a bunch of cheats those welfare moms are. The rest of the story? The mom was one of 110,000 funded of whom 109,999 *didn't cheat.* The $40,000 was out of $198,000,000 of funding, or less than **2/100ths of one percent!** And then, no one ever asks how much the agency spent to find and recover that $40,000. Given the norm, probably about $200,000. Why do we allow this to happen? Because no government agency official wants to be seen as advocating a lax policy that could allow anyone at all to cheat, and, in reality, the $40,000 is a *lot* of money to most voters–no matter that it is an infinitesimal percentage of the total. So we let it go, and waste a whole lot of money chasing very little.

Thus, not-for-profits spend a great deal of time and money being accountable for the real or imagined sins of others in order to cover the derrieres of the funders. Since there is a political liability for the funders if the public perceives that $1 is misspent, the funders want to control *everything*.

These three rules have done more harm than all the budget cuts not-for-profits have endured since 1981. They have prevented stability, empowerment, and dignity in our nation's not-for-profits–and steadily eroded our confidence in our ability to manage our own affairs.

● **FOR EXAMPLE:** To demonstrate this evolution (and its downfall), I'll use as an example a group of not-for-profits that was created solely to respond to a succession of federal laws in the 60's and 70's, who influenced health care policy for a while, and faded away with the end of federal largess in the 80's: Health Planning Agencies. (The reader should note that I was integrally involved in health planning from 1974 through 1982 as a volunteer, staffer, and executive director, and thus have a somewhat biased view of what happened.)

Most of you will never have heard of HSA's (Health Systems Agencies) or their predecessors, CHP's (Comprehensive Health Planning Agencies), but both were funded primarily with federal funds, and grew out of federal concern about rising health care costs, duplication of health care services, and a need to control both. CHP's which were funded from 1968 to 1974, were to enable consumer participation in health policy. In over 200 geographic health planning areas of the country, CHP's were to develop health care plans, and were to have limited regulatory authority over hospital and nursing home expansion. HSA's (1974-1984) were the second generation of such agencies with more money, expanded staffs, a mandate for "consumer" majorities on all boards and committees, and enhanced regulatory powers. The result of this program was over 200 new not-for-profits with anywhere from 4 to 200 staff each, over 100,000 volunteers on boards and committees, and an entire federal and state bureaucracy (I have heard numbers in excess of 350 federal staff when all the regional people were accounted for) just to keep tabs on the locals.

Why? To fulfill the federally-designed mandates of cost containment, increased access for care, and consumer empowerment. Did it work? No, and in large part because of the three rules. WHAT WE SAY GOES turned out to be the most deadly: the federal government decided in just one of many broad, national regulations that there should be no more than 6.1 medical surgical hospital beds per 1,000 population. As a result, HSA's were to turn down applications from hospitals for construction that exceeded that amount, and the funding of the HSA's was in part contingent upon achieving that goal. Now this policy did allow for some local variance, but it had to be rigorously justified, and never adequately took into account important issues such as patient preference, rural accessibility, and relative quality of hospitals. Since these issues are common sense ones, even to non-professionals, the regulation was derided, resented, and disliked by almost all of the citizen volunteers upon whose service the entire system depended.

WHAT IS YOURS IS OURS and YOU CAN'T DO WELL WITHOUT DOING GOOD also had their own impact: HSA's could not raise funds without penalty–whatever money they raised was subtracted from the next year's budget allotment. They could not keep assets–the assets were really the Feds although HSA's were "independent". The end of the HSA's? Since the Feds funded the program, but never really made it a local one, when David Stockman and President Reagan attacked the program and tried to zero out its budget, even local volunteers were hesitant to come to its defense. The HSA's were dead in the water.

This program cost millions upon millions of dollars, and had good people–at the volunteer, board, and staff level–committed to its success, but it went aground on the shoals of too much distrust of local control, an overzealous accounting mechanism, and a high resistance to change.

As long as we don't demand some common sense in government, we'll have to live with the ludicrous level of oversight that reduces all regulations to catching the 3% of us who are crooks and/or idiots and punishes the 97% who are honest and have a brain cell or two. In this environment, you can't blame the state or federal employees who are caught in the oversight squeeze; they have to assume guilt until innocence is proven, and thus they are never going to fully trust us.

Now, how can we go about breaking both you and your funders out of this relational purgatory? We must, you know, if we are to bring the industry into the 21st century in some sort of reasonably effective shape. That's really what the rest of this book is about. Hopefully, by giving you some idea of the world you will be working in, by increasing your skill base, by giving you tools, by showing you how other agencies have broken free of the cycle of co-dependence (and that is exactly what it is), you'll be better able to do it yourself. Let's start with an examination of the environment you'll be working in.

B. WHAT THE NEXT TEN YEARS WILL BRING

Given the pace of changes throughout the world in the past few years, it is obviously difficult to predict what will happen in the United States, particularly with our economy and deficit being so dependent on the world economy as a whole. Additionally, the change in national administration that occurred in 1993 will have an impact on our industry in ways no one can yet foresee. However, there are some givens that you, as a manager and policy maker for a not-for-profit, can assume will impact on your organization and its capability to perform its mission.

*1. There will be no increase in federal or state spending above
    inflation.*

The size of the federal deficit combined with the popular phobia regarding new taxes makes it arithmetically impossible to have either major new domestic initiatives or significant increases in spending. The Bush Administration continued the process initiated by President Reagan of turning over more and more responsibility for social program funding to the states. Unfortunately, many state governments are now in a deeper financial crisis than that suffered by the federal government, and states are required to balance their budgets each year. This translates to funding streams that, at the *very* best, keep up with the rate of inflation.

The reader should also be aware of three important points regarding this prediction. The first is that even though the *overall* rate of funding will remain constant at best, the level of support for the specific programs that your organization provides will vary greatly depending on the political winds. For example, the largest percentage increase in social funding in the past five years from the Feds has been in areas that prevent or treat substance abuse—in response to the national movement toward semi-temperance. Another example is funding for AIDS research, prevention, diagnosis, and treatment, which has flowed to entities as widely varied as health departments, hospitals, child welfare departments, drug centers, medical schools, and arts organizations. If your area of service is in vogue, you will prosper; if not, you will be hurt even more deeply.

The second point is that, while the rate of funding for your organization may stay constant, if you are like the majority of your peers, this rate of payment is probably already woefully short of meeting the needs in your community, and may not even be paying your full cost of service. Thus, the fact that your funding may (at best) stay steady should not be a great deal of comfort. You and your organization will have to look to new sources of income to meet the increasing needs of your community for services. Moreover, if your organization, particularly those in human service or education, gets paid on a fee-for-service basis, where you bill the city, county, state, or federal government for services *after* those services are provided, be prepared to be able to come up with more "working capital", the money that you need to pay the bills between the time you provide a service and when you get paid. Why? Because you will be providing more such services, and thus floating more receivables, and the government agencies will be paying you later. (One high official of a state welfare agency told me recently, "We postpone payment one day, just *one* day, and we save $22 million." That's real money, even in today's inflated environment.)

The third point is related to the second, and it has to do with the need to go outside and look for new sources of funds. The traditional place that not-for-profits do that is in fundraising and foundation applications. These will be much, much more competitive in the next few years as governmental resources stay static in the face of growing demand. Be prepared to improve your fundraising and grantwriting skills dramatically or to fall by the wayside.

2. The "Boomers" hit 50.

This is not a prediction, this is simple fact; but how will you react to it in your organization? Look at it this way—the largest single age cohort in American history (also the best educated, most wealthy, and latest to have children) will be in the middle of middle age. Some of the boomers, depending on national economic conditions, will begin to retire, and certainly they will have more time on their hands as their children leave home. Will this impact on people demanding your services? Perhaps, but it will certainly be a huge pool of potential board members and volunteers with time and expertise to donate, and who will have significant assets in their estates.

3. Demand for services will grow, both in terms of volume and in meeting recipients' needs.

The volume of demand will grow irrevocably, irreversibly, and probably faster than you anticipate, in almost every area of not-for-profit service. If you are in education, the national concern with the decay in our educational structure will lead to further privatization, competition from private industry, and demand for special services. If you run a religious organization, the continuing return to the church will lead to increased need for services and facilities, as well as increases in competition for dollars, as many ministries vie for the same funding sources. In the arts, a better-educated public will want more theater, music, displays of fine arts nearer and more accessible to them. If you provide a social service, whether to youth, seniors, the homeless, or the mentally or physically disabled, the need for your services will grow faster than the population as a whole.

The reasons for the increase in demand outstripping simple demographic growth are multiple. First, we as a society have turned to not-for-profits increasingly for the past thirty years, and we are used to seeking help there. Second, social services are now chronically underfunded, especially in the areas of low-income housing and job-creation assistance. As a result, large numbers of homeless and "underclass" citizens are in need of services provided by not-for-profits. Thus, you should not simply use census projections to predict the need for your services.

Demand will also be higher for very specific, highly technical services that target and meet the needs of small groups of recipients. For example, many city hospitals are placing physical rehabilitation units away from the main hospital to allow suburban residents easier access to this highly lucrative service. (The hospitals also often enjoy lower cost for the space in which they provide the service.) Another example would be an increase in home-based intermittent nursing care, what I call a "convenient necessity" for many families with infirm members living at home. Whatever your area of service, you will find more sophisticated consumers (and their advocates) demanding more targeted services that are often very expensive to provide.

4. A More Competitive Environment.

This competition will show up in everything you do. You will be competing for clients, students, patrons, or parishioners; for funding from traditional sources, for funding from new sources, for donations, for United Way dollars; for visibility; for donated services such as air time and advertising; for volunteers, and for staff. Since 1980, both for-profits and other not-for-profits have entered into areas that were once "your" territory; in a sense challenging the monopoly that you once enjoyed. "Monopoly!?" Absolutely. How many times when asking for funding have you heard the question, "Does this program duplicate anything already serving the same constituency?" Many times, I'm sure. The reason: funders did not want to encourage "duplicate" funding, i.e. competition. Imagine the same scene with your city council only approving one fast food restaurant, or one grocery store in town—to avoid duplication. They would be run out of office for obstructing commerce, interfering with competition, and in general for being too regulatory. But in the not-for-profit arena this has been considered appropriate.

No more. Funders are looking for the best productivity, the most mission for the money. Volunteers are looking to spend their time wisely. Quality staff want to work with organizations that are financially viable as well as state of the art in terms of service. Businesses who donate services want to associate with top caliber organizations, not ones who will have their work, finances, or reputation show up in the scandal sheets.

5. Accelerated Use of Technology.

This is not news, but the not-for-profit sector has lagged far behind in using the available technology—in part because the sector is so dominated by social service/educational types, as opposed to techies. But your field, like any other, needs to adapt, and the costs of that adaptation are coming down every day. Remember that it was only in the 80's that most of us sat down at our first computer and began playing with a rudimentary spreadsheet or accounting program or word processor. User-friendliness of computers and the availability of "off the shelf" software have both increased dramatically, at the same time that the price of computers has dropped by 90% or more in the past five years. The benefits of using technology are evident everywhere, from faxes to cellular phones to beepers to E-mail. The question is: will you and your organization make use of it to provide the most services for the least dollars? The capital investment is so low now (as of this writing $1,200 would buy a 486 computer with a huge hard drive, lots of memory, a great deal of pre-installed software and a printer) that the largest expense is in the staff time invested to learn how to use the machines—and that is dropping rapidly as well.

Put simply, rapidly advancing technology is a fact of life, it is economical, and it can help. The not-for-profits that survive into the 21st century will use that technology to further their mission. Those who don't will be left behind.

6. Continued Integration of New Populations.

The United States has always been a melting pot, with an increasingly complex mix of cultures, backgrounds, and ethnicities coexisting, cohabitating, and sometimes even cooperating to build the country. While the popular vision is that the last great wave of immigration ended with Ellis Island in the 1930's, the truth is that more people immigrated to this country during 1991–1992 than came through Ellis Island *in total* during the 20 years of its highest activity. Not only that, but these people came from a wide array of places: Mexico, Central America, Southeast Asia, Eastern Europe, the states of the former Soviet Union, and Western Asia.

Additionally, the past twenty years have seen an increasing demand on the part of all ethnic groups for recognition and sensitivity to cultural uniqueness. This means not only acknowledging the legitimacy of someone's background, but as a provider of service, taking the time to learn enough about a person's background to be providing services in a way that meets their needs.

● **FOR EXAMPLE:** I have a former client organization in Los Angeles that provides primary health care to part of South L.A. They print their handouts, warnings, and health information in 28 (that's *twenty-eight*) different languages, and have staff fluent in 20 languages, plus sign language. Why? Because health information is no good if the patient can't understand it. Additionally, for each ethnic group in the Center's service area, the health professionals retain a cultural liaison who meets with them regularly to help them understand the cultures and what barriers those cultures may have to the utilization of Western medicine. As a comparison, the Los Angeles Public Schools have students whose native languages number *over 70*.

● **FOR EXAMPLE:** In child welfare, caseworkers need to be assured that, when they meet with parents, their advice and/or instructions are understood and obeyed. In one case I am aware of, a Caucasian caseworker went into an Hispanic home to investigate an allegation of abuse. She met with the mother, interviewed the children, and found no foundation for the abuse allegation, but did have some ideas on pre-school and infant care for the mother. The caseworker set up an appointment with the mother for the next day with the infant development counselor, and received repeated assurances that the mother would be there, had the necessary transportation, etc. The mother never showed. Why? Because, in this case, the *father* who (in many Hispanic homes) is the final authority, had not been included in the decision, had not given his agreement or assurance, and thus the mother did not attend the meeting.

Cultural competence is a key to continued success, not only with those your organization serves, but also with your staff and board.

If you are from an area of the country that is culturally homogeneous, don't assume that this issue does not pertain to you. It does. Every area has its minorities and, even in the most rural areas, people from different backgrounds are migrating in. Look at it this way: in a more competitive environment, with more demands on your organization, can you afford to turn away *any* client, *any* volunteer, *any* donor, *any* potential staff person, simply because you didn't take the time to get to know them? I think not.

7. More Accountability.

This is a good thing—if it is handled in an atmosphere of making sure that your organization is accountable for what you do, how you do it and how much you spend—but it can easily turn into a witch hunt (see my earlier discussion of the basic tenets of funders).

The United Way of America scandal, Jim Bakker's PTL notoriety, and abuses at many local charities over the years mean that your organization will be subject to (and must be prepared for) close and largely unsympathetic scrutiny of everything you do, every dollar you spend, every raise you give, every program you cut or expand or reduce or propose.

You have to know what you are doing, why you are doing it, how it will help further your mission, and what the alternatives are. Simply saying, "We've always done it that way" is not enough. Be prepared to defend your actions based on reasoned decisions that are regularly reviewed.

RECAP

In this chapter we have reviewed how not-for-profits came to where they are today, how your funders really think of you, and the seven trends that I believe you are going to have to accommodate to stay viable over the next ten years.

   With these predictions in mind, the next question is: how do we adapt and accommodate to these conditions? Even more difficult is the answer to the next question: how do we adapt and accommodate to conditions that may exist in five years that no one can even foresee today? How do we stay close to our mission, stay solvent, stay flexible, and stay sane, all at the same time? I'm not sure that all of those things are possible, particularly the part about retaining your sanity, but the next few chapters will detail my observations about the key characteristics of the best, most flexible, and yet most focused not-for-profits in the country. By trying to emulate their successes and integrate their strengths with yours, your organization can do much to reach the next century in excellent shape.

3. What Works: The Characteristics of a Successful Not-for-Profit

OVERVIEW

Since 1982, I have had the opportunity to train thousands and consult for hundreds of not-for-profits. These consultations often included management reviews, strategic planning, and new business development. In the course of this work, I had the opportunity to talk to staff, board, community members, and the people that the organization served in depth. As a result, I have had the good fortune to not only work for many consistently excellent not-for-profits, but also to talk about their strengths and weaknesses with the people who are most important to their success. It is an examination of these strengths, how they work, and how they can work for you and your organization that make up the rest of this book.

What is striking in these consistently successful organizations is the similarity of the key characteristics of what they are and how they do their job. Over and over, I see the same core foundations on which the organization functions. It doesn't matter whether the not-for-profit is a church, a school, a museum, a hospital, a trade association, or a rehabilitation facility, these key characteristics shine through.

This chapter will, in effect, preview the remainder of the book. I will lay out for you the nine characteristics of success that will overcome the problems and environmental changes that we reviewed in Chapter 2. Each of the chapters that follow will detail the ways to attain these characteristics.

I have attempted to distill the key characteristics into the nine below. Any such distillation is fraught with peril: I may group things in ways that don't exactly fit your organization; I may not emphasize a particular item enough. I have tried to put the key components in a logical and workable form, breaking them not only into different segments, but separating them in such a way that I hope you can study each, apply the information to your organization, and then put all the pieces back together to make a cohesive whole.

With the exception of the mission, which should always come first, you should not read these characteristics as individual items, with varying degrees of importance. They are *all* important. Moreover, they work together as a group, like the parts of a fine symphony. Ignore one or more parts and the whole is greatly diminished. Bring them all together and their synergy outstrips the sum of their individual contributions.

Here are the nine key characteristics:

1. A VIABLE MISSION: One that is definable, understandable, supportable, and needed. Without the mission, what's the point? Unfortunately, at too many not-for-profits, there is no point, because the mission has become secondary to survival. In Chapter 4 you will learn how to write and use an effective mission statement.

2. A BUSINESSLIKE BOARD OF DIRECTORS: One that knows (and understands) the organization's mission, knows the community, deals with policy issues, and is the check and balance on the staff and funders. A board needs the information, experience, character, and support to know how to decide key issues quickly and effectively, and, in today's tough environment, they need to know when to say no to a good idea. In Chapters 5 and 6, I'll show you how to assess, recruit, and retain just such a board, one that will give you more outcome and policy guidance and less day-to-day manipulation than you thought possible.

3. STRONG, WELL-EDUCATED STAFF: Ones who are advocates for the mission, who manage from the bottom-up and who are constantly trained. There is no investment more necessary or more neglected than staff education and training. Chapter 7 will show you the way to treat your staff: from the bottom up. You'll learn how to effectively manage and motivate your employees, and how to get them involved in the outcomes of your organization.

4. A TIGHT SET OF CONTROLS: These include personnel, finance, operations, quality control, and maintenance policies. Good controls free the organization to work on its mission rather than watching its back all the time. In Chapter 8, we'll look at nine different types of policies, and I'll show you where most groups make mistakes—so you don't have to.

5. A BIAS FOR MARKETING: Organizations that understand that *everything* that they do is marketing, and who see every act, from service provision to how the phone is answered, as a marketing opportunity to pursue their mission. Our marketing discussion will be in Chapter 9, where you will learn who your markets really are, how to give those markets what they want, and how to provide a marketing edge for everyone in your organization.

6. A VISION FOR WHERE THEY ARE GOING: This is so simple, yet so often ignored. A strategic plan, both the process and the document, are keys to success. Without a plan, the only way you get anywhere is by accident. Isn't what you do too important to be left up to chance? Of course it is, and Chapter 10 will show you why you need to have a plan, what kinds of plans there are, and will lay out a process for you to get a usable, meaningful plan.

7. FINANCIALLY EMPOWERED: Organizations that have diversified income, income from non-traditional sources, an endowment, and therefore, the ability to impact on their mission without waiting for help. Sure, you say. All of that would be nice if it dropped in my lap. Well, it doesn't happen on its own. These organizations make it happen. In Chapters 11 and 12 we'll look at the characteristics of financial empowerment and how to apply them in your organization.

8. SOCIAL ENTREPRENEURS: Organizations that are willing to take risks to perform their mission; to try (and often fail) and try again; to look at markets and provide services to support their mission rather than create bureaucracies to continue past (and often outdated) practices. Chapter 13 will give you the best ideas on how to motivate your staff, board, and community to take prudent risks on behalf of your constituency.

9. RAPID RESPONSE TO CHANGING CIRCUMSTANCES: What percentage of your services were you providing in the same way (same time, same place, same method) five years ago? Don't look now, but the world has changed—a lot. Has your organization the ability to change with it? Chapter 14 will discuss how to be a change facilitator, pointing out why people are resistant to change and how to affect change in a mission-based manner.

Others have noted that there are consistent and key characteristics in organizations that thrive. Tom Peters and Robert Waterman in *In Search of Excellence* laid out "Eight Basic Principles" including two that are very similar to those above: "Staying Close to the Customer" and "Hands-on, Value-Driven". In Waterman's later book, *The Renewal Factor*, he discussed the key factors that kept excellent organizations constantly renewing themselves. These included "Tight Controls" and "Flexibility", two of the characteristics that I cover here.

In the following chapters, we'll discuss the important parts of each of the nine characteristics noted above.

Finally, a word of advice: as you look at information in the following chapters, information that expands on each of these nine core characteristics of not-for-profit success, ask yourself: How does my organization measure up? Do we *really* do all these things, or only pay them lip service? As you continue through the remaining chapters, be brutally frank with yourself: this is not a time for self-delusion. That will only lead to ignoring real problems and deferring any needed changes.

RECAP

In this chapter, you have seen the nine characteristics you and your organization need to embrace, adopt, and maintain. These nine characteristics, when achieved as a group, can improve your ability to do your mission, improve your organization's long-term viability, and assure the people you serve that you will be there to serve them for the long haul. These characteristics don't show up on their own, and they can't be developed overnight. Moreover, once you attain them all, only hard work and discipline will keep them in place.

4. The Mission is the Reason

OVERVIEW

Let's be realistic: if you are a staff person of a not-for-profit, you are not in this for the money, nor for a low-stress, short-hour job. If you are a volunteer, you are not working with this not-for-profit so that you can miss time at home or at work, or avoid getting eight hours of sleep at night.

You came and you stay because of the *mission*—what the organization *does*.

If that is true, why is the mission even an issue in this book? Why take up time and space on a topic that we all agree is key? There are more reasons than you might imagine, and in this chapter we'll cover each of them and provide some examples and ideas for you to better utilize your mission as you move your organization ahead.

In the following pages, we'll first examine the need that you have for a mission statement and how to review and rewrite your mission statement to help you become the organization that you want to be, not merely continue to be the organization you were in the past. We'll then look at the ways that mission statements are misused, underutilized, or completely forgotten. Finally, we'll discuss how to use your mission statement as a tool for policy, management, and marketing; in short, how to be mission-based every single day.

A. THE MISSION STATEMENT IS YOUR LEGAL REASON FOR EXISTENCE

The mission statement is not only the reason you work or volunteer for your organization, but it also has important legal implications for staff and board. If you do not perform your mission, the IRS can take away your tax-exempt status under section 501(c) of the Internal Revenue Code. If you bring in too many of your funds from Unrelated Business Income (defined as "income that is derived from activities that do not importantly contribute to the mission of the organization") you also stand a chance of losing your tax-exempt status, as well as bearing tax liability for any profits from such unrelated businesses.

Many not-for-profits are technically in violation of their mission statement and have Unrelated Business Income that they don't even realize. Usually this is due to having a prehistoric mission statement. For example if, in 1960 you were set up to provide a service in County A but now, as your community has grown, you provide services in County A, B, and C, and if your mission statement specifies only County A, you are technically getting unrelated business income from all of the activities that you perform and are reimbursed for in Counties B and C. The same issue arises for not-for-profits who were originally set up to provide only mental health services but now do substance abuse, were formed to help the African-American community, but now assist people from all ethnic backgrounds, or were formed to help senior citizens, but now find it useful to provide day care to the elderly *and* the very young. (Note: for those of you concerned about Unrelated Business Income, it is covered in detail in Chapter 12.)

All of this is to underscore the importance of having a mission that you know, that you can live with, and that accurately portrays not only what your organization does now but what you want it to do in the next three to five years.

B. WRITING OR REWRITING YOUR MISSION STATEMENT

You all have a mission statement. It is in your articles of incorporation and in the forms you submitted to the IRS to receive your tax-exempt status. It may also be restated in your bylaws. Every three years (at the same time that you will be writing your strategic plan that we will discuss in Chapter 10) you need to revisit your mission statement. You need to take the opportunity to get staff and board input into what your mission should be. In most cases it will be exactly the same as it is now, only you will have a renewed sense of its urgency as a result of the discussion. There are, of course, a number of steps that I suggest you take in reviewing your mission statement. These are:

1. FIND YOUR CURRENT MISSION STATEMENT

If you are like most of your peers, you may have more than one mission statement. There may be different language in your bylaws, articles of incorporation, or applications for funding. Gather them all up and review them.

2. NOTE ANY SUBSTANTIVE CHANGES

Have you started to provide services in a new geographic area outside of any listed in your mission statement? Have you added services or a new kind of clientele? Make sure to add these to your statement.

3. HAVE A BOARD/STAFF REVIEW

At a special meeting or at your strategic planning retreat, go over your current mission, consider any substantive changes, and then talk through whether your current mission statement is inclusive enough for the kind of organization you are shaping. Does it accurately reflect your core values? Does it restrict your flexibility? DON'T try to rewrite the mission as a group. You will still be there agonizing over syntax and comma placement in 2105. Do talk through the key points or values you want to include, things like "accessible to all parts of the community", "highest quality of service", "sensitive to different cultural values". Then redraft your mission statement and take it back to the board for review and adoption.

Once the mission is rewritten, have it formally adopted by the board of directors or voted on by your membership (meeting whatever stipulations are in the bylaws) **and then send it, with the minutes of the board action, to your state attorney general and to the Internal Revenue Service**. This is critical, as the IRS will judge you under the Unrelated Business Income Tax provisions of the Code based on the mission statement that they have *on file*. If you don't send the amended mission statement to the IRS, they will never know, and will judge you on your old, outdated mission statement.

Now let's turn our attention to the ways that people misuse or underutilize their mission statement. I have already noted that the mission statement is a resource that you need to use. Unfortunately, it is a resource that is very underutilized in most not-for-profits.

C. THE FORGOTTEN MISSION STATEMENT

What good is your mission statement if no one knows about it? You and your board and staff may review the mission statement every year or two, but if you are like most not-for-profits, that's the extent of your use of your mission. I think you need to be reminded of it regularly. We need the mission as a beacon, to guide us when we get distracted by the day-to-day ups and downs of life.

> ● **FOR EXAMPLE:** All three of my children at one time or another played non-competitive youth soccer. Since the oldest played, the middle and youngest started at the earliest age allowed: age four. Watching soccer played by four-year-olds is more amusing than exciting, and when our middle child started playing, I decided to keep busy by analyzing a little of the group dynamics of the games, practice, and coaching.
>
> Questions sprang to mind. How do you motivate four-year-olds to keep their minds on the game? To compete? To even take the ball away from someone else when all they've heard from parents up to that age is "Share now, Susie." At the first game, I wondered, what does the coach say before the game? Will he say "Win one for the Gipper?"; or get technical and say "Remember play 17! Trevor go left, Andrea go right, pass to Sarah and she shoots!"?
>
> Not a chance. What he did, and what all soccer coaches of very young players say is: "Look at me, now WHICH WAY ARE WE GOING???" And most (sometimes all) of the children think and point to the goal and say "THAT WAY!!!" And then the parents line up along the side of the field and remind the kids which way to kick the ball. Why? Because kids get easily distracted, by picking a flower, seeing a friend from school on the other team, waving to Mom or Dad, and often kick the ball toward the wrong end of the field.

The point of the story is that we, in our organizations, often also get distracted from the goal and from our mission, and it is not as easy for us to refocus on the point of what we do as it is for the kids on the soccer field: you can pick them up and show them where the goal is. For you, your "goal" is the mission statement, and it needs to be as visible and readily available as the goal on the soccer field.

Remember, distractions are a natural part of the busy world we live and work in. Thus we need to model ourselves after the parents at the soccer game, and constantly be reminding each other that the mission *is* the point. By using the mission statement in management and board decisions, by posting it clearly, by incorporating it into personnel evaluations, you can reinforce and remind people all of the time that your mission is paramount. Otherwise, your mission is forgotten among the ashes of the fires that you are putting out each day.

D. THE MYSTERY MISSION STATEMENT

Can you recite your mission statement right now? Probably not, and that's OK for now. But do you at least know the key elements? Does your mission statement specify a particular group of people, geographic area, or type of service? Or some combination of all three? You do need to know that. When was it written? When was it last reviewed by the board and the staff?

One thing is important to remember: most mission statements are written to be broad statements of charitable activity—usually drafted by attorneys to be as broad as possible, or by advocates of a particular crusade who don't want to offend anyone. They often say, in effect *"XYZ of YourTown is a not-for-profit dedicated to be all things to all people everywhere for ever, charitably."* That's fine, but realize that along with that broad, all-inclusive mission can come considerable disagreement on *how* to achieve or at least pursue that mission.

> ☞ **HANDS ON:** Try this. At your next board meeting, and next senior management meeting, ask everyone to get a piece of paper out and write down in one sentence *the single most important thing your organization does.* Now have everyone read their answers off and write them on the board, or on a flipchart. Compare the answers. How many duplications do you have?

If you are like the overwhelming number of not-for-profits, you'll have few if any duplications. Why? Because *everyone* in the organization comes to it from a different background, perspective, or priority. For example, if you are a human service provider you have staff who are *doing* while your managers are *managing*. It sounds obvious, but look at how their perspectives will be different. The staff will look at the micro (how the mission affects their job and their part of the organization) and the managers *should* look at the macro (the organization as a whole, or at least their larger part of it). You may well have board members or volunteers who have been recipients of one (but perhaps *only* one) of the services you provide, and their perspective on what you do is colored by their individual and often very personal experiences.

This difference of perspective is a key, and too often overlooked fact in not-for-profits. We are likely to assume that every one of us comes to the organization because we agree on the mission and good works the organization does. Not so. We come together to support what we perceive the mission to be, and it is that mission (our perceived one) that we will advocate for and work toward. Obviously, this phenomenon results in a likelihood that we don't agree on the mission, and that can lead to either major conflicts or major strengthening.

Let's look at some real-world examples of this phenomenon.

● **FOR EXAMPLE:** An Association for Retarded Citizens (ARC) in a midwestern state was a model of a mission-oriented not-for-profit. It was formed in the 1950's by parents of retarded children as a volunteer organization dedicated to fighting for funding. Over the years it had evolved to provide direct services to persons with developmental disabilities, their families, and employers who employed people with disabilities. The ARC ran twelve residential sites, a vocational workshop, early childhood assessment programs, and recreational outings, as well as support groups and outreach into the community.

Economically, 72% of its funding came from state and federal funds, usually in the form of purchase-of-service, and mostly for less than the actual cost of service provided. The ARC made up for these underpayments by running a traditional (and profitable) "sheltered workshop" where developmentally disabled people did assembly, packaging, and manufacturing for for-profit businesses with assistance from supervisors. The ARC depended on the workshop profits to subsidize many of its other programs.

Then came a change in the philosophy of working with the developmentally disabled, an idea called "supported employment". In supported employment, agencies like the ARC work with employers to find real jobs in real employment settings, and if the person with the disability needs some assistance, they get the job along with a job coach, who is on site with them some or all of the time to assure that they stay on task and do the job as it needs to be done.

For the sheltered workshop this policy was a potential financial disaster. Gone were the least disabled (and thus easiest to work with and most productive) employees. What would be done to keep the workshop profitable? Both the workshop director and the ARC Executive Director knew that without the profits from the workshop other services would have to be cut. This would, of course, have an impact on service array, service quality, staff morale, and eventually, community support and donations.

What should they do? Mandated by the state rules to move people "out into the working community", the ARC was faced with an agency-threatening dilemma, unless the staff and board could adjust and adapt. But they didn't want to just react, they wanted to respond in a way that they could all support.

The ARC Board President called a board/staff retreat to discuss the issue, and started with a review of their mission statement.

"The Mission of the ARC is to work for persons with mental retardation, other related disabilities and their families to help them achieve their highest potential in school, work, community life and recreation."

Even with this broad mission statement there was stinging disagreement about how to proceed. Some participants wanted to close the workshop, noting that supported employment "works for everyone", no matter how disabled. Some were hesitant about setting a policy (promoting and providing supported employment) that would potentially put clients into a more "risky" job in the real community. Others raised the overall economic impact of potentially reduced profits on the rest of the agency's service array.

The solution? Support the mission. The key phrase? *"Work for persons with disabilities."* To the board and staff, this meant allowing clients to choose their options, and thus keep both options open. What this resulted in was keeping the workshop open as a work-training, transition, and work location, with the eventual goal of having each person with a disability work in the setting they most liked. To keep profits up, they brought in non-disabled staff to supplement the workforce. Thus the program and the financial viability were preserved, and the solution worked well in light of the mission statement.

Those readers who are professionals or volunteers in the field of developmental disabilities may disagree with the ARC's choices, but the point here is that they let the mission guide them, and didn't just react without thinking.

● **FOR EXAMPLE:** A not-for-profit performance auditorium in the South was in crisis. Like all major performance centers, The Hall, as we shall call it, had gone through tough financial times along with the arts community in general. The Hall not only housed the local symphony, ballet, and opera companies (renting to them at a steep discount), but also reached out beyond its traditional white, upper middle class clientele to the minority and lower income communities by holding a wide variety of bookings, special performances for children, etc. The financial mainstay of The Hall, however, was its series of Broadway touring productions. The profits from these productions kept The Hall open, and allowed it to subsidize the "fine" arts and community outreach.

But ticket sales for the core Broadway series were down. The Hall needed renovations and upkeep that had been neglected for years. The outreach program had brought new not-for-profit community groups asking to book the hall, at a discount, of course. The performing arts not-for-profits (symphony, ballet, and opera) were in a financially precarious state as well, and could not afford to pay the full cost of the rental of the site, and considered The Hall the only dignified place to perform.

What should be done? The board looked at their mission to gain guidance into what their priorities should be:

"The mission of The Hall Inc. shall be to improve the community and cultural experiences of the people of [this state], to foster improvements and expansion of the arts and to maintain The Hall as a community resource for future generations."

Now, this broad mission provided some guidance, but there were other barriers to a quick fix. First, several members of the board were also members of the symphony, ballet, and opera boards. Thus, their perspective was that The Hall's board should focus on the phrase "foster improvements and expansion of the arts" which to them meant continuing to subsidize their performing arts groups. Several board members were highly successful CEO's who focused on the "maintain The Hall as a community resource for future generations" part of the mission as a mandate to first and foremost break even financially and keep The Hall in excellent physical condition. The third group on the board were community representatives who wanted more access for their own constituencies.

The solution? There was no perfect one, but all of the people around the table understood finance well enough to know that without financial stability, there can be no social good. They agreed to prioritize their social and cultural obligations and budgeted an affordable amount to subsidize each performing group. Then it was up to staff to sell the Broadway series to meet the budget needs. They also set up a five-year capital endowment campaign to facilitate income from a non-arts source each year. Did they satisfy everyone? Not really. But they did acknowledge all of the perspectives around the table and tried to accommodate as many as possible, based on the mission statement.

The important points in these stories are many. First, even with a well-written and up-to-date mission statement, your organization will continue to have healthy (I hope) debate on how to implement the mission, and on what your values are. That's fine. If it is kept on a healthy, positive basis it can help the organization mature and keep up with the times. Second, without some common framework around which to discuss, there would have been no starting point for the ARC's or the performance hall's discussions. Their mission statements provided that framework. Third, everyone at your board table and staff meetings comes to the organization with their own history, perspective, and agenda. That can be an enriching fact or a divisive one, depending on how the executive director and board chairperson handle it. Use people's diversity of opinion, experience, and perspective to strengthen your organization; don't require everyone to think and act alike.

E. GETTING MORE FROM AN UNDERUTILIZED RESOURCE

Staff and board members of a not-for-profit have a responsibility to get the most good out of the limited resources that they have. But isn't it ironic that in the day-to-day race to secure more of those resources to allow more of the mission to be realized, people usually forget to use *the mission itself as a resource*?

The mission statement can be a management tool, a rallying cry, a staff motivator, a volunteer recruiter, and a fund raiser. You already have invested in getting the mission statement right for your organization, your community, and current times. Now use that resource in these other areas:

1. Management Tool: The mission statement should be a regular part of staff and board discussions of questions such as: "Which of the three options that we have before us is most responsive to our mission?" or "Will this type of funding gain us dollars but distract us from our mission?" Use the mission statement to make better management and policy decisions.

2. Rallying Cry and Staff Motivator: The mission statement can be used as a rallying cry and motivator for staff, volunteers, and board in tough times.

☞ **H ANDS ON:** Try this: when the going gets particularly tough, when morale is low, or it seems people have given up hope, ask your staff or your board to list the good things that have happened in the last three weeks or months as a result of your organization being in business. Get personal, talking about the impact of your organization's services on individuals. Then turn it around, and ask them what would have happened if you hadn't been around as an organization. Refocus on the mission statement as a higher calling, a cause worth working and sacrificing for. Note: you can't use this exercise every day, as it will lose its impact. Save it for when you *really* need it.

3. Volunteer Recruiter: Remember the response when President Kennedy called for the formation of the Peace Corps? Or the Red Cross volunteers who flocked to south Florida to help after the devastation wrought by Hurricane Andrew in 1992? Or perhaps the questions you ask when people ask you to serve on a board, or special committee? *Mission*, what the organization *did,* was the key in all of these. Kennedy called for assisting in less developed countries as a way of non-military goodwill in an era of military confrontation. After Hurricane Andrew, the Red Cross made it clear what people could and should do to help hurricane victims. When you are recruited for a board job, you ask what services the organization provides, what it *does.*

4. Fund Raiser: Here, as in the volunteer recruitment area, what you do, what good works are done, and why you do it are all key questions in a donor's mind. The *what* of what you do is up to you, but the *why*, the mission, is the linchpin, and should be the first rationale for funding. Donors, particularly big ones, like to see organizations that are focused on their mission, not just taking money for any and all purposes.

F. THE MISSION THAT IS EVERYWHERE

Excellent organizations know their mission. It's on the tip of everyone's tongue, and you can ask nearly everyone in the place what their mission is and they will repeat it verbatim and give you reasons why *they* are the essential link in the chain to get the mission realized. How does this happen? Like the children on the soccer team, it is tough to focus people and it is easy to get distracted. A unified reason for being does not happen by accident. It happens through meaningful repetition. The mission needs to be visible *everywhere*.

Assuming that you have agreed to your revised mission statement, do the following:

▶ Have your mission statement drawn up in an attractive format (most popular word processing programs are now essentially desktop printing programs and have a wide variety of fonts, backgrounds, and graphics available). Then matte and frame it and place a copy of the framed mission in your reception area, staff lounges, and where services are provided. DON'T just copy the mission and have people tape it to the wall. Do this right. Also, DON'T have the first time that the staff people see the mission be the framed copy on the wall. Make sure that they have seen and discussed it in advance.

▶ Put the mission statement in every document you print. It should be inside the front cover or front and center in at least the following:

> ▶ *Your Annual Report*
> ▶ *All marketing and public relations material*
> ▶*Your Board Manual*
> ▶*Your Staff Personnel Policies*
> ▶*Your Staff Orientation Manual (with heavy emphasis on why the mission is so important)*
> ▶*Your Strategic Plan*

▶ Use the mission daily as a tool (see above).

The mission that is everywhere is more likely to become part of the culture and part of the mindset of the people who work and volunteer for your organization.

G. PUTTING ACTIONS BEHIND YOUR WORDS

Using the mission statement is a great thing, but a perilous risk if not handled correctly. Once you hold the mission statement up as the Holy Grail, and take time and resources to print it and use it at meetings, you hold yourself to a higher standard, one that invites criticism and interpretation from a variety of places ("Well, *that* decision certainly does not support our mission" from whoever loses in a choice made by management or board).

The cure for this is threefold: leadership, time, and training.

● **FOR EXAMPLE:** Everyone knows of Ross Perot, the computer services billionaire who ran for President of the United States in 1992. Perot made his money starting and growing Electronic Data Systems (EDS), a computer data services firm that was the first, and for a time the largest processor of data in the world. Perot built his organization by doing a number of things, including emphasizing customer service, teamwork, loyalty to each other and the organization, and by having a simple mission and set of values for everyone to work by.

EDS's mission statement was short and simple. Perot had it reduced to a wallet-sized card which every employee carried so that they could produce it quickly to use in management discussions. For EDS employees, this worked.

At the same time, General Motors was a giant going nowhere. The new GM CEO, Roger Smith, saw the need for more and more information management to tie together the far-flung outposts of his automotive empire, and he contracted with EDS to set up and run the system. Smith got to know Perot, and he admired the lean, can-do attitude that EDS employees exuded and demonstrated in their work for GM. So, Smith proposed that GM buy EDS, in the hopes that the EDS culture would prove to be a "virus" that would spread throughout GM. He, and the senior GM management team, analyzed what to do to hasten this spread of entrepreneurial spirit, and they focused on the mission statements that everyone on the EDS team whipped out at the drop of a hat. They paid a consultant to come up with a new mission statement for GM, distributed the cards to everyone, and waited for the new "Entrepreneurial GM" to emerge fully-clothed. It didn't. Not only did the two cultures clash, but the inevitable battle and eventual falling out between Perot and Smith has attained the status of corporate legend.

Why didn't the EDS-GM marriage work? There are probably 50 major reasons, and entire books have been written on this subject. Suffice it to say that you can't change a culture by handing out a wallet-sized card with nice words on it that no one has invested in (remember: a consultant had written GM's mission statement).

Back to our keys to success with the mission: leadership, time, and training.

1. LEADERSHIP

You need to be seen *living* the mission statement. Once you publicize and invest in your mission statement, you hold yourself up to a higher standard. *You* have to use the mission daily, visibly, and consistently. *You* have to embody its ideals. If the mission says to be culturally sensitive, *you* have to be the most educated and sensitive person in the organization. If the mission says for the organization to be an advocate for children, or a service provider to the most disadvantaged, or an educator of the best and brightest, *you* have to articulate and be a living symbol of the mission. People will be skeptical of the need or value of a revamped mission, and you have to live the mission. Do it, don't just say it.

2. TIME

After leadership the next key is the hardest, giving it time. You will need to work for many months and even years before the mission becomes ingrained. If you decide to do this, and you must, you need to lead the charge for a long, long time. As new staff and board people come on, they will know no other organization than one driven by the mission, and it will begin to be culturally ingrained.

3. TRAINING

Next, there is the need for training, training, training. There is no substitute for training. As we will see in later chapters, investing in your workforce is key and 40 hours per year per person is the minimum acceptable amount. Make at least some of that training be about the mission, why it is there, and how to use it. Remember, if someone has never managed or provided direct service with a clearly articulated mission before, this is new. Don't expect them to know how to do this automatically. Give them a chance to learn, practice, review, and learn more.

● **FOR EXAMPLE:** In the period from 1986 to 1993, Michael Jordan of the Chicago Bulls in the National Basketball Association was, by a wide margin, the best basketball player in the world. And yet, to stay there, he practiced every day. But in the work world, we say, "Oh, I went to a supervision course once, I know how to do that", or "I took accounting in college, I remember that." Wrong. People say, "I've got thirty year's management experience, I've seen it all." Remember, OJT (On-The-Job Training) is not practice, it's the game. When you screw up it is for real. If it's just experience you have, it's almost certainly based on outmoded philosophies, techniques, and technologies. Make learning for yourself and for your staff a life-long pursuit. Train, train, train.

RECAP

In this chapter, we have covered the crux of your organization—the mission.

We've reviewed the way to write or rewrite a mission statement to bring it up-to-date and why a forgotten or mystery mission statement is of little or no use. We've looked at methods of utilizing your mission as a management, motivation, and policy tool. We've suggested methods for you, your staff, and board to *live* the mission, not just parrot it.

As you finish this chapter, look around your organization. In how many places can you see and read the mission? Is it on the walls? On people's bulletin boards? Why not? Ask the first five staff you see what the mission is. Listen to their answers. Are they the same? Why not? Look at your marketing material. Is your mission on each and every piece? Why not?

I hope we agree that the mission is a key element in your success. You need to review it, revise it with help from the board and as many staff as you can, publicize it, use it daily (starting with your own activities), and train staff and volunteers in how to use the mission as a management and service provision tool. That's the starting point, and if you start here, the rest of what's in this book will be a lot more useful to you and your organization.

5. A Businesslike Board of Directors

OVERVIEW

Whether you are a staff member or a board member, you know that the board of directors is a key component of your organization. For starters, you *have* to have one; it is a legal requirement in state and federal statutes. Secondly, the board can provide an excellent source of judgement and leadership, a connection with the rest of the community, and a partnership with staff that can strengthen the organization and its services. In other words, the board *should* be a key resource for the organization. Unfortunately, it is often anything but.

Too often boards either totally dominate an organization, thus blocking the staff's ability to do their jobs, or are so subservient to staff "expertise" that the staff in effect manipulate the board at will. Neither are effective uses of resources, and both are counterproductive.

In the worst case, both problems—-board dominance and staff dominance—occur in the same organization. How can that be? Simple, the staff *think* the board is dominating while at the same time the board members *think* the staff is running roughshod over them! Gridlock in governance!

How do you optimize your board as a resource? How do you analyze what your organization needs from a board and then go out and recruit one that meets those needs? What should the respective roles of the staff and the board be? In this chapter I'll tell you about those things as well as about how to reduce your board's liability. In Chapter 6, I'll show you how to get the most effective board, why board people *really* serve and how you can meet their needs and wants, and how to evaluate your board. With the things you learn in this chapter and the next, you can really turn your board into the effective policy setting and check-and-balance resource that it needs to be.

A. BOARD EFFECTIVENESS

The first thing you need in order to make your board a better-utilized resource is a benchmark of effectiveness against which to measure.

An effective board has most, if not all, of the following characteristics:

▶ *It understands the organization's mission, and acts to implement that mission for the benefit of the organization's constituency, consistently and professionally.* If it is to be effective, a board must first and foremost understand and support the organization's mission (see Chapter 4). It must also be consistent in the development of policy to implement that mission. If it favors one method of implementation one week and another the next, it will be doing more harm than good.

▶ *It acts as a policy setter and check and balance with the staff.* With one exception (a startup not-for-profit where the board often *is* the staff) the board must act as policy setter and check and balance *only*. It must not allow itself nor any of its members to get seduced into trying to run the day-to-day activities of the organization. If the board is responsible for hiring staff, running the organization's day-to-day activities is what it hires them for. The board should set the broad policy and let the staff implement it. The board has more important things to do; things that only a board can do.

▶ *It works primarily with the Executive Director and evaluates the Executive Director at least annually.* Rule Number 1 of not-for-profit management:

**The Executive Director works for the board
and the rest of the staff work for the Executive Director.**

The board cannot be effective if it allows itself to be bogged down in both personal and personnel issues that are most appropriate for staff to handle on their own. Thus, board members who allow staff people other than the CEO or executive director to call and complain are asking for more trouble than they want. I know that this is not always easy, particularly in small towns where everyone knows everyone else, but it is *the* prime rule of not-for-profit board/staff management. As with any relationship, the one between the board and the exec can only flourish if both parties let the other know how they are doing. Many board people tell me that they are not an expert in the exec's specialty (i.e they aren't a minister, teacher, or social worker), so they can't evaluate him or her. This, while understandable, neglects what the board *does* know and *can* evaluate. The board can evaluate how the exec interacts with and supports the board, how close the staff come to staying within the budget, completing tasks in the long-range plan, achieving fundraising or outreach goals, reducing staff turnover, etc, etc, etc. The board can and should set measurable goals for the exec and then evaluate his or her ability to meet those goals. Moreover, the board should set these goals and conduct this evaluation annually at the very least. To board members that are reluctant to evaluate, I say this: *You* want to be evaluated in *your* job. If you want to keep your exec, provide the same courtesy: let him or her know how they are doing.

▶ *It changes over time, filling its membership fully by recruiting new members to meet the changing needs of the organization.* Your organization does not look like it did five years ago in terms of funding, programs, or staff. But it may very well be identical or close to it in board makeup. If the board is a resource, shouldn't its constitution change with the changing needs of the organization? Of course it should. Boards should *not* be perpetual. You should build board turnover into your bylaws. My suggestion is a three-year term, with a maximum of two successive terms before a particular board member goes off for at least a year. Thus, one-third of your board is up for renewal each year, and this gives you a chance to evaluate them and recruit both new people and new skills regularly. Also, a three-year term works well with my recommendations on strategic plans (see Chapter 10), which include a planning retreat every three years or at least once in every board member's term of office. We'll cover the issue of how you assess what kind of board you need and how you recruit board members later in this chapter.

▶ *It elects qualified officers, and appoints qualified committee chairs.* As in so many of life's endeavors, the difference between success and failure can often be leadership. Think of some of the great leaders of key organizations in our past: Presidents like Washington, Lincoln, Franklin Roosevelt; visionaries like Martin Luther King Jr., Susan B. Anthony, and countless others led their groups at a time when they were most needed. Just because you may not be involved with a national or trend-setting organization does not mean you don't need leaders on your board or to head your committees. It

also does not mean that all your leaders need to be officers or committee chairs, but it certainly helps. Effective boards have people in
officer and committee chair roles who know their job (and its limitations), get it done effectively, and are willing to commit the time to
do so. They show up with their homework done, lead their groups
through the decisions that need to be made, and represent the organization without bias with funders, donors, the media, and the public.
Your organization needs a leadership development track, where new
members are assessed after a time and potential leaders are put onto
an "officer track", assigning them first to committee chairs, then
officer slots, and finally, if appropriate, the board presidency.

▶ *It supports the organization in public.* Elaine was elected to the
board of the XYZ agency four months ago. She has been to every meeting
and has had, in her own words, "a steep learning curve" about the agency,
its works, its staff, and its funding problems. Elaine is at a social engage-
ment at a friend's house when she is approached by Phil, whom she has
not seen since her election to the board. Phil mentions that he has heard
that Elaine is now on XYZ's board. Elaine's response:

> *"(sigh) Yes, I got talked into being on the board. I'm not sure that I*
> *won't regret it, what with all of their financial problems. I had no*
> *idea how big XYZ is, how many staff and services they have, nor*
> *how financially fragile they are. I mean, they are good people and*
> *all, but they are working under tremendous strain. I don't really see*
> *how they are going to continue at their present pace or their present*
> *funding. But I am learning a lot, and I guess I'll be able to help at*
> *some point, once I figure out what is really going on."*

or

> *"(smile) Yes, I started about four months ago, and talk about an*
> *education! I had no idea how big and diversified they are. I'm really*
> *impressed by the staff. They are good people and are doing miracles*
> *with, shall we say, minimal resources. I'm learning a lot, and hope*
> *that I can really contribute once I get my feet on the ground."*

As a staff member, which answer would you like to have your
board members giving? As a board member, do you hear yourself
echoed in the first or the second answer? And, just for discussion, what if
Elaine's friend Phil happens to be on the United Way allocation committee for this year, or is an officer at XYZ's bank, or is a potential referral
source for new clients? What message do you prefer he get?

We'll deal more with this in Chapter 9 on Marketing, but it is critical that board people realize that they are "on the team" and must support the team—even if they don't agree with every decision made at every board meeting. Once board members start to criticize board decisions or complain about the agency outside of the boardroom, the ability of board members to act as an effective team starts to go down the black hole of internal conflict.

B. BARRIERS TO BOARD EFFECTIVENESS

What are the main barriers that get in the way? It's always beneficial to highlight the most common places that boards trip up. A board *cannot* be an effective resource for the organization if:

▶ *The members of the board don't know basic and up-to-date information about the organization's mission, programs, and purposes.* This sounds so elementary on the face of it one would think that *of course* people on boards have that kind of information. Don't be so sure. Board members come to the table with different ideas and backgrounds, and their perceptions of the mission (as we discussed in Chapter 4) may be as different as night and day. This also extends to the programs. They may not even be aware of some programs' existence. Thus, orientation, on a consistent basis, is a key to board effectiveness.

☞ **HANDS ON:** At *every* board meeting, reserve 15 minutes for ongoing board orientation. Cover a single program, a new state law effecting your organization, or new developments in your field. Orientation should be a continuous, never-ending process. Too often it is only done at one meeting at the beginning of the board member's term, provided in a language (your jargon) that the board member does not yet understand. Think back to your own orientation when you joined the staff of your employer. How much do you remember? Not much, and you have worked there 40 hours a week ever since. Now add to that only "working" a few hours a month as a board member does, and you may get the picture about why they don't keep 100% up to speed. Help them keep current by dedicating 15 minutes per meeting.

▶ *It doesn't get accurate and timely information from staff.* There is no excuse for inaccurate information going out to the board, and even less excuse for not sending information to them in advance. If board members are to set policy, and to be a check and balance for

the organization, they need to see the meeting materials in advance—
and that does not mean ten minutes in advance of the meeting. As a
rule, three days is the minimum for materials to be *in the hands* of
board members before a meeting.

Another part of this barrier is not telling board members about
key or controversial issues until they read it in the paper. This is, to
understate the issue, not smart. Whether the news is good or bad, if
you are a staff manager, let the board members hear it from you, not
from the grapevine or the press. If the news is good, the board member feels like an insider. If it is bad, you get to tell them the whole
story first, not after they have read (and been prejudiced by) whatever spin the paper puts on the story. Keep your board well informed.

▶ *It frequently lacks a quorum.* How can you take action without a
quorum? You can't. If the board members are not there, three things
happen. First, board people who are not present cannot add their contributions to the discussion and decision. Second, if a bare quorum is
present, decisions that are made will not have the strength of a wider
board ownership, and may later be subject to being overturned, or at
least not supported fully. Finally, board members are liable for actions
taken in their absence (see Board Liability).

I tell executive directors all the time what I was told (and did
not like hearing): *if you don't have quorums it is your fault!* Because
board members are people like all the rest of us. They make choices
about how to spend the 24 hours they are given each day. All of us
have more things to choose from than we have hours to do them in.
Thus, going to a board meeting is a choice, one that competes with
family time, work time, TV time, socializing, or sleep, to name a few.
As a staff member you are *competing* for your board members' time
and you have to *earn* their attendance by meeting their needs and
wants. You need these people at the meetings. It's your job to entice
them there and to keep them coming.

☞ **HANDS ON:** You also need a tool to help you entice by enforcement. All boards should have attendance requirements that are discussed during recruitment, and enforced rigorously. For example, if
you have 12 meetings a year, each board member must come to 9 per
year, or not be renewed for membership. Missing three in a row is
cause for probation with one more miss leading to termination. If this
sounds tough, it is designed to be. You are a mission-oriented business and you can't get your business done without board attendance.
Be up front with your board people and let them know you cannot

have them be casual about attendance. They need to be on or off the board, not both.

Board members are liable for actions taken at meetings that they miss. That fact alone should entice them to come to meetings. We'll discuss this fact more in a few pages.

▶ *It is not given anything meaningful to do.* I make the assumption that you want talented and accomplished people on your board, ones who can contribute to your organization with their skills, experience, and expertise. Given that, why would you not give these people anything to do that challenges them? Too many boards are perfunctory: call the meeting to order, take attendance, review the minutes of the last meeting, approve three committee reports, and go home. As the commercial said, all too well "Where's the beef?" If you treat your board like they are incapable of doing real work, the good board members will leave, and you won't have a quorum, yet again.

▶ *The board leadership is weak.* Weak leadership often results in internal strife, chaos, and lack of direction. Also, boards sometimes need strong leaders to stand up to strong staffs. Finally, weak leaders do not inspire good people to keep coming to the board meetings, to contribute, or to take risks on behalf of the organization.

▶ *Its meetings have no agenda and are not well-facilitated.* The lack of an agenda is an open invitation to anarchy and meetings that go on for centuries. You simply must have an agenda and stick to it. The agenda needs to be mailed out in advance with meeting materials, and, if possible, the agenda should be somewhat standardized from meeting to meeting.

Facilitation is another issue. It is a skill, one that your committee chairs and board president need. It requires that they encourage people to speak and allow them to contribute, but at the same time, keep the meeting on track and bring each issue to closure in a timely fashion. That's a big order, and too big an order for a lot of board presidents I have observed.

▶ *Its committee structure is not effective and every policy decision comes before the full board for lengthy debate.* There is simply not enough time in a single board meeting (no matter how long it may drag on) to get effective policy and oversight accomplished by the board as a whole. To use the board effectively, you need a committee structure that allows for persons on (and sometimes not yet on) the board to use their particular expertise and focus on a particular issue, such as finance, personnel, fundraising, or planning. Then, once the board delegates the details of a particular area to the committees, the board discussion should be limited and, in most cases, perfunctory. If every issue that is discussed at committee meetings is completely rehashed at the board level, why have committees? In the next chapter, we'll discuss what committees you need and how to constitute them so that they can be effective. Board members must let the committees do their job, or else the board won't be able to do its job.

▶ *The staff lacks the skills to support the board, or worse, makes a systematic effort to ignore the board or undermine its effectiveness.* The staff have a role in making the board work well: they need to be supportive, but guiding, and we'll review the key functions in a page or two. But if the staff don't help make the board effective, it won't be. If they undermine the board by trying to seize or hold power, the checks and balances get negated and there is a terrible risk of the organization not keeping to its mission, not keeping up with changes in the community, and thus being out of touch. Additionally, if staff are not supportive, good board members will either walk out or will attempt to take over the day-to-day activities of the organization, both of which are situations you want to avoid.

C. BOARD MEMBER RESPONSIBILITIES

In attempting to mold a better board, we need to define the specific responsibilities that it has. As we have already noted, the members of the board of directors are the representatives of the community; they protect the community's interest while advancing the organization's mission in the same fashion that a for-profit corporate board represents the stockholders and promotes the corporate goals.

Even with this philosophical background, it is important to list specifics. The board is responsible for seeing that the items listed below are accomplished; but it may not actually do each of these things personally. If there are staff, certain tasks, such as filing IRS forms, are left for them to do, but board members are still responsible for ensuring that they are done.

Other authors have talked extensively about the roles of boards, particularly Brian O'Connell's excellent *Board Member's Book*. In this text, O'Connell notes the need for clear definition of roles, particularly between boards and staffs. On the other hand, Barbara Burgess, writing in *The Nonprofit Management Handbook*, lists three governing functions of boards:

"To preserve the integrity of the trust;
To set policy;
To support and promote the organization."

While I agree with this list, I think we need to expand on the roles a bit. A board of directors must:

▶ *Fulfill all of the IRS and state not-for-profit reporting require-ments.* This includes taxes, FICA, annual reports, UBIT estimations, and operating under Section 501(c) of the IRS code.

▶ *Set policy and establish organizational goals.* Boards are respon-sible for broad policy and must do long-range planning to set those policies in place.

▶ *Hire the executive director.* No one else can or should do this important job.

▶ *Evaluate the executive director's performance in writing at least annually.* No excuses, accept no substitutes.

▶ *Ensure that fiscal policies are in place and followed.* We'll talk more about controls in Chapter 8, but boards should be very con-cerned about financial oversight and that means good cash, receiv-ables, payables, and budgeting policies.

▶ *Help develop and adopt budgets.* The board must have the final say about how the resources of the organization are allocated and this is most clearly embodied in the budget. Staff (at all levels) should help draft the budget, but the board has the final say.

▶ *Review and amend bylaws every two years.* This assures that they are up-to-date with current regulations and that they reflect current board thinking on attendance, board selection, standing committees, officers, etc.

▶ *Ensure compliance with funding source's policies and regulations.* Every not-for-profit has at least one major source of fund-ing: government, United Way, foundations. Every funding source has a different way of monitoring expenses and auditing past work. When you sign a contract to take someone's money, you also agree to comply with their regulations. These may include such diverse items as having a drug-free workplace, not discriminating in employment, or keeping all records related to the contract for five years. Read the fine print before you sign, then make sure that you can meet all of the provisions. If you are a board member, and you don't fulfill your contractual obligation, it's your head on the platter.

▶ *Establish personnel policies and monitor their compliance.* Organizations have people problems more often than any other kind. Have good personnel policies, review them every two years with a professional, and build in checks and balances to ensure that they are followed *to the letter every time.*

▶ *Nominate and elect officers.* Most bylaws have the board do this function at the annual meeting.

▶ *Represent the organization in public* within the constraints of the media policy.

▶ *Help recruit new board members.* The board needs to replenish itself. Good recruitment calls for a board/staff partnership, but board involvement is key.

▶ *Oversee fundraising and/or raise funds.* Not all boards take active roles in fundraising. That may be left to a committee, or it may not now be a significant source of income.

▶ *Perform volunteer program work.* If the organization has a volunteer component, I strongly urge board members to at least try some hands-on volunteer work to get to know the organization better. Sometimes it is an integral part of the leadership track.

D. STAFF RESPONSIBILITIES TO THE BOARD

As with any other relationship, "it takes two". Staff have to support the board if the board is to be effective; it is not only the board that must contribute to the overall relationship. What follows are the minimal expectations that the board should have of its staff.

▶ *The board should expect accurate, timely, honest, and focused information.* The board needs to be able to rely totally on the staff to provide it with honest and unbiased information and to provide that well in advance of meetings. The hired staff are professionals, and the board should solicit their advice and ideas. Too often, I see board members who want "just the facts, ma'am," like the Dragnet cops, and feel that if they ask for any suggestions from staff they will be overrun. I disagree. The board hired the staff as the paid experts. Let staff contribute to the discussion, but make sure that everyone is aware that the board has the final say.

▶ *The board should be regularly informed of new developments.* As the paid experts, the staff needs to inform the board of new developments in the organization as well as in the field in which the organization operates, such as health care or special education.

▶ *The board should expect staff to gather information, analyze, and make recommendations to the board.* The staff should be technical advisors to the board. As noted above, the staff must be the responsible conduit of information to the board. The staff also need to focus the board on what is essential. Here the staff walk a very thin line, one where they are right on the edge of controlling rather than assisting. If the only information that they provide the board is self-serving, or only supports the staff position, the staff has not done their job. In fact, they have violated their trust.

▶ *The board should expect staff to report fiscal information regularly.* We had a not-for-profit organization a few years ago in my home town that went out of business very suddenly. Staff (over 100) came to work one morning to find the doors locked with a sign saying, "Out of Business". The organization had run out of money and no one—other than the Executive Director and the Financial Manager, both staff members—had known it was in trouble. It was a major scandal for our small town and when I ran into some of the board members, I asked them what had happened. Their (admittedly lame) excuse was that they had not seen financials for a year! I had no sympathy for the board members, none at all. Not providing regular (as in monthly) financials, annual budgets, and cash flow projections to the board is totally unprofessional for staff. Board members, if financials stop being regular, start *demanding* them. This is cause for *extreme* concern and urgency of action. Find out what is going on and accept no excuses. You need to see the financials.

▶ *The board should encourage staff to make optimum use of the board as a resource.* The staff have a responsibility to be familiar with the skills, connections, and talents of the board and to make use of these to the best interest of the organization.

▶ *The board should expect staff to develop a process for and to educate all new board members, and to orient all board members on an ongoing basis.* As noted earlier, board members only come to one or two meetings (including committee meetings) a month, so they need regular orientation in addition to their initial overview of the agency.

▶ *The board should expect staff to provide support for board recruitment and development.* The process I lay out later in this chapter will demonstrate a board/staff partnership in this key area.

▶ *The board should expect staff to support board committees and provide them with the information and expertise they need.* Just as with the board as a whole, someone needs to provide support to the committees, to get them information, and provide technical assistance and advice.

▶ *The board should expect staff to attend all meetings of the board unless excused.* I am also a strong supporter of board meetings being open to staff—it breaks down the mythical barrier between the board and staff and lets staff know what goes on. I am also a strong advocate of staff, other than just the executive director, making presentations to the board. For example, the financial manager can present the financials, the program director can present items about the programs, etc.

There is a great deal on both plates, but if the staff do their part, and the board does its part, the relationship will truly benefit the organization.

E. BOARD MEMBERS' LEGAL LIABILITIES

In addition to a long list of responsibilities, boards also have legal liabilities as a result of their board membership. Board members are fiduciaries—defined as a person, association, or corporation that has a duty to act for another in a specified area—and as such they have a fiduciary responsibility to the organizations they serve. In financial terms, this means that board members are responsible for the proper utilization, management, or investment of property and other assets placed in their trust. They are legally responsible for the management and control of the organization—and the resulting actions or accidents.

This is a pretty heavy responsibility, but does not mean that a board member should worry about liability for every corporate loss or mishap that occurs. Most states protect the not-for-profit board member from liability for errors of judgment as long as he or she acts responsibly, in good faith, with the best interests of the corporation foremost.

All of this must be balanced with the board's overall role. As I have said repeatedly, the board should be interested in results, not details of operation. The board's involvement in programs and operations should be limited to setting overall policy and monitoring results, unless there are extenuating circumstances.

● **FOR EXAMPLE:** A medium-sized, not-for-profit school found that it was unable to pay its bills. In order to stay afloat, the director began borrowing heavily from employee withholding (FICA) taxes. The board had no idea this was going on until the Internal Revenue Service contacted the board president and demanded payment of the back taxes. By the time the board of directors took action the school had closed, and the few remaining assets had been liquidated to pay creditors. The IRS, of course, still wanted its money. They took the board to court to pursue the payment of the taxes by the fiduciaries, arguing that the board members were ultimately responsible for the financial actions or inactions of the organization. The lawsuits dragged on for years and there was always the nagging concern that the board members would be held personally liable for the organization's outstanding debts. The answer? Yes, they would, and to the tune of thousands of dollars for each board member.

This is not a scenario you want to repeat. But it is a true story, and one that I hear repetitions of annually. To avoid this and other embarrassments, you need to be aware there are two common violations of fiduciary duties (or of being prudent):

1. Failure to follow fundamental management principles. This happens when a decision is made that a prudent person would not make if provided the same information. It occurs when a board:

▶ *Doesn't develop plans or budgets.*
▶ *Doesn't read staff reports to see if there are problems.*
▶ *Doesn't pay attention to problems raised in reports.*
▶ *Doesn't demand a reasonable standard of reporting and control (like the board of the organization that went out of business overnight).*
▶ *Ignores repeated warnings from staff, volunteers, or outside experts.*
▶ *Does not attend meetings.*

2. Operating the organization in a way that benefits the board members directly. This is known as self-dealing or inurement of benefit. You need to have strong conflict of interest policies and enforce them.

F. AVOIDING LIABILITY

Let's focus on some proven ways to avoid liability:

▶ First, if you are a board member, take your responsibility as a board member seriously. Come to the meetings, read the material in advance, and be willing to ask questions.

▶ Take the time to read and understand the organization's bylaws and mission and act in accordance with these documents. If actions conflict with either the bylaws or the mission, speak out.

▶ Stay informed of what is going on within the organization's programs and administration.

▶ Set policies only after reviewing the facts carefully. Never make decisions in a vacuum; demand documentation.

▶ Read the financial statements before each meeting. Demand a format that can be understood, and training in how to use the reports in your role as a board member.

▶ Make sure that your organization has a long-range (three- to five-year) plan and that board and staff contribute to its creation and revisions.

▶ Make sure that minimum statutory or technical requirements are met: filing annual reports, timely payment of withholding taxes, contracting with a CPA for an independent audit of the agency's books annually, meeting the legal and regulatory requirements of the agency's funding sources, etc.

▶ Demand minutes from all meetings that list who voted which way on all significant items. List dissenting members by name.

▶ Adopt and enforce a conflict of interest policy that discourages any business transactions between directors and the corporation, unless conducted openly and with stringent safeguards.

▶ Know the state laws regulating voluntary organizations to ensure compliance. The board's attorney should review these laws closely to determine how the state handles the issue of board members' liability. A report to the board should be made on these issues.

Following these suggestions should greatly reduce the risk that board members face and make it an acceptable risk for them to continue service on the board.

Finally, remember that many states have laws that reduce the board members' individual liability for actions taken in good faith. Make a good faith effort, and you will be in much better shape.

RECAP

In this chapter we have set the stage for building a better board of directors for your organization. You have learned about what makes an effective board, and the barriers to that effectiveness. We have reviewed the responsibilities of the board to the organization, and listed the expectations that the board should have of the staff. We also went over the legal liabilities of the board and suggested ways to reduce and avoid liability.

Having a board that meets the demands of your organizations is essential. But how do you find out what kind of board you really need? Once you know, how do you recruit those people, and more importantly, retain them on the board for years to come? All of those important questions are answered in the next chapter, where I'll show you how to build a better board.

6. Building a Better Board

OVERVIEW

Now that we know the things that a board should do, and how it can be the most effective, what kind of board should you have? Many not-for-profits are happy simply to fill the available slots, never going beyond the basic membership criteria that their bylaws may require. But there is more that you can do. To get the most out of the board as a resource, you need to have the people on the board that the organization needs now, and for the coming years. These needs will change as the organization grows and matures, and the board recruitment program needs to change as well.

Also, you need to find the best board members, and keep them on the board for their full terms. You invest time (and thus money) in orienting and educating board members, and you want to get a good return on that investment.

In this chapter I will show you how to figure out the board that you need, how to predict when the needs will occur, and how to develop a consistent and successful recruitment program. I'll also show you why your board members serve, and how to meet their needs and wants to keep your board full. Finally, we'll look at how to develop an effective committee structure, what committees you should have at a minimum, and how to support them.

By the end of this chapter, you will know how to build a better board and, by doing that, you will strengthen your organization and your ability to do your mission.

A. TYPES OF BOARD MEMBERS

Let's turn our attention to the kind of board you want to have. To do that, we need to first examine the kinds of board members you currently have. I have grouped them into the following categories for the sake of discussion. Each category pertains to the main function that these people *want* to serve.

FUNDRAISING. Primarily concerned with seeking donations in the community. Leaves most management and policy decisions to the staff. Loves to run fundraising events of all types. Gets satisfaction from the amounts raised. You need these people on your board, even if you don't get a great deal of your income from donations today. In later chapters I will argue that you should have an endowment, and then you will need them badly.

MANAGEMENT BY DETAIL. Wants to be involved in the day-to-day (and sometimes hour-to-hour) management of the organization. Must be informed of each and every decision and activity. These people can be the death of an organization, unless it is in the startup phase.

POLICY. Primarily concerned with the overall policies of the organization and how it is run. Not usually involved in day-to-day activities of the organization. Find these folks and work to keep them as long as your bylaws will allow.

PROGRAM ZEALOTS. Passionately concerned with the programs of the organization, sometimes to the exclusion of all other considerations, including funding, political concerns, and compromise. These people are hell in budget discussions where resources are allocated, but they are indispensable if you need to lobby a government agency for new or increased funds.

TITULAR. Primarily on the board for name recognition and "clout" on letterhead. Hardly ever take the time to come to meetings. These people you can no longer afford. They are liable for actions taken in their absence. It's not fair to you or to them. Get them off.

WARM BODY. Primarily come to board meetings because they think they should, or because over the years it has become habit. No active involvement in policy, promotion, or program. These members often are recruited to fill generic slots, not because of their interest. They sit at the meetings and vote "aye" to any motion, look blankly at the financial reports, and then may ask a question totally unrelated to the issue at hand. Again, these people take up valuable seats. Get them off.

The point here? That board members serve for differing reasons, and you need to be aware of who is there for what. Additionally, board members come to fill certain of their own needs and wants. So what are those wants, and how do you fill them? Again, I've put the wants of members into broad categories.

B. BOARD MEMBER WANTS

RECOGNITION/STATUS. If your organization is well-known and/ or respected—a goal every not-for-profit should have—serving on your board may be a mark of distinction and prestige. Also, some people serve to meet people for future sales for their own business. For example, some insurance firms encourage agents to get on three not-for-profit boards as a way of making contacts for future sales.

OBLIGATION. This person may be obliged to serve by reason of employment. For example, many banks strongly "encourage" their lending officers to be on boards as a way of underscoring their (the banks') good citizenship.

GENERAL SOCIAL PURPOSE. This person may serve to satisfy his or her desire to help the community at large. These people need to feel that their contribution (whether fundraising or policy) is real and is affecting the social good.

FOCUSED SOCIAL PURPOSE. This person is a strong advocate of either your particular services or your particular clientele. An excellent example is the parent of a retarded child serving on the board of an agency that serves persons with retardation. Or it could be a former staff person who has left the organization, but is still very committed to the cause. These people often come with a great deal of information and knowledge in your field, but can also slip into "program zealotry" (see above).

DESIRE TO GET BOARD EXPERIENCE. This person may be interested in understanding board dynamics and the operation of your agency.

Whatever the wants of your board members are, find out and meet those wants as much as you can. That's the way to keep them coming to board meetings.

C. BUILDING A BETTER BOARD

Now that you understand why your board members come to serve, how can you build a better board? First, you need to look at the needs you have in terms of expertise on the board. Then you should assess when those needs will become critical. For example, if you have, in your strategic plan, a goal to add a new building in three years, within a year you need to recruit a board member with construction experience, and perhaps someone who can help you through the maze of financing options.

Finally, you need to develop and implement a recruitment program that fills slots in an orderly and planned manner.

In assessing the type of board member expertise you need, you should pay attention to three things:

1. *Your organization's current programs (what you are now).*
2. *Your strategic plan (what you want to be in three to five years).*
3. *Your funding sources' regulations (what the payers require).*

The criteria of need can be objective, such as "race", "age", or "county of residence", or subjective, such as "community leader" or "political connections". The following checklist allows you to:

1. *Assess those criteria important to you.*
2. *Add your own criteria.*
3. *Assess your current status.*

Use the checklist as the basis to assess your recruitment needs.

CHARACTERISTIC/ EXPERTISE	ON BOARD ?	NEED THIS SKILL			
		NOW	1 Year	2 Years	3 Years
GENDER					
ETHNICITY (various)					
FUNDER'S MANDATE					
AGE GROUP (various)					
LOCATION (county, city, etc)					
ADVOCATE					
LEGISLATIVE					
CLERGY					
CUSTOMER					
LEGAL					
ACCOUNTING					
FINANCE/BANKING					
MARKETING					
PERSONNEL					
CONSTRUCTION					
FUNDRAISING					
SMALL BUSINESS					

As you can see from the checklist, the types of board members that you will need vary greatly and can change over time. I served on a board that, at the time I joined, had no one with finance, architectural, or building skills, and yet the organization had just acquired a 60-bed residential facility and was planning on buying or renting 20 small homes within the coming five years. We needed people with those skills and recruited them. Eight years later, as I went off the board, the skills needs had changed again from property acquisition and financing, to fundraising, marketing, and property management. Your needs will change too. Don't make your categories for board service static. Review them regularly, at the same time you review your strategic plan.

D. BOARD RECRUITMENT

Now that you have established the board that you want, and the schedule on which you will recruit those skills, you will need to organize a consistent recruitment program to constantly be prospecting for high quality board members. As I noted above, the quality of the board member is as important as the "slot" she or he fills.

There are five keys to good board recruitment and retention:

1. CONSISTENT RECRUITMENT.

This means that you don't just deal with board recruitment the week before the Nominations Committee meets, or the afternoon before the annual meeting. Finding quality volunteers to sit on your policy-setting board is a constant job, and the process should encourage consistent effort.

2. THE RECRUITMENT EFFORT IS A JOINT BOARD/STAFF TASK.

Board members need to be involved in the job of recruiting and assessing potential board candidates. So do staff. The effort should be split between the two groups, but if both aren't involved, the outcome will not be optimal.

3. PROVIDE WELL-DEFINED AND CLEARLY STATED EXPECTATIONS OF THE BOARD MEMBERS.

There is no substitute for clearly stating to potential board members the expectations of them. That way, if they don't feel that they can meet those expectations, they can decline an offer to serve, and save you the trouble of recruiting another person later. Examples of such expectations would be:

▶ *You must attend 10 of 12 monthly meetings.*
▶ *You must serve on one board committee (most meet monthly) after your first six months on the board.*
▶ *We expect you to read your board mailings before you come to the meeting.*
▶ *You must work at our annual XYZ (fundraising) event, and either sell 20 tickets or donate $100 dollars yourself.*

4. ENFORCEMENT OF THESE EXPECTATIONS.

Having rules and then not enforcing them is a waste of time, effort, and political capital. If you have these expectations, and board members can't or won't meet them, let them know that they will either be voted off the board, or not nominated for renewal. When you let people know in advance, and in writing, about your expectations, then there is little area for them to complain. That doesn't mean that they won't complain or that "firing" a board member is ever easy. It's not, particularly if your culture has not enforced any expectations on them in the past.

5. EVALUATION OF RECRUITMENT EFFORTS.

How many of the available board slots did you fill? Did you double up on the important ones? How many of your recruits stayed the first full year? How do you know these things? You track your efforts. As with any good process, you learn from your mistakes only if you know about them. You can build on your successes, but only if you are aware of them. Evaluate, evaluate, evaluate.

E. BOARD ORIENTATION AND EDUCATION

1. ORIENTATION

There are some essential parts of good orientation.

First, and unlike the way that most organizations orient board, orientation should be a never-ending discipline. It should occur at every board meeting and, in the best-run organizations, extends to brief, focused discussions at committee meetings as well. However, the process does have to start somewhere, and that somewhere is at the interview for potential candidates. At that time, not only does the future board member get an oral briefing on programs, funding, and philosophy, he or she should also get that key document: the board manual. After someone is elected to the board, they should get a number of things provided in addition to the board manual: the current budget, the most recent two audits, the last three or four monthly financial statements, and all of the organization's promotional material. If you also want to provide information on key funding sources, fine.

Second, new board members need a personal oral orientation to the organization. That usually means a tour of the facility(ies), hopefully at the time that actual services are being provided. The board member may also choose (or be required) to serve as a volunteer for a short time as a hands-on practicum. A week or so after the tour, the board member should be called to see what questions have popped up.

☞ **HANDS ON:** One technique that I have seen work is to assign a senior staff person (not the executive director), and one veteran board member to each new board member as their "buddies" for six months. These people sit with the new member at the meetings, take them to lunch once or twice to check on whether they are getting what they need, are available by phone to chat, etc. It's a method to increase the likelihood of meeting the new member's wants and assuring that problems or questions are resolved early. This buddy system does not need to last long—three to six months—but it really works.

Third, make sure that at their first meeting, the board people are introduced to everyone. That's the job of the board president.

2. THE BOARD MANUAL

The board manual (I don't like the term "orientation manual" because board members should regularly return to this document for reference—even after they are veterans) provides board members with an organized, single reference source for questions about your organization. It should include at least the following:

▶The organization's bylaws and charter.
▶The organization's Mission Statement.
▶A table of organization with a listing of all key staff people and a brief description of what they do for the agency (DON'T send job descriptions unless requested).
▶A list of current board members with their addresses, place of employment and title, work and home phone numbers, what officer or committee chair positions they hold.

▶A list of the board committees, with a listing of current members and a brief explanation of what the committees do.

▶A flow chart of funding, where it comes from, where it goes. Pie charts are particularly good for this purpose.

▶A list of programs with a two-sentence description of each program.

▶A listing of frequently-used acronyms/jargon and their meaning.

▶A list of board responsibilities (adapted from earlier in this chapter).

▶A list of staff responsibilities (adapted from earlier in this chapter).

▶A list of officer responsibilities (see next section).

F. COMMITTEES OF THE BOARD

As we noted earlier, you need a structure of committees to make the board work. The full board does not have the time to review every single issue in detail. Thus, the board needs to delegate the "grunt" work to the committees. Your organization needs to determine what type of committees it needs to serve your board of directors. Some committees may outlive their usefulness over time. Others, such as your Finance Committee, will always be needed. Standing committees are those committees that are established on a permanent basis and may be described in the bylaws. Ad hoc committees are those assigned to carry out specific functions, make recommendations to the entire board, and then disband.

It is important to note that committee membership does not need to be solely comprised of board members. Committee members can also come from the pool of potential board members and from persons who have a specific interest in helping the organization. This is an excellent training ground for board membership.

1. AN EFFECTIVE COMMITTEE STRUCTURE CAN:

▶ provide expertise to the board by gathering a group of experts on a given subject in a committee where they can share ideas and make recommendations based on the issues at hand.

▶ alleviate the board's dealing with every detail of operation. Working committees take assignments from the board, deal with them effectively, and return with solutions to recommend to the board. Committees will also come before the board with ideas and recommendations that their committee members have developed.

▶ permit broader participation by all board members.

The president, in consultation with the executive director, should make all committee assignments based on each board member's expertise, special talents, and personal preference. This should be done on an annual basis. Each board member should know several weeks before the first board meeting of the year which committee(s) he or she will serve on for the year. Board members should be notified in writing on which committee they will serve, who the chairman is, when and where the committee usually meets, and who the other committee members will be.

> ☞ **HANDS ON:** Some board members will not be happy with their committee assignments. One way to solve this is to ask each board member which committee they would prefer to serve on before the decision is made. At the last board meeting of the year, provide each board member with a written checklist of available committee assignments that must be returned to the president by the deadline noted. (Make it clear that it is not always possible to place them on the committee of their choice, but every effort will be made to do so. If they do not submit the form by the deadline noted, their assignment will be made by the president.) Then, based on this and the organization's needs, make assignments.

As we noted in our discussion of board responsibilities, every board member should serve on at least one committee. Don't, however, ask new members to serve right away. Let them ease into their duties for five or six months and then give them an assignment. Try to keep committee membership small and focused. Five to nine people seems to work well for most groups. An odd number of members provides a tie-breaker if you need it.

Finally, I recommend having all committee appointments be one year in length. That way, the president and the committee chair can constantly be improving the committees, adjusting to the changes on the board, on the staff, and in the industry. This does not mean that a particular board member might not serve on one particular committee for six years it just ensures the maximum flexibility for the president.

2. WHAT COMMITTEES NEED TO OPERATE

Committees, like boards, need certain things to operate effectively and efficiently. As I have noted repeatedly, an effective committee structure is crucial to an effective board, so staff need to assure that the following elements are present:

> ▶ A clear understanding of the committee's role and what its limitations are.

▶ Quality, supportive staffing.

▶ A committee chairperson who is:
   * *a leader*
   * *knowledgeable*
   * *experienced in group leadership*
   * *able to encourage participation by all committee members*
   * *capable of facilitating a meeting and keeping members on track without inhibiting valuable new discussion*
   * *able to bring the group to a timely conclusion and/or a decision.*

▶ Committee members who:
   * *complete their assignments on time*
   * *do their homework between meetings*
   * *are reasonable and thoughtful*
   * *understand the importance and impact of their decisions.*

One last suggestion on committees. If you find that committee reports to the board are simply the basis for rehashing everything at length again, you are not using your committee structure well. I understand that some critical issues will deserve a great deal of board attention and time, but if you see that you are simply holding the committee meeting over again at the board meeting, work to cut short the debate and have the board accept or reject committee recommendations, not reinvent them. One technique that works well for board members who feel the need to know everything about everything is to invite them (in public at the board meeting) to attend the committee meetings and have input there.

RECAP

In these two chapters we have reviewed the ways to strengthen your most underutilized resource: the board of directors. I have tried to offer suggestions on ways to get the board you need, and to keep the board members involved by giving them what they want, how to develop and maintain a working recruitment process, and how to develop meaningful committee structures.

In other chapters we will refer to the importance of the board, how financial reporting to the board should be done, and how staff can market to and with the board. We'll also cover the policies that the board should help adopt and enforce, and how the board should be involved in strategic planning and social entrepreneuring.

The importance of the board to an effective not-for-profit cannot be overstated. You need to utilize the board as a resource: it will help you get more mission for your money which is the ultimate bottom line.

Finally, if your board "culture" is not even close to the one described in this chapter, you need to make a decision as to whether you want to change it now, later, or ever. Making major cultural changes in a volunteer body is never easy, nor is it painless. For staff, there is always a concern about their own job if they "shake up" the board too much. All of that is understandable and needs to be taken into account.

I guarantee that if you can incorporate the board functions and outlook described here, you will have a more effective board, but it is up to you to decide whether that should be your primary area of change, or whether you need to attend to the other issues described in this book first.

7. Managing Your People

OVERVIEW

An essential component of successful not-for-profits is building and retaining a strong staff, one that knows the mission, knows the field of endeavor that the organization is embarked on, and manages all of its resources to accomplish the mission. These resources, of course, include the mission and the board, but they also include volunteers, the cash and fixed plant of the organization and, of course, the staff, which is the subject of this chapter.

In the following pages I will walk you through the information you need to become a more effective manager of your staff, valuing and empowering them. We'll look at a management style that is literally upside-down, and at some competing management styles and their advantages and disadvantages. We'll look long and hard at ways to communicate better. I'll show you some new thoughts on delegation, how to double your outcomes in evaluations, and how to set up a staff reward program that really rewards rather than punishes. By the end of the chapter, you will have a clearer understanding of how to manage that irreplaceable asset, your staff.

First, some facts to set the framework from which I will advise you. As I noted in the second chapter, you are increasingly going to be in competition for good staff. I don't need to tell any of you who try to hire occupational, physical, or speech therapists about that kind of competition, but in most other fields it is true as well. Second, you can't pay, and probably never will, like the private sector, whether for a secretary, a driver, a line staff person, or an administrator. Thus, you have to give folks who work with you something more than just a check to keep them coming to work for you.

To a certain extent this something is your mission statement, and we discussed this at length in Chapter 4. But beyond that, it is your culture, the way you and all the staff treat each other and hang in there together as a team that will keep people wanting to be employed by your organization.

A. THE INVERTED PYRAMID OF MANAGEMENT

So how to do all of these things and still maintain your role in management? How do you treat people well and motivate them to produce at the highest levels every day? There is a way to do this that is not rocket science, and is well-tested by some of the best organizations in the world, both for-profit and not-for-profit. It goes by many names, but I like to call it the *inverted pyramid.*

Managing by inverted pyramid style should not be foreign to the not-for-profit culture. It means that you value the people you serve the most, and that the people who provide them the direct service (your line staff) are the most important staff. Inverted pyramid managers realize that without line staff, they would not have a job (no one to manage), and that even the *executive director's* job is to find, manage, and facilitate the application of resources so that line staff can do *their* job.

The term inverted pyramid comes from the organizational chart that most organizations have. Yours may currently look like this:

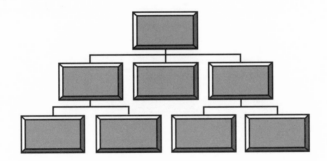

In this organizational model, the executive director is at the top of the heap, with associate or assistant directors, and assorted middle management between the exec and the line staff, who are portrayed at the bottom of the pile.

This style of hierarchical management was developed for the military and for large corporations when mass production, mass control, and rigid lines of authority were in vogue. It has continued to this day for a number of reasons:

▶ *It shows the executive director on top—in the classic dominating and control position.* Think of all of the language we use about our careers: "Climbing up the ladder", "getting to the top", "top dog", etc. All of these refer to and reinforce our vision of being atop the heap, king or queen of the mountain. It emphasizes dominance.

▶ *It puts staff in a subservient position.* In this organizational chart, the staff have to "look up" to the exec, again emphasizing dominance of one person over the other.

Now, what is *not* on this chart? A number of things that are very important. First, I rarely see traditional organizational charts where the people an organization *serve* are mentioned. They are assumed, but not shown and the place where they are assumed to be is at the bottom of the pile. These people are the patrons, patients, clients, students, parishioners of a not-for-profit—the most important people in the organization—the recipients of the mission. Second, there is no value placed on the most important staff—the staff that interact with those clients, parishioners, students, etc., every day. Third, this chart symbolizes management as a controlling function rather than as a supporting one.

Let's examine the same chart in the fashion that I would have you use.

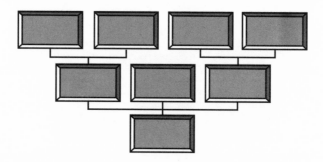

Note that the box that the executive director would occupy is at the bottom, and the line staff at the top, with the people that you serve at the very top. This symbolism (and that is all it is if you don't live this style of management all the time) is important, because many organizations need to rethink what is the most important thing that they do, who is most important, and where their internal priorities are.

Let's look at the major tenets of my version of the inverted pyramid, and then examine some examples.

▶ *The only reason there are staff is because there are people to serve.*
▶ *The only reason there are managers is because the staff doing the service need support.*

The executive director is not the most important person in the not-for-profit. He or she may be the most *powerful*, but not the most important.

If all staff realize that management exists to find and manage resources that allow line staff to do their jobs, then the priorities become much clearer, the roles begin to change a bit, and the organization starts to head in the correct direction.

▶ *Managers are enablers, not "restricters".*

Good management should be a supportive, assistive function rather than a harsh power game, telling people why they can't do things. As an enabler, your role is to support your staff in accomplishing the goals of the organization. This support means doing what it takes to get the job done. It includes fighting for resources for your people, fixing things that aren't right, getting distractions large and small out of the way, and participating in budget and planning activities, no matter what your level in the organization. This fundamental principle allows you to see your job in very human terms. Your job as a supervisor is to take some of the load off of the people who you supervise and let them do their jobs.

▶ *The supervisor/supervised relationship is two-way.*

The relationships you develop with your staff, like any other relationship, are two-way. That means that both the supervisor and the supervised have a responsibility to make things work. Additionally, the supervisor—instead of spending time restricting and controlling—should be facilitating getting resources to the employees providing the service. As we all know, relationships will not work if you always talk and never listen, if you only give ideas and are never receptive to those of your staff, or if you make all the decisions and don't delegate. More on these later.

▶ *Treat others the way you would want to be treated.*

Honesty, fairness, and consistency are the key characteristics of a successful manager. Honesty means not promising to do something you cannot deliver ("I'll get back to you on that tomorrow"); fairness means treating all of your staff equally (what goes for Sam has to go for Sally); and consistency means asking for rules to be followed and then enforcing them when you say you will. Say what you mean and mean what you say.

▶ *Be a leader, but willing to follow.*

This means that you are a leader who takes risks on behalf of your staff. It also means you let your staff take the lead when they are right. (This happens more than you or I want to admit.) It also means being very human and part of the team, so that you pitch in and do the most menial task when it is necessary to help support your staff. If there is a rush item to get out, like a mailing, and everyone is hustling around, pitch in: stuff envelopes, run copies, lug boxes, drive the van. We all know that you are very busy, but these small efforts go a long way with staff people; they remember them and it makes you more accessible to them.

▶ *If you are going to help your staff, you need to keep in touch.*

Knowing what is going on with your line staff has never been more important. The further you are from line work, the more important it is. Make the time to work with line workers. My rule is one day per quarter at the very least, and more if the size and locations that you operate allow it. This task (which too many managers think is a waste of time) is, in truth, an essential component of the job. The most popular term for this was coined by Peters and Waterman in *In Search of Excellence*. They called it "Management by Wandering Around". They talked about keeping in touch by being on-site, on the factory floor or at the place that service is being provided. In addition to just being there, I have seen over and over the positive effects of having management do some line work at regular intervals.

> ☞ **HANDS ON:** Do a monthly stint as a volunteer, a quarterly day as a line worker, or simply have breakfast or lunch with line staff once a week. You've got to keep in touch with your people, and that means starting by understanding what they do. For example, if you run a hospital, work as a security guard, or as a volunteer who greets new patients for a day. If you run a human service organization, open a case, be a meals-on-wheels driver, sit in on an encounter or support group. If you run a school, teach an hour a week or a day a month as guest teacher. The essential philosophy: This is *not* taking time away from your job, *THIS IS AN ESSENTIAL PART OF YOUR JOB!!!* You will learn more about your organization, how it really runs, and what staff really need to get the mission accomplished than you would ever believe.
>
> Many of the senior staff at McDonald's work one week a year behind the counter at a restaurant, to keep in touch. It doesn't matter that most of them worked at a Mac's as a teenager, they need to work on-site *now* to know what works and what doesn't *now*.

▶ *When you and your staff are praised, pass it around. When you are criticized, take the fall.*

You are responsible for the results of both you and your staff. But, when someone praises you (individually or as a group), pass the praise on directly: "Well, thank you, Mayor, for those kind words, but I am just the exec. The real work, and thus the real praise, should go to our outreach staff." Pass the praise around.

Also, go out of your way to compliment deserving individual and group efforts. Positive reinforcement is always appreciated. This can be constant and informal or may include employee recognition, which we'll discuss later in this chapter.

The reverse is true when you are criticized—as an individual or as your part of the organization. If you are the head person, you take the fall. Never, ever, ever, blame someone else. There are three reasons for this. First, even if whatever went wrong is really not your fault, you are in charge. The captain on the bridge is responsible for the actions of his or her people. Second, nothing you do will bring more loyalty or build more morale than stepping in front of the blame bullet for your staff people."Well, (board president,) I know we missed the deadline. I'm doing all I can to minimize the damage, and I've already apologized to the effected people. It won't happen again."

Finally, it's always easy to blame your staff for something that doesn't go right. But remember, *it really may be your fault*, as a result of your not clearly communicating instructions or picking the wrong person to complete a task. We'll look at delegation and communications in a few pages.

The inverted pyramid works, slowly but surely. However, to make it work, it has to be *lived*, every day in every way. Once you set yourself up as believing this philosophy, it is easy to fall off the pedestal. If you just flip your organizational chart on its head and don't follow it up with real and consistent actions to support the concept, you will lose ground with your staff.

With those tenets in mind, let's look at a couple of applications of the principal of the inverted pyramid and how it works.

● **FOR EXAMPLE:** My wife Chris is a special education teacher in our local public school district, assigned to one of the 5th-6th grade centers. All teachers are required to come in for planning days and meetings a few days before the children return in the fall, and these are not days that most teachers look forward to. The schools are still hot, the meetings are dull, the kids are not yet there, and there is too much to get done in too short a time.

This particular fall, Chris went in for her planning days with even more trepidation. The 5-6 Center she was assigned to was new, she knew only some of the staff and didn't know the principal at all, although she had heard through the grapevine that the principal was "incredible".

After her first day of meetings, Chris came home, totally pumped up and excited. She almost couldn't tell me the story fast enough. "It was incredible. Our principal (Phyllis) was amazing. She came into our first all-faculty meeting and said:

'I am the principal here, but I am not the boss. I am the person who assures that you get the resources you need and the necessary environment to allow you to teach to your maximum potential. You, as teachers, are what this school is all about: teaching children. My job is to get you the resources you need, as well as remove the distractions you don't need. If you need supplies, see me and I'll get them. If you need a disruptive child removed from the room, I'll do it. If you can't get parental support, I'll help you. My job is not to sit on you, it is to help you teach.' "

Chris went on: "You could have heard a pin drop. No one had ever been talked to by a principal like that before. I actually heard our union rep say as we walked out, 'Who needs money if we're treated like that?' "

Chris has taught at that school for four years as of this writing, and Phyllis has done everything she said and more. She is everywhere at once, talking to kids, encouraging teachers, giving praise, getting resources, helping out when teachers are sick, sending handwritten thank-you notes for exceptional work. When Chris was in the hospital, Phyllis was there for her, and the first to offer to help me with our kids.

The school is a great place to learn. Not only do kids like it there, but the kids' test scores are up, there are innovative teaching techniques being tried, and parents from other 5-6 centers are trying to get their kids transferred.

This example shows what can be done in a short time with a commitment of one person. Admittedly, Phyllis had a clean slate (a new faculty) to start with, but she also had to overcome tradition, past morale problems, and inertia. She did it by letting the teachers know in word and deed that she valued them as professionals and as individuals. What more do any of us really want?

● **FOR EXAMPLE:** As a result of my work, I travel a great deal. I usually stay in hotels that are the choice of the conference planners at the conventions where I speak, or at hotels close to clients with whom I am consulting. In both cases, someone else decides where I stay.

When I am lucky enough to check in to a Marriott I know that everything will work, that I will be treated like a valued customer, and that whatever I need will be provided. This is particularly important when I am conducting training, as I need to assure that the overhead projector, microphone, and room temperature all are working well (and in many places this is an iffy proposition at best), and that other last-minute details are attended to. What I don't want are hassles, bad attitudes, or to be told "can't" or "won't".

In the fifteen years that I have been travelling, I have probably stayed at 70 Marriotts, and I have never, ever, met anyone (bellhop, waitress, housekeeping staff, convention worker) who works in any of those hotels and who has not greeted me with a "Good morning, sir, how are you today?". And it was said like they meant it. I can recount dozens of times staff went out of their way to make me feel special or to willingly and immediately fix a small problem that I had. Like the night I arrived at one Marriott in Washington D.C. at 2:00 am after interminable travel delays, only to find that my reservation was for a different Marriott across town. What did the clerk do? Dismiss me and tell me to go elsewhere? No, first, he called the other hotel to assure that my room was still available, and then, sensing my exhaustion and frustration, offered me a room at "his" hotel—even though they had no rooms at my reserved rate. I gratefully accepted the latter offer, and five minutes later was escorted into a three-room suite, complete with fruit basket! Or the time I was off to a meeting and walked by a pleasant matronly housekeeping supervisor who greeted me with a cheery "Good morning", then told me to wait while she very tactfully straightened my tie, and added, "Go get 'em!" What a great way to start my day!

Both of these people made my stay memorable, by doing a little extra that they were both encouraged and empowered to do. The desk clerk had the authority to upgrade my reservation (or actually to give me one without a reservation), and the housekeeping staff person was simply motivated and pleasant.

Marriott as a corporation believes in the phrase of their CEO: *Take care of your employees and they will take care of you.* They constantly train and motivate their line staff, drilling into them the concept that they, and not the management, will make the hotel succeed or fail. They have the line people surface ideas on ways to make the guests more comfortable. The company invests in its people and it pays off.

Other examples abound in the proprietary world. When was the last time you met a curt or unfriendly UPS or Federal Express delivery person? Or talked to a brusque sales person from Land's End? You won't. Why? Because these organizations value their people, they tell them so all the time, and they show them by their actions. *All* of the staff at the Disney properties are provided "costumes"—not uniforms—and even the trash collectors at their parks go through a solid week of training in how to interact with customers *before* they get their trash collection training.

Think of each of these and other organizations like airlines, restaurants, and the like. Who do you deal with nearly all the time in these organizations? *The lowest paid people in the company.* At the airline, it's the ticket agent or the baggage clerk or the flight attendant. At a hotel, it's the concierge or bellhop or desk clerk. At a restaurant it's the greeter or server. It's these people who really shape your experience with the company. And, in successful companies, it is these people who are the most valued.

Who are these people in your organization? Who do your clients, donors, volunteers, and referral sources deal with most? If you are the exec (unless you are a one-person shop), it's probably not you. Treat the people who actually *do* the mission with respect, and you'll get a lot more out of them.

B. STYLES OF SUPERVISION

There are four broad categories of management style listed below. In truth, we all fit into at least one, and probably more than one at various times. As you read these, think about how each does or does not fit into our inverted pyramid model.

▶ *Attila the Hun*

We've all worked for Attila, or a direct descendant. This person is *the* boss. No question about it. He or she maintains a "directing behavior", lays down the law and expects it to be followed to the letter. He or she looks at their staff as stepping stones *up* the management ladder. "Attila" is quick to criticize and judge and has never heard of the words "thank you". Attila is obeyed but usually not respected. Attila also gets results, at least in the short term, but when Attila is not present, a great deal of staff time is spent griping.

▶ *One of the Gang*

This manager usually comes "up from the ranks" but never adjusts to the new role. He or she wants to remain one of the gang so they try to minimize or eliminate the distinctions between them and their staff. They never understand that once they cross the bridge to become a supervisor, they never again are peers. They can still be friends with those that they supervise, but they can never be pals. This person has difficulty in completing performance appraisals, and usually cannot discipline at all. Morale is good if you work for one of the gang, but productivity tends to slip, as this person may be liked, but is hardly ever respected.

▶ *All Business*

This manager is thoroughly professional, but distant. He or she does not fraternize or socialize with the troops, and places great emphasis on plans, goals, objectives, budgets, and performance.They never take the time to truly get to know their people, and this is a key to good communications and effective delegation. I cannot envision this manager stuffing envelopes or filling in at the reception desk in a pinch.

▶ *Coach/Conductor*

Both a coach and an orchestra conductor get the job done, but through the actions of others. The coach and the conductor know that they don't play, that others do, and that their success is contingent upon the success of their team. He or she cajoles, praises, and disciplines when it is necessary. This manager exemplifies team spirit with enthusiasm, but maintains a long-term view of the organization. A coach/conductor helps his or her staff to grow and attain their maximum potential.

Obviously, I would prefer if all of us were coaches or conductors. But it would be naive to assume that everyone can adopt that style. Besides, in the real world, we all need to be Attila once in a while—hopefully for only short periods at long intervals! The most important thing is to adapt your style to let people know you value them. If you are demanding, fine, but be demanding of the right things: things that focus attention on mission and line staff and quality of outcome, not things that inflate your ego or make people cower before you.

Your style as a manager, as well as your priorities in terms of staff and mission, are inherent parts of bringing about the organizational direction that will allow you to succeed.

C. COMMUNICATIONS

To succeed with your staff, you will need to be able to communicate with them: to find out what they need to get their job done, to delegate tasks, plan budgets, figure out what to buy for lunch—all these things require good communications. It often seems that *Communication* is a five-syllable word meaning trouble; as in, "What we have here is a failure to communicate". I can hardly think of one of the not-for-profits that I have consulted with over the past ten years—even the well-run ones—who didn't complain about inadequate (or poor or awful) internal communications. This seems to be an area where everyone would like to see improvement (or is unsatisfied with the way things are now). Why?

There are a number of reasons. First, many people assume that they need to know everything that goes on in the organization. They don't, but that is irrelevant.They *feel* that they should be better informed, and thus will be discontented until they *feel* that they are being at least adequately informed. (Often these people will simultaneously complain about too many meetings, too many memos, and not enough time to do their "real" jobs.) The second reason is that many not-for-profits are changing quickly and growing rapidly. As a result the staff, particularly those who have been employed for a number of years, often feel that they "used to know everything and everyone around here" and now feel isolated. This problem is most acute if the organization has multiple buildings or sites.

Obviously, the issue of communications is essential, not only to good operational management, but also to good morale. Good communications is as much perception as reality, and it is based on the following tenets:

1. TRUST

If the staff don't trust the management to give them full, accurate, and timely information, the rest of these techniques are a waste of time. The staff people will still complain about the lack of communication from top management.

● **FOR EXAMPLE:** A client agency of mine was having problems with employee morale. The Executive Director had been on the job two years and had instituted a number of staff and organizational changes which I felt were terrific, but which had met with traditional resistance to change from many staff. This agency provided distinctly different services at two separate sites, and thus staff didn't all get to see each other a great deal.

The agency was planning to construct a new building to house some of its services. At the time the events described here occurred, the agency had developed architectural plans, had acquired a site, and had a date for the initiation of construction, and a target for completion. They also knew the budget, and which major components of the agency would move to the site upon completion.They were to build the building as a shell first, then later divide the shell into components to house various programs.

As soon as the site had been purchased, all staff who had not been in on the early planning were informed of the project. Approximately two weeks later, I was scheduled to come in to run some focus groups of staff to discuss the results of an employee survey that our firm had administered for the agency. In the survey, communications had come up over and over again as a real deficit in the management area.

During my discussions with staff, one staff person I'll call Linda and

I had the following conversation:

LINDA   "Senior Management never tells us anything 'til after the fact."

PCB   "Give me an example."

LINDA   "Well, take this new building we just heard about. We just haven't been told anything about the project, and it's important to us."

PCB   "Of course it is.   What did the management staff tell you specifically?"

LINDA   "Well, I know that the building is being built at the corner of Adams Street and 15th, and that it will house the Intake, Client Assessment, and Rehabilitation Divisions."

PCB   "Did they tell you anything else?"

LINDA   "No, nothing."

PCB   "No information on schedule, budgets or anything else?"

LINDA   "I do know that they are laying the foundation next week and that we are scheduled to occupy next April. I think my division will move in first."

PCB   "Sounds like you know everything there is to know about this project."

LINDA   "Well, they always tell us so late...."

You get the picture I'm sure. Linda did not trust the management staff, for whatever reason. And, no matter what the management people told her, no matter if she was included in senior management meetings, she would not be happy. If, however, she had trusted the senior management, she would have had a different outlook on the same information.

2. ALL COMMUNICATION IS *TWO-WAY*.

The most important part of communications is not what you say, but what your staff hears. It is not what you "send," but what your staff "receives". It is not what you "write," but what your staff "reads". All of us have the "mystery filter" in our houses; you know the one that comes between you and your spouse or you and your kids. It's the filter that comes between your mouth and their ears, and results in the conversation: "No, I didn't say *that*, what I said *was*, etc., etc. etc." There is little protection against poor communications, but we can do more to check on what people heard so that we correct the initial miscommunication.

☞ **HANDS ON:** To vividly demonstrate this to your management staff, try this exercise. At a staff meeting, read off the following list (exactly) *without warning*. Read it slowly and deliberately:

BED, REST, SLUMBER, SNOOZE, PILLOW, SHEET, NAP, MATTRESS, SNORE, DREAM.

Now ask the staff to write down as many as they can remember. Give them a minute or two. Ask how many people got 6 words (ask them to raise hands). Some will have gotten 6. Ask if anyone got 8. Compliment them. Ask who wrote down the word "BED", the first word you read. About half will have. Compliment them. Ask who wrote down "DREAM", the last word you read. About the same number will have. Now, and this is the key, ask those who wrote down the word "SLEEP" to raise their hands—and keep their hands up. If your group is like the dozens I've done this with, over half will have written down SLEEP, and *you never read it! Have everyone look around to see how many hands were raised.*

Make the point with your staff that the reason that they wrote down "sleep" was that they associated it with the rest of the words you read, and that they felt so strongly that they heard it, that they *wrote it down*. Now, if you were to have gone back to them in a week and asked for notes on what you said, they would have "proof" (documentation) that you said "SLEEP" because they wrote it down!

We need to assure that our instructions and communications are understood.

Let's examine the issue of communications from the viewpoint of results. When does one of your staff fail to complete a task correctly? When:

▶ *They don't know what they are supposed to do.* None of us is very good on this one. Think about it; you tell your staff something and then ask, "Do you understand?" or even worse, "You understand, don't you?" Now, who is going to say to his or her boss, in effect "No, I don't understand; I'm stupid."? We don't give people much of a chance to say no, or to ask for help.

▶ *They don't know how to do the task.* Same issues as above.

▶ *They think they are doing it right, but haven't received any feedback.* If you are not around to talk to or observe staff while they are working on the project, you can't guide them away from mistakes. Thus, little problems become big ones. If people are not given some supervision or have not been observed, the first time they do a job, they may very well, with good intentions, do it completely wrong, and in a way that could have been prevented if you had been around enough to catch the little mistake before it got to be a big one.

▶ *They don't know why they should complete the task.* The *why* is so important. Telling people *why* they need to do something puts it in context, it gives the assignment a rationale, a purpose, and a priority. In terms of accurate communications, think of the difference in the message sent by someone saying, "Please put together a spreadsheet of our cashflow projections" or saying, "Please put together a spreadsheet of our cashflow projections because I need to present them to the finance committee on Thursday night." The first assignment gives the bare bones. The second gives context, and would probably lead to a clearer, more complete (and neat) cashflow being presented. Tell people *why* something needs to be done. Don't assume that they don't care about the why. Let them make that choice.

▶ *They hear something different than what you say and you are not in control of what your staff hears.* Remember our list *without* the word "SLEEP"? Need I say more?

In order to get over the worst of these, when you give instructions to someone, particularly on something new, follow this order:

1. *Explain* how to do it.
2. *Demonstrate* how to do it (if possible).
3. *Request* an explanation of how to do it.
4. *Invite* the employee to demonstrate it for you (if possible).

Now, you can't just treat staff like little kids and say, "What did I just say?" in a condescending voice. But what you can do, is ask "Please tell me what we just agreed you'd do, so that I can make sure I didn't tell you wrong." In an inverted pyramid management scheme, and if you agree that you are responsible to get communications across, ask for feedback with the assumption that you have not communicated whatever needs to be communicated accurately or thoroughly. At the end of meetings, ask everyone at the table to reiterate what it is that they agreed to do at the meeting, and by when. Don't *you* tell them what they agreed to; you want to hear it in their words.

D. DELEGATION

There is enough good material on delegation to fill three shelves at your local library, and we all know that good managers are ones who delegate effectively, so I won't try to convince you that you should be delegating more. Rather, I'll try to pass on some ideas on how to delegate better. Delegation is particularly tough on first-time supervisors who still want to "do" rather than "manage". After all, if you hadn't been good at the "doing" you probably wouldn't have gotten promoted. But since you now are a supervisor, you have a different job, and not enough time to both do and supervise.

You need to delegate the jobs that your staff can do now or learn fairly quickly. To be successful, you need to attend to the following rules:

▶ *Delegate authority with responsibility.* This is critical: your employee must feel that she or he has the authority to decide as well as to do. If you require them to get back to you on every little detail, you might as well do it yourself, and your staff person will be very frustrated to boot. The further toward the line staff that decision authority can be pushed, the better.

▶ *Challenge your staff supportively.* Don't just give them a job, a deadline, and then kick them out the door of your office. Learn how to offer support and advice without having them lean on you for everything. Also, push them a bit, forcing them to try new tasks if you feel they can learn them. Back off in the level of supervision as quickly as you can, but let them know that you are there as a safety net.

▶ *Know your staff.* This is critical for good supervision, delegation, and communications. You just have to take the time to know your people. Learn their pitfalls. You have to have this information if you are going to use your people to their maximum potential. Being on-site and available allows you to know your people.

▶ *Recognize that mistakes will (and should) be made.* It's how we learn. Honest mistakes, honestly made are OK. Don't let people make the same mistake twice. Be reassuring and helpful, noting that you also have made your share of goof-ups. If people don't make mistakes, and don't learn, they won't ever grow. Adopt the maxim: "DO SOMETHING!" as your credo, and you'll have gone a long way toward better delegating.

▶ *Admit that other people can do some things better than you can.* It really is true. You'll be amazed at how well other people can do what you have always done, often without your help. It will be different, but often—if you are really honest—better than the way you have done it in the past. Remember, be a leader but willing to follow.

☞ **HANDS ON:** Try this with your staff. Make a copy of the figure below. Hand it out at a staff meeting and tell people *exactly* the following: "Take this, add one line and turn it into a six."

IX

Give the staff people a minute or two to get the right answer, and perhaps 1 in 10 will. The answer, by the way, is SIX.

I used to use this exercise to teach people to learn how to solve problems in different ways. But, in 1988, my then six-year-old son Benjamin was talking to me as I was preparing for a presentation. He was asking the age-old question, "What do you do at work, Daddy?" and I was trying my best to explain the job of management consultant to not-for-profits in terms that he could understand. While talking, we came upon a copy of my training material that included the "IX" exercise. Aha! Here was a way that I could at least distract Benjamin from my inability to give him a satisfactory answer about my occupation. "Benjamin," I said, showing him the IX, "Take the pencil and with one line, turn it into a six." With no hesitation at all, he grabbed the pencil, added an "S" before the IX and said, "Like this?" I was floored. I mean, I knew he was smart, but only about 10% of adults get this at all, much less immediately. What was going on?

What was going on, of course, was that Benjamin, as a first grader, had never learned about Roman numerals. When he looked at "IX", he saw "icks", not a "nine," which is what adults see. In short, we, as adults have *too much information, too much education, too much knowledge* to solve this problem. Later that week, I was visiting Benjamin's classroom, and I asked the teacher if I could repeat the activity with the class. Of 30 kids in the room, all 30 got it immediately.

The point here is, don't assume that because you have a college diploma or a masters or a doctorate or 20 years on the job, that you can solve every problem better than someone without those degrees or experience. Sometimes you'll be *too smart to solve the problem.*

> *Postscript:* As I was preparing this manuscript, Benjamin, now 11, asked me how the book was coming, and if there were any stories about him in the book. I told him yes, and summarized the story for him. When I finished, he asked to see the problem; for me to let him do it again. He couldn't come up with the answer. I laughed and asked him what he saw on the page, and he said, "Dad, how can you turn a nine into a six with one line?" I showed him, and informed him that he now knew too much to solve the problem: he had learned about Roman numerals. At this point Benjamin's seven-year-old brother Adam walked in. Benjamin (who like all big brothers thinks he knows it *all*) handed Adam the "IX" and asked him to turn it into a six. You guessed it. Adam, with no hesitation, replayed his brother's actions from five years before. He grabbed a pencil and wrote a "S" in front of the "IX". I still treasure the memory of the look on Benjamin's face as he realized he did not automatically know more than his little brother, just because he was four years older.

Communicate clearly. Back to communications, again. Remember:

1. *Explain* how to do it.
2. *Demonstrate* how to do it (if possible).
3. *Request* an explanation of how to do it.
4. *Invite* the employee to demonstrate it for you (if possible).

Good delegation is the path to supportive management: you help people grow by good delegation. They wither without new challenges.

E. EVALUATION

I make the assumption in writing this section that you already have an evaluation policy and an evaluation tool in place. If you don't have such a policy, you need one, starting today.

At a minimum, you and your management team should provide a written and oral evaluation of every staff member, volunteer, and board member every year. Why? Because without evaluations, without confronting the bad and acknowledging the good, people don't grow. It is also the only documentation that you have of a person's capability (or lack thereof), their contributions to the organization, etc. It is the easiest management task to procrastinate on, but it is an essential component of good management.

That having been said, there are some keys to the way we encourage a staff evaluation process to be established and conducted. These may be different than you have seen before, but they are well-tested, and they work.

▶ *All Evaluations Should Be Two-Way.* As we discussed in the opening pages of this chapter, the relationship between a supervisor and the supervisee is just that, a relationship. It will not work if both parties don't participate and try to make it work. For example, if the worker does not get clear instructions from the supervisor, or does not get them in a way that can be understood and followed, then the worker will fail to do the job up to the supervisor's expectations. In a normal evaluation setting, that problem would be the employee's fault, with no encouragement to the worker to point out the supervisor's communications problem. Therefore, your employee evaluations should have parts where the employee is evaluated, goals reviewed, etc., as well as parts where the supervisor is evaluated in terms of interaction with and support of the employee.

There is no question that for many supervisors this is a *terribly* threatening change. Supervisors are used to doing the evaluation, not being evaluated. For staff, this can be very nerve-wracking as well. Evaluate my boss? No way! But it does work, can work, and should work in an organization that sees management as support, and staff as critical. We'll cover *how* you do it in the methodology below.

▶ *Evaluations should be oral and written.* You write them out so that you have to think about them, so that people can read and think about them, and so that you have documentation of what was said. You do them orally as well so that each person has to face the other with both the good and bad parts of the evaluation. It opens yet another channel in the communications array.

▶ *There should be no surprises at evaluations.* If you and your staff are communicating well and regularly, if you are dealing with the good and bad immediately rather than waiting for an annual review, then there should be no bombshells between supervisor and worker. If there are big surprises, then the rest of the communications system is breaking down, and you should use the evaluation process as an early warning sign of that breakdown.

▶ *Set and evaluate goals for both people.* Three or four goals for the next evaluation period are important. If accomplished, they provide a feeling of satisfaction and accomplishment. If not, they provide a challenge for improvement. Again, the goals should be for the supervisor *and* the worker.

▶ *Evaluations never should be just numerical.* I feel that the biggest mistake that we all have made in the past ten years in the area of evaluations is the trend to totally numerical rankings or ratings for evaluations. I understand the need for quantification in many evaluation/compensation systems; you need a number to calculate a bonus or a raise. But numbers without context are meaningless. They provide no guidance for the employee, and a record of no value in the future.

● **FOR EXAMPLE:** Agency A has a form that asks for a supervisor to rate an employee in ten categories such as "Enthusiasm", "Attendance", "Work Quality", "Interaction with Clients", "Interaction with Staff", etc., on a 1 to 10 scale with 10 being "Exceptional" and 1 being "Totally Unacceptable". Thus, a supervisor can go down the list and rank John or Mary a 7 for "Interaction with Staff" and a 5 for "Interaction with Clients" and be done with the whole rating in a minute. Now, the supervisor gives the evaluation to John or Mary and tries to compare the rating with last year's. John went from a "7" to an "8" in "Work Quality". But why? The supervisor cannot *really* remember. Worse, if next year there is a new supervisor, he or she will have absolutely no background as to *why* John was rated an "8" as opposed to a "7", or a "2" for that matter.

I strongly prefer written evaluations, with questions that require thought and answers in complete sentences. If you must use a quantified scale, fine, but require written justification for each numerical rating.

▶ *Include the mission as an evaluation criterion.* Everyone should have as part of their evaluation criteria an item with wording to the effect of: In what ways did [the person being evaluated] pursue the mission or embody our mission and values this year? This, once again, reinforces the mission statement as a focus for the work ethic at your organization.

▶ *Develop criteria that are important to the organization and to the individual job being evaluated.* Don't rely on standard evaluation forms. Work with your people to establish criteria that reflect your culture, mission, and values, as well as critieria that are focused on the job being evaluated. For example, I feel that people who supervise should have a component of their evaluation that deals with how the people they supervise have evaluated them. This supports the theory of management as a support function. Another example would be to limit an evaluation criteria for "Interaction with customers" to only those who *have* such interaction.

▶ *Separate evaluation from compensation, in terms of timing.* Discussions of money muddy the waters between a supervisor and an employee. Have the supervisor deal with the money portion of this well before the evaluation of work effort, and have it out of the way.

G. CHANGING THE WAY YOU EVALUATE

You may evaluate once a year, twice a year, or quarterly. Never do it any less than annually, and, if you really want to impress your people, do it twice a year. No matter how often you do it, here are some suggestions on how to implement a two-way evaluation system.

1. PLAN AND CONSULT

Before instituting such a major change as going to two-way evaluations, some planning and consultation are necessary—or you will wind up with people very, very upset. Start by establishing a staff committee (of all levels of staff) to review both the evaluation tool and the evaluation process. Discuss the importance of two-way evaluations, what they are and are not, and set the criteria for evaluation as well as the process. If you tie the evaluation process into your compensation package talk about how that will happen and how worker evaluation of supervisors will not be held against the worker in the compensation area (there are protections against that outlined below).

Write up your new evaluation policy, the reason why it is being instituted, and transmit that to staff in writing and in meetings. I strongly encourage you to stage a role-playing exercise at this point so that people can see how the process is supposed to work. Have two staff act out the entire process.

Try the process for a year, monitoring it closely and then evaluate and amend it. Understand that it will take time for some staff to adequately trust their supervisors to be willing to take the risk of offering criticism. It will also take time for some supervisors to be able to accept constructive criticism from their workers. Give it time, but monitor the implementation carefully. Have intermittent meetings with supervisors and workers to discuss the program and how it is going, comparing your findings to the original intent.

2. A SUGGESTED EVALUATION PROCESS

▶ The clerical staff (Personnel Director, etc.) should provide both the supervisor and the worker with their copies of the evaluation form ten days prior to the evaluation being due. Each person then fills out his or her part of the form in writing. The supervisor also at this point fills out any salary or bonus recommendation in line with the organization's compensation policy, and hands it in to the appropriate person to implement. That way, the financial part of the evaluation is done and delivered *before* the supervisor gets evaluated by the worker, reducing the chance of retribution by the supervisor if the evaluation from the worker is not perfect.

▶ The supervisor and worker meet in private, exchange forms, and go over the evaluation as well as the goals that they had set at the last evaluation. They discuss the reason for each criteria rating and, in general, how they are doing as a team.

▶ Both supervisor and worker now set their goals for the next evaluation period. This is best done by themselves and then discussed at a second meeting.

▶ After meeting to discuss the goals, the supervisor may, as appropriate, inform the worker of compensation changes, or bonuses.

▶ It is critical that the supervisor and worker informally review the progress toward the goals two or three times during the next evaluation period. I recommend that they both put the times for such an informal review on their calendars to remind them.

H. STAFF RECOGNITION

An often forgotten component of inverted pyramid management has to do with staff recognition—celebrating and rewarding the kinds of behaviors that you want to see the most. There are virtually unlimited ways to do this, but most organizations that try this have problems that could have been avoided. The most common is to adopt another organization's program without checking with their own staff first!

Three critical rules for staff recognition programs:

1. The "rewards" should not be punishment. Don't assume that what you think is a nice reward is received the same way by those whom you are trying to honor. Reward (and punishment) is a very subjective thing

● **FOR EXAMPLE:** A few years ago, I was running a two-day retreat for a state human service department at which the Director and the 15 "highest" level staff were participating. One of the Department's training staff who specialized in working with hotels had made all the hotel and meal arrangements, and she was on-site for the two days of the retreat, ready and able to assist us if needed. The staff person, whom I will call Leslie, was a very capable and pleasant person and had mentioned to me that, among many other things, in 20 years with the Department she had never actually met a Director. She also had reserved another training room right down the hall from our meeting room in which she would set up camp to help us if we needed her, and in which she would eat.

Following the afternoon session, the participants broke for dinner in the hotel restaurant, while I remained behind in the meeting room to summarize our afternoon activities so that we could proceed without delay when we reconvened. Leslie had made dinner reservations for all the participants, plus me, and now I realized that since I would not be at dinner, there would be an empty seat at the table. I saw the Director walking by in the hall and ran out to stop her, and suggest that since Leslie had done such a great job on the arrangements that it might be a real treat for her to be invited to dinner with all the Department senior staff. The Director agreed, and said that she would set it up. I returned to my work feeling that I had really done a nice thing for Leslie, and that she would be very pleased by the opportunity to visit with the Director and other senior staff.

Ten minutes later Leslie stuck her head in the door and said, "Well, I *won't* be down the hall for dinner, if you need me. I have been told to eat dinner with the 'mucky mucks.'" She walked out of the room with a long face looking completely depressed. I immediately realized that my "reward" to Leslie was actually a punishment. While I might want to meet the people at the dinner table, the thought of spending an hour with the "big bosses" terrified Leslie. It was the worst thing I could have done to her. I later apologized to her, and we still joke about the incident when we talk.

2. The system must be seen by staff as fair and impartial. There is no point to this if the staff people feel that the system is rigged, and that only the "boss's favorites" will be chosen. You simply must have a system that *is* and, more importantly, *will be seen as* impartial and fair.

● **FOR EXAMPLE:** In another statewide agency, a good friend of mine took over as Director, following an "Attila the Hun". My friend, who we'll call Greg, as one of his early actions, asked line staff to develop a rewards program that was fair, meaningful, and easy to administer. The results? There is a rewards review committee made up of ten line staff (the total staff of the agency is over 2,000). This review committee has volunteered, and also has made itself *permanently* ineligible from receiving the rewards. Each month, this committee reviews nominations for Employee of the Month, nominations which can be submitted by peers or supervisors. Employees who are selected get a number of things: their picture in the foyer of all agency offices that month, a plaque given to them by Greg, and other "perks" that *they get to choose*. The system has worked wonders in the two years that it has been in place. It has all the parts essential for success: peer review, impartiality, and rewards that *really* reward.

3. The system must be understandable and support the mission. You can't have a reward system that requires a degree in astrophysics to understand. You also need a reward system that rewards behavior that supports the mission. That's why soldiers get medals for valor, and police officers and fire fighters get awards for saving citizens' lives; it's the kind of action that we want to encourage in those professions.

In order to do all these things well, have a group of employees from all levels of the organization study the idea of rewards and get back to you with a program. They may even tell you that staff would prefer *not* to have rewards, preferring to remain anonymous, or to have the funds that a reward program would use go into the programs instead. Don't decide from your senior management seat what is meaningful for line staff. You may well waste time, money, and morale.

RECAP

In this chapter we have reviewed top-quality management characteristics for your not-for-profit. Quickly, these are:

▶ Living the *Inverted Pyramid.* Valuing your staff, remembering that increasing the importance of your staff who are closest to the people you serve will improve morale and productivity. You need to live this attitude, not just put it on your table of organization. You need to be your staff's best advocate.

▶ Using the *Coach/Conductor style* of management. Remember that neither the coach nor the conductor play. You have to get your outcomes completed through the actions of others. You have to know your people and their capabilities in order to have them come together and achieve a common, desired outcome.

▶ Understanding that all *communications* are two-way and that what someone hears is more important than what you say. If you believe, as I do, in the inverted pyramid, you need to act as a facilitator, as a supporter. That means you need to communicate in the way that your people hear best, not in the way that you feel is most important.

▶ *Delegating* effectively is a strength, not a weakness. You need to remember that you cannot do it all and, in fact, that others can often do it better than you.

▶ *Evaluating* in the best manner: two-way. You and your staff should both evaluate the relationship, and your contributions to it. These evaluations will improve your management skills as much as they will help your staff people.

▶ *Rewarding staff* for their desirable behavior. All of us like to be rewarded. Just remember to make rewards real rewards and not punishments. Ask what people would like and try to give them that, instead of something that you would like to have.

Mr. Marriott had it right: "Take care of your employees and they will take care of you." You need your staff to be motivated and committed. You know you can never pay them enough, so keeping the good ones takes a different kind of compensation: what they do and how you treat them. Hopefully, this chapter has provided some insights and some tools for you to apply to that end.

8. The Controls That Set You Free

OVERVIEW

All managers, whether for-profit or not-for-profit, worry. They worry about things going wrong, people messing up, accidents happening, checks not clearing, wrong items being ordered, low quality services being provided, supervisors not following disciplinary procedure, and the thousand little and big things that can occur without warning.

Over and over in my work, managers and executive directors tell me that they worry about not being on-site all of the time because "people won't know what to do if something goes wrong, and I'm liable if they screw up". This, of course, chains the exec to his or her desk, because it assumes that the staff people are incompetent and unable to handle all but the most ordinary and routine situations.

If you agree with my suggestions and theories on delegation that were laid out in the last chapter, you know that you can't reach your potential as a manager nor as an organization until you delegate well, at all levels of the organization. But how can you do that and still sleep at night? You can, with good controls in place, good training on how to use those controls, and accountability to make sure that those controls are used each and every time.

Let's first define controls. Controls are sets of policies and procedures that standardize actions in your organization and clearly lay out accountability and responsibility in key areas of the organization. You want controls that protect you, but do not overly hamper your flexibility and creativity, and admittedly that is a balance. Too much control and people have no room for personal creativity and contribution, too little control and people lose the guidance and checks and balances that come from well-written, balanced policies and procedures.

This chapter will help you sleep better. Why? Because having good controls is the best sleep medicine I know. In the following pages I will give you my insights on how to write good, solid management control documents, ones that guide your organization, reduce risk and waste, and let you manage rather than administrate. We'll first look at how to develop controls, and then review the following types of controls:

▶ *BYLAWS*
▶ *CONFLICT OF INTEREST POLICIES*
▶ *FINANCIAL CONTROLS*
▶ *PERSONNEL POLICIES*
▶ *MEDIA POLICIES*
▶ *VOLUNTEER POLICIES*
▶ *QUALITY ASSURANCE POLICIES*
▶ *PROGRAM POLICIES*
▶ *DISASTER POLICIES*

Finally, we'll examine how to train and enforce the standards and controls that you have set.

A. THE CONTROL DEVELOPMENT PROCESS

The process for control development and management is daunting if your organization has none in place, but can be broken down into segments and taken one step at a time. The process that is suggested below will be inclusive, bottoms up, and as relatively painless as possible. I would suggest looking at the list of policies that you need and putting them into priority order for development. Try to develop the policies that you need within the next 12 to 18 months. If you already have some or all of the controls that I will discuss, you can review your current policies and consider the items that I suggest for inclusion.

1. Get examples from other organizations. There is no point in reinventing the wheel. Ask your trade association or other not-for-profits in your community for copies of their policies. Note the strengths and weaknesses, but do not automatically adopt their system; it may not be the best for your organization.

2. Write the policy in draft. You have to start somewhere. Write the policy in draft for your organization, or have a staff person do it. Then review it with a board/staff committee and, in the case of certain policies, such as financial or personnel, with a specialist such as your banker, CPA, or a board member who is also a professional human resource specialist. Make sure that someone on the committee is a person who will actually use the policy day-to-day. For example, if it is a disciplinary policy, include a line supervisor, middle manager, and senior manager on the policy development team.

3. Float the policy for comment. Let *everyone* who may have to work with the policy have a chance to comment. This means letting your funders see quality assurance policies; your entire board review conflict of interest and media policies; your bank, CPA, and funding auditors look at your cash controls; and your staff see discipline, reward, and compensation policies.

4. Implement the policy. Start by printing the new policy and then hold orientation and training sessions for all staff and/or board who are affected by the policy to make sure that everyone understands why the policy is there, how and when it is to be used, and their responsibilities and authority under the policy. Repeat these sessions until everyone has been trained and then repeat as a refresher course, particularly for conflict of interest, interviewing, hiring, discipline, and firing, at least once a year.

5. Review the policy regularly. Each policy should be formally reviewed at least every two years. Dating the copy of the policy on file will help remind you to update it.

> ☞ **HANDS ON:** In many of your policies and procedures you will have forms: evaluation, cash receipts, travel reimbursement, timesheets, and the like. Make sure that in every case you include a sample of the form *filled in* as an example. I have yet to see a form and instructions, no matter how clearly written, that were not misinterpreted by someone. Having a filled-in form as an example, in addition to blank ones for immediate use, allows the potential user to have a clear idea of how to use the form. It will reduce frustration and save a great deal of time.

6. Enforce the policy. There is no point in doing this if you are not going to enforce your expectations that people follow them. State clearly in the policies that failure to follow them will be cause for discipline for staff and for removal for board and volunteers. Put similar wording in the personnel policies and board and volunteer manuals, and make the following of policy a criteria in your evaluation process.

The development of good policies may seem to you to be tedious and bureaucratic. Tedious, yes, bureaucratic, no. This is good management, excellent stewardship. Why should you take the time to do control and policy development when you have so many other pressing things to do? Because having good controls will free you up to do good mission. Good controls emancipate managers from constant worry about people making avoidable mistakes, they allow you to delegate fully, and to use your time, energy, and talents on *managing* the organization rather than *administering* it. This is a crucial difference.

In *In Search of Excellence* Peters and Waterman noted that those organizations that had good controls could free their managers to be the visionary leaders that were necessary to achieve and maintain excellence— the "simultaneous loose-tight" organization. Waterman later expanded on this characteristic in his book *The Renewal Factor*. Other management gurus have noted the same correlation: if you are sitting around worrying about cash controls, personnel management, or discrimination suits, you are wasting time. Those things can be (for the most part) controlled by having and enforcing good policies.

Again, this is not bureaucracy, or a waste of time putting things on paper: this is good, solid management. It can turn into bureaucracy at its worst; a constricting, top-down controlling, initiative-limiting mess, but it shouldn't. You need to work with your people to design the controls, and do it with an attitude that "these will help us do our job better, will take a lot of the questions out of routine procedure, and will free us up to be creative to do more of our mission".

B. TYPES OF CONTROLS

There are numerous sets of policies and controls that you can develop. The list below is not intended to be all-inclusive, but it is extensive. It covers the types of policies I have seen organizations develop poorly, or sometimes, not at all. Sometimes the latter is better than the former, because poorly-written controls can be very dangerous.

At the very least, you need the following policy documents:

▶ *BYLAWS*
▶ *CONFLICT OF INTEREST POLICIES (usually in your ByLaws)*
▶ *FINANCIAL CONTROLS*
▶ *PERSONNEL POLICIES*
▶ *MEDIA POLICIES*
▶ *VOLUNTEER POLICIES*
▶ *QUALITY ASSURANCE*

▶ *PROGRAM POLICIES*
▶ *DISASTER POLICIES*

Each of these areas will be discussed in some detail in the following pages. Note, however, that I *do not* claim to be an expert in each of these areas. Many are highly technical and have to do with your compliance with state and/ or federal law. You will need to consult professionals in your community to assure that you are in line with local, state, and federal laws as well as with your funders' regulations and your contractual obligations.

What I will try to do is to point out key items that people forget to put in, and to point out places where we have observed flaws in policies at many organizations.

☞ **HANDS ON:** Policy development is one of the areas where my technique of recruiting a "professional volunteer" works best. The purpose of the recruitment is to get a real expert to look at your problem—in this case your policy—without requiring him or her to make a long-term commitment as a board member. What you do, taking your personnel policies as an example, is go to the CEO of your bank, or of another large company that has supported you in the past, and say "We're reviewing our personnel policies this year and wondered if you had a staff person who could provide us with his or her expertise in personnel issues for three or four two-hour meetings over the next three months?" Then the CEO gives you the name and feels like he or she has made a "donation", the expert gives their time, but doesn't feel like they are saddled with a long-term commitment, you get your expertise for free, and the expert may, in fact become enamored of your organization and agree to help again, serve in another capacity, or donate to your fundraiser! Try this, it works.

C. BYLAWS

Bylaws for a not-for-profit are required by statute in all 50 states, and by IRS regulations. You have them, but how recently have you and your board reviewed them? Here are some things you should check for:

▶ *Mission Statement:* You should review this every two years. You should file any substantive changes in your mission statement with the IRS and with the appropriate state official in your state (usually the Attorney General or Secretary of State). For much more on missions, see Chapter 4.

▶ *Board Selection and Term:* Have the board turn over. My

suggestion is that each board term be no more than three years, with two consecutive terms before a member has to go off. Perpetual boards tend to perpetuate past policy—long after it is out-of-date. The selection of the board can be from the membership, by the membership, or by the board itself, depending on your state and funding streams' requirements. For much more on boards, see Chapter 5.

▶ *Quorum:* Don't box yourself in by saying that you need 8 members for a quorum (on a 15-member board). What if, due to unforeseen but reasonable circumstances, four board members resign, and you have no one to replace them with for six months? Suddenly you need 73% (8 of 11) rather than 53% (8 of 15) to do business at a board meeting. You need to say "A quorum of the board shall be constituted by more than 50% of the board members serving as of the date of the meeting."

▶ *Dissolution Clause:* Make sure you have a clause detailing what happens in case your organization closes. You need to state that you will pay off your liabilities and that the remaining assets will then be distributed to one or more 501(c)(3) corporations. You can specify the corporation if you wish.

▶ *Standing Committees:* I urge people to name the standing committees and their responsibilities. For more on Committees see Chapter 6.

▶ *Intentions and Restrictions:* Without being too wordy, you should state particular intentions and restrictions. If, for example, there is a second signature requirement on checks over $5,000, say it here. If, as I hope you do, it is the intent of the board that the committees will have a great deal of authority, say so here. If it is the intent of the board to delegate certain authority to the executive director, say so here.

D. CONFLICT OF INTEREST POLICIES

While these are usually included in your bylaws, they are more than important enough to discuss as a separate item. Remember in the first chapter, I briefly discussed my prediction that you will operate under more and more scrutiny during the next ten years, scrutiny from the public, the press, your funders, and your donors. One of the areas where not-for-profits are most vulnerable is in the writing and interpretation of their conflict of interest policies. Don't forget, it's not the facts that count if you wind up in the local paper as having had board members who benefited financially from their board position, it's the *appearance of impropriety* that will sink you. You want to design your policy to prevent the appearance of impropriety, to prevent actual abuse, and to be enforceable should someone try to self-aggrandize.

There are three schools of thought on these policies. They can be categorized as follows:

1. Overkill: In an effort to prevent any and all appearances of impropriety, the policy says that no board or committee member can provide any service to the organization for compensation and if a relative of theirs is under consideration for such a service contract that they not only cannot vote on the issue, but that they have to actually leave the meeting until the discussion is concluded.

This is a bit much. If you live in a small town like I do, there are only so many qualified people around, and automatically excluding them from providing services to you will not only prohibit you from using some valuable resources, it will also almost certainly be a disincentive to serve on the board.

2. Underkill: The policy says that the board shall not personally profit from its relationship to the organization, but has no clear guidelines as to what that means, how to assess it, or how to enforce a violation. In essence, it trusts the board members to do what is right.

This is living in la-la land. Board members are like all the rest of us: 97% honest, 3% not so ethical. You need to use common sense, and have policies that prevent abuse, while at the same time not insulting the 97% of the board that is honest and upstanding.

● **FOR EXAMPLE:** A number of years ago, I was on the board of a social services provider, and became Vice Chairman of the Board, and thus by default the chairman of the Finance Committee. This organization was then 20 years old, and had only had one Executive Director, who had run the organization from its infancy through the stage of having well over 100 employees. The board, when I arrived, was a loose confederation of original board members, titular members (local state representatives, alderman, etc.), and family members of persons served by the organization.

At the time I became Finance Committee Chair, I was also the newly-hired Executive Director of a health planning not-for-profit, and in my new job had undertaken a complete overhaul of the financial controls, board policies, and other internal procedures. I had researched the issues thoroughly and tried to also use this fresh knowledge in my board and Finance Committee work. Our Finance Committee examined the financial policies and made many changes, including requiring at least two bids on contracts over $1,000, and reviewing insurance purchases every three years.

About two months into my term as Chair, our comprehensive insurance package came up for renewal, and the Executive Director called to tell me that I needed to sign off on the contract. I asked her if we had bid the insurance out, as called for in our newly rewritten financial policies. Her shocked reply was: "No, of course not. George (a board member for 10 years) gives us a great rate on the premiums, so we always go with him. We're *not* going to bid this." I informed her that I differed with her, and that if we were going to have policies they needed to be followed for everyone, every time. Besides, if George were giving us such a great rate, he'd certainly retain the business. The Exec was very uncomfortable with this idea, noting how dedicated George had been to the organization, how his daughter was one of our first clients, etc., etc., and in general setting George up for immediate canonization by the Pope. So I added, "I know you and George go back a long ways, and that he has been a great help to us. Let's blame this on me, and I'll even be the one to tell George in person, OK?" Fine, she said, still not very happy. We set the meeting with George for the next day.

George arrived at our meeting assuming it was merely a formality and that I was there just to sign off on his contract and to pass him a check for the first month's premium. After initial formalities, he slid the papers across the table to me, and I slid them back, saying: "George, this is *absolutely* no reflection on you, but as you know we now have a financial policy that requires us to bid out all contracts over $1,000. Since this premium is over $35,000 we need to bid it out. You are very familiar with our insurance needs and may have put everything we need in the material you have today. So, I can either take the papers that you have as your bid, and hold them until we get two competing bids, or you can rework them into a more 'bid-like' form. I have a request for proposal (RFP) here for you to look at if you would like. We have been very happy with your service and hope that you will bid for the work, but I'm sure that you understand our need to get the best price we can."

George looked at me for a moment, then smiled slightly, but didn't say a word. He simply crossed out the premium amount on the contract, *reduced it by 20%,* and slid it back across the table! I could hear the Exec gasp and saw her flush red as I tried to keep from getting angry. The best response I could muster was "Should I take that as your bid?" "Nope," he said, "I've provided good service here for ten years. I don't do bids. This is a one-time offer. Take it or leave it."

"We'll take it!" said the Exec. "Wrong. We'll leave it." I said. I handed George the RFP and walked out of the room.

The point? George, good old George the board member, the parent, the supporter of our organization, had been *stealing* from us for years by inflating the premium way over the market price. He got away with it because the organization never bothered to check, and he knew about our lax policy. Once we had reasonable checks and balances, he was forced to play fair. Oh, and the Exec never forgave me for *embarrassing* her in front of George!

3. A BALANCED APPROACH: You need to attempt to reach a balance between overkill and underkill. I suggest the following components of a conflict of interest policy:

1. Bid out contractual work. Set a threshold, and get bids on things over that amount: contracting, equipment, supplies, food, anything. You'll need to learn how to write out your needs in an RFP, and once you learn how, and get in the habit of doing it, you will not only save money, but you will avoid anyone saying that a board member got a "no bid" contract.

2. If a board member bids on a contract, they should only get it if it is the lowest bid. This is somewhat restrictive, but again avoids potential bad publicity.

3. In discussions where a board member has or feels he or she may have a conflict, the board member should disclose that conflict or potential conflict immediately. After such disclosure, they should be able to participate in discussion, but should excuse themselves from voting. Their participation in the discussion may bring important insights to the table, and, as long as everyone is aware of their conflict, should not be inappropriate.

4. Include your staff in your conflict policies. We always focus on board members and forget our staff. What if the husband of your Vice President of Finance owns a computer firm and you need computers. Can he bid or not? You should specify. Can staff work on their own after hours? Can they consult with other agencies? You should spell it out.

You may need to be more stringent if you have had a bad experience with your board, or if there has been a scandal at another organization in your community, but try to attain a reasonable balance. Put your policy in your bylaws and have a training session with your board and staff about what it means. Repeat that training annually.

E. FINANCIAL CONTROLS

Good financial controls can be very technical and certainly should be designed to meet your organization's unique needs. Thus, you will need to rely on your CPA and your funding source for help on these controls. I will, however, highlight the major areas that need your attention. The keys to financial policies are to have good oversight in reporting, good theft prevention by reducing temptation, and good records to allow for easy auditing and analysis.

▶ *Cash Controls:* You should already have cash controls in place, where one person logs in checks and cash, another deposits, and a third reconciles the bank statement. Even if there are only three staff, this is possible. Try to achieve it. Note: everyone who handles any cash, or checks should be bonded. It's cheap.

▶ *Payables Controls:* The person who receives goods or services from vendors and checks them in should not be the person who writes the check to the vendor. This will help prevent collusion and overpayment.

▶ *Debt Policy:* You need to spell out your policy on debt. Can the exec add to the line of credit without board approval? Can the executive committee approve a payroll loan without board approval? Be specific here. In Chapter 13 we'll discuss Social Entrepreneuring, and in that chapter I'll tell you why prudent debt can be a good thing. But you want a policy and you want it to be specific.

▶ *Check Signature:* Most boards let the staff write checks within the budget, but sometimes it takes two signatures above a certain threshold, such as $1,000 or $10,000. Some organizations make payroll exempt from this provision. How high or low your threshold is, and how many signatures you need will in some part depend on your organization's history, the community practices on the issue, and the requirements of your funders.

● **FOR EXAMPLE:** A few years ago, my consulting firm received a check from a small town in Alabama for a subscription to our six issues per year newsletter. The check was for one year's subscription—

$12. It had five—that's right, *five*—signatures: the mayor, the town treasurer, the town deputy mayor, the town clerk, and the police chief. I swear this is a true story. Now after all of us had stopped laughing, I asked our staff: "The question is, in this town, who stole how much and how recently?"

We never found out the answer to the question, but the point is that you need to be reasonable. That town spent probably $50 in someone's time running that $12 check all over the courthouse getting five signatures. If you have had a bad experience with a former staff person, take extra precautions, but not absurd ones.

▶ *Reporting:* Your policies should note who gets which reports how often. For example, your board may get quarterly financial statements, but your executive committee and financial committee get monthly income and expense statements, cash flows, and an aging of payables and receivables. You need to have reporting requirements and formats that meet the needs of the people reading the reports. That means that different groups will get different reports. How do you know what they want and need? Be a good marketer: ask them. For more on this see Chapter 11.

▶ *Confidentiality:* A lot of people forget this. Your financials are your business. You need a statement that specifies that this information is not to be shared outside the agency except with auditors, funders, and others who need the information, and only with the express written approval of the board. You don't want your numbers floating all over town.

F. PERSONNEL POLICIES

I know that this will seem like a cursory discussion of an all-too important issue, but it is intentional. Not having personnel policies, or not following them, are, in my view, the biggest liabilities you have. Angry staff sue their employers more and more. We are, after all, a litigious society. We as not-for-profits also don't pay our staff enough, and probably never will. The one major area where angry, underpaid staff can sue us is in personnel: discriminatory hiring, sexual harassment, unjust termination, the list goes on and on. You simply have to have policies that *meet the current law and regulation* and are *followed to the letter every single time.*

Additionally, there have been some major changes in the law in the past few years, not the least of which is the Americans With Disabilities Act (ADA). Getting your personnel policies right is a job for a professional, and someone on your staff or board should be or become such a professional. Invest in training for these people: send them to seminars, buy them manuals; help them to get it right and keep it that way. Also, train your supervisory staff on your discipline process at least annually.

I intentionally did not include even a brief checklist here for fear that some reader would think that it was all-inclusive and get into trouble. Please talk to an expert.

G. MEDIA POLICIES

The media love to sell papers, magazines, and air time. That's their business. You want to avoid being part of that sales effort by not becoming a negative story in the scandal sheets. The public's and thus the press's zest for scandal is one of the reasons that you need to develop such detailed policies in all areas of the agency: it helps avoid the things that the media love to run on the front page or the evening news; "Board Members Get Sweetheart Contract", "Staff of Agency File Discrimination Suit", "Executive Director Had Vacation on Agency Funds". *No one* wants to wake up to see or hear those stories about the organization that they work for.

But what if you do? What does one do when the reporter calls for information on a story, good or bad? Your media policies should tell you. I strongly suggest that your policies include at least the following:

1. External Flow Control. You need to have one person designated as the spokesperson for the agency. Usually this will be the chief staff person, but, if you are large enough, it could also be the Public Information Officer. In some cases, you'll want to have your Board President be the spokesperson. But the rule is: Limit the voices talking to the press. You want one message and one only. This rule is particularly important to impress on your board members, as they can be easily contacted and are often susceptible to press badgering as they are only volunteers and may not know the whole issue.

2. Internal Information Flow. Keep people informed; staff, board, the people your serve, funders, and donors. Get your side of the issue to them and quickly—before the papers hit the stands if possible. Keep your staff fully informed of what is happening, and how it will affect them and their programs. Use these opportunities to remind them *not* to talk to the press on their own.

While we are on the subject, remember these rules of dealing with the media—in good times and bad:

1. State facts only, not assumptions. For example, if a reporter asks: "Doesn't your new program provide services in a discriminatory manner?" don't answer yes *or* no. An appropriate factual response (if true) would be, "Our Board has a long-standing non-discrimination policy in all aspects of service provision, hiring, and employment. That policy includes our new program."

2. Don't be afraid to say "I don't know, but I'll get back to you" and then do. It is better to check your facts and call back, but always do call back. Also, always get back to reporters by *their* deadline, even if it is inconvenient. They'll run the story anyway, and put their slant on it, so return their calls, and try to get your two-cents-worth into the story.

3. State and restate your concern for the people you serve, your prior awards and positive press. Then state how this issue, whatever it may be, will not affect the long-term program(s).

4. Don't try to be a "spin doctor". Most reporters are pros, and know a spin when they hear it.

H. VOLUNTEER POLICIES

Volunteer policies do not need to be tedious or long, but at the very least they need to cover orientation with an explanation of your mission and a description of all of your services, job descriptions, descriptions of responsibility and liability, and a list of the staff positions that the volunteers relate/report to. These policies can then be distributed to staff and volunteers and all can better understand the role volunteers play in your organization and how each individual participates as well.

I. QUALITY ASSURANCE

A passion for quality is not only good marketing, it is also good mission. No matter what service you are in you need a quality assurance (QA) program. The recent interest in Total Quality Management (TQM) and Continuous Quality Improvement (CQI) has provided a whole new generation of references on quality and a great number of very qualified consultants in the area as well.

In some areas of service there are quality boards that certify the quality of the organization. Programs like the Joint Commission on the Accreditation of Healthcare Organizations (JCAHO) and the Commission on the Accreditation of Rehabilitation Facilities (CARF) are two good examples of such organizations, and there may be equivalents in your field. Additionally, you may have a trade organization that has developed standards of excellence for your field. For example, the National Society of Fund Raising Executives (NSFRE) has standards for its members that it publishes. Your trade association may do the same.

At the very least, you want to set some standards for yourself to try to meet and exceed. These are not just goals and objectives in the planning sense, but standards of quality. For example, if you are a mental health assessment facility, you might have a standard that says that all new patients in crisis will see a counselor for initial assessment within three hours of a call, 24 hours a day. If you are a church, you might have a standard that one or more of your ministerial staff will attend every church activity to facilitate counseling and fellowship. If you are a museum, you might not display any new works that have not passed a rigorous peer review of experts.

Your goal should be to do what you do better and better. You want to earn a reputation as a quality program, and that reputation is tough to earn and tougher to keep. Setting standards in writing will help you, your management team, your staff, and volunteers achieve those standards.

J. PROGRAM POLICIES

Program policies are essential tools for you to convey your mission and your values to your staff, volunteers, funders, and service recipients. These policies may be short and general or long and detailed, but they should outline both the steps involved in any and all service provision, and the philosophy of that provision. For example, an arts association may have a set of hands-on art exploration programs for young children. The association would need to put down both its philosophy of "having children explore various creative media in a wholesome safe environment", but also such finite details as the need to register children, have emergency phone numbers if the children are dropped off, and perhaps (in this sad day and age of fear of child abuse) always having two adults in the room with the children. They might also put into their protocols to have the child's name added to their mailing list for future announcements of similar classes.

A second example: a health clinic might have very specific health care protocols for admission, screening, lab work, information gathering, insurance billing, and the like. These go a long way to ensure that staff understand each and every facet of what they need to do with each and every patient.

☞ **HANDS ON:** Don't assume that *anything* is too minute or too obvious to write down! That is why it is so critical to develop these with a group of line staff as well as with managers. I once saw a set of program policies for a health clinic that had such items as the information required on check in, directions on how to offer coffee or tea in the waiting room in English and Spanish, what to do with blood tests, etc., etc., but forgot to direct the nurses to take the temperature and blood pressure of the patient! When a new LPN came on board, she was trained in the policies, and it wasn't until the patient charts were reviewed a week or two later that people noticed that these key items were not being assessed. When asked why not, she said, "You have great procedures, and I was just following them. It didn't make a whole lot of sense, but I'm new and didn't want to make trouble."

Don't fall into this trap. Let your staff know that policies are not substitutes for common sense.

K. DISASTER POLICIES

Fires, earthquakes, tornadoes, floods, power outages, and hurricanes all occur, and regularly. I know that you have fire evacuation procedures for all of your buildings, and I hope that you have fire drills for any residential facilities you may run. But do you have disaster procedures? Perhaps not, and you need them. Make sure that your policies have at least these parts:

▶ *Disaster preparedness.* What's included will depend on where you live and work. Are you in a hurricane-prone area? One that is regularly visited by tornadoes or earthquakes? If so, consult your local disaster preparedness agency and get up-to-date advice on being as prepared as possible. This may mean something as simple as laying in a supply of water, food, flashlights, and batteries, or as complex as reinforcing your structures.

▶ *Post-disaster planning:* What will you do *after* a disaster? If you lose a building to a fire or a flood, how do you get back up and running in as short a time as possible? You do this with a plan that has a checklist of things that need to be attended to, people to contact, and alternate sites for provision of services outlined.

● FOR EXAMPLE: During the final preparation of this manuscript, the school where my wife teaches had a fire, destroying about 15% of the school, with extensive smoke and water damage to the rest. The fire occurred on Friday night, ending about 4 a.m. on Saturday. By Sunday evening, with a superhuman effort by the administration and school district maintenance staff, the following had occurred: The entire school (a large school, with 450 students) had been cleaned and most areas repainted; all the carpeting had been removed, cleaned, and replaced; all the affected areas of the school had been rewired; alternate sites and transportation for 100 students had been secured; a gym site for the entire student body had been found; medical forms had been prepared to let students and faculty know what cleaning materials had been used in case of allergic reactions; insurance had been extended to the new sites; press conferences had been held; and every student in the school had been called. By Monday evening, when an open house at both sites was held, all the lost student materials had been replaced, the new classrooms (at the different site) were set up, every book in the library (which had had smoke damage) had been cleaned and reshelved, and all the computers and audio-visual equipment in the school had been cleaned and returned. Classes resumed Tuesday, 76 hours after the fire was out.

There were 1000 other things that these people did which I have not recounted, but the key for them was that they had a plan for what to do in case there was severe damage to a school. The plan was not all-inclusive, and they had to ad lib a lot, but it kept them on track, and ensured that their efforts were focused and directed.

You need disaster policies, and not just for fire drills.

L. TRAINING AND ENFORCEMENT

While policies can be a great management tool, they are a lot of work to create and to keep up-to-date. As I have noted repeatedly, they are also worthless without training staff and board people in their use. Again, you need to have in-service training on every policy with all staff when it is first in place and then with affected staff each year. Only by repeated exposure to the policies will staff people get it right, and at the same time, ways to improve the policies will be found.

Policies must also be enforced. There is no point in spending the time and money to develop these guidelines if you aren't going to discipline staff and board when they don't follow the policies. Make it clear at the outset (at the training) that a wide array of staff and board were involved in development and testing of the policies, and you expect them to be followed. Then note clearly that failure to follow the policies will lead to disciplinary action. And when someone does violate them knowingly (and someone *always* does, just to see what will happen), discipline them. You'll be amazed at how many fewer violations you'll have in the future.

RECAP

Have and use good controls! But remember that while controls are great, they should not discourage innovation, experimentation, and the taking of risk. Staff should know that policies are not excuses for total brain shutdown, and that common sense is still expected.

In this chapter we've reviewed why it is critical to your success and your ability to manage to have good, well-written, and up-to-date policies and procedures. We have reviewed the essential kinds of policies and gone over the key things that I have seen many organizations forget to include. Remember, good controls are a key to good management and mission success. Without them, you will almost surely have staff or volunteers do something, major or minor, that distracts you from your job: managing the organization. With controls, there will be less of that, although even the best controls are valueless if people ignore them. That is why we went over the issue of regular training as a key to implementation of your policies, and enforcement as a way to insure that they are used.

One more time: good controls set you free from administration—they allow you to be a manager. The time and money spent to develop and update them will be returned to you tenfold. Do this. Without them, your organization is a multitude of accidents waiting to happen.

9. Developing a Bias for Marketing

OVERVIEW

This chapter is central to your success. If you don't know who you are serving, if you don't know what they want, if you don't know how to ask them how to improve, if you don't know how to let people know that you are around, how can you stay in business? You can't. You need to adopt a culture of marketing and this chapter will show you how. We'll talk through the benefits of marketing, and then go through each of the seven key steps in the marketing process, which are:

1. *Identifying Your Target Markets.*
2. *Assessing the Market Wants.*
3. *Developing the Service.*
4. *Pricing the Service.*
5. *Promoting the Service.*
6. *Providing (distributing) the Service.*
7. *Evaluating the Marketing Effort.*

After that, we'll look at the best ways to ask your markets what they want, and then show you the ways to evaluate your marketing efforts. By the end of the chapter, you'll have a new understanding of who your markets *really* are, what they *really* want, and how to satisfy their wants.

A. WHY MARKET?

Marketing is so essential, so integral to your success, and yet, in many ways, so foreign to not-for-profits. Let's start this critical component with a short quiz.

▶You are a not-for-profit, so you don't have to worry about marketing, right? *Wrong.*

▶The people who you serve are your primary markets, right? *Only partly.*

Successful not-for-profits know that their continued success, even their continued existence, depends on living, breathing, eating, and sleeping this slogan:

EVERYTHING
THAT EVERYONE HERE DOES
EVERY DAY
IS MARKETING.

This means the way the phone is answered, the way the staff dresses, the way the trash is picked up and the lawn is cut, the quality of your printed material, the knowledge of the board, to say nothing of how services are provided. All these activities go into the marketing mix. You have to assume that every interaction with a client, patron, donor, funder, community member, or politician—even those that you are totally unaware of—has an impact on some part of your organization: a decision to come to you for services, a decision to refer someone else to you, a decision to donate, or a decision to fund.

This maxim is not just applicable to management, or to service provision staff, but to every employee and volunteer that is associated with your organization. Remember the story I told in the chapter on boards about the new board member who attended the cocktail party? She had two ways of presenting her new experience, one positive, one less so. It is important that everyone understand that their role in the entire enterprise is essential—and part of your team marketing effort.

● **FOR EXAMPLE:** During the late 1990 buildup to the Gulf War, Americans saw interviews with dozens of young military personnel. Often they were asked: what are you doing here? Regardless of their job; cook, truck driver, munitions handler, mechanic, they answered: "Driving Saddam Hussein out of Kuwait." No matter how menial their task in the huge war machine, these soldiers, sailors, and airmen had been taught that their small component was critical. I remember hearing a dock worker who spent his 105-degree days offloading cargo at one of the ports saying, "Hey, no one eats, moves, or fights without supplies, and no supplies get to nobody[sic] without me. That means I'm winning the war!" And he meant it. You want to work on that type of ownership with your staff. They need to understand that what they do does affect the whole, even if on the surface there is not a direct impact on your services or your funding.

In the discussion on management of people (Chapter 7) I talked about the fact that the lowest paid people in your organization are the most important: they are the ones who have the most direct contact with your clientele and the public and the most impact on your marketing potential: directly or indirectly. These people need to be involved in your marketing, in the planning and execution of your marketing plan. They need to understand their critical role in the marketing of, and therefore the future of, your organization.

B. MARKETING BASICS

Marketing is so often considered a "dirty" word in not-for-profits. It is unseemly, and after all, you are not in *sales*, right? Wrong. You need to attend to your markets (and there are more of those than you think), find out what they want, and give it to them within the limits of your resources.

Let's start by looking at a basic marketing flow chart on page 112.

As you can see, the entire process starts not with developing a product or service and then trying to sell it, but instead with choosing your target markets. Now, what do we do in our organizations? Usually we say: "We're here to provide services and we know how to provide them. So we'll let you know when we're open and y'all come!" This is known as *product-driven marketing*: we believe in our product (or service) and we believe that it will sell itself.

Let's go through the parts of the marketing diagram one box at a time.

1. IDENTIFYING YOUR TARGET MARKETS

Fact: the not-for-profit industry is the only industry in the world that regularly gets together in groups to berate and complain about its best customers. Think about it. Your best customer is the group or groups that send you the most money. For most readers, that is some branch of the local, state, or federal government. Do you see them as customers? If you are like 99% of not-for-profit managers, you see them as the *enemy*. This, to say the least, is a self-defeating viewpoint. You, your staff, and board need to start thinking of your largest funders as your best customers: and then start treating them that way.

But, before we discuss how you can do that, I need to realign your

MARKETING FLOW CHART

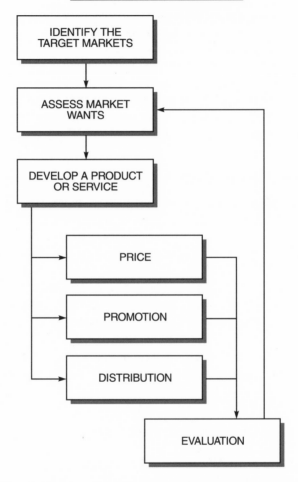

thinking about who your markets really are. Stop and think for a minute. Who *are* your markets and how can you identify them? Look at the following chart for a start in breaking down the concept that the only market you have that counts is your clientele.

I've divided the not-for-profit marketing mix into three main categories:

▶ *Payer Markets:* These are the people who send you money. They may be the federal, state, or local government, donors, foundations, users, or others. Each of these should be considered a different market

segment. For example, if you get money from three different state programs, each program should be assessed as a different market segment. I also include in the payer markets a box for "referrers". These are the critical people who send other people your way. They might be a mental health counselor, a social worker, a friend, a physician, or a minister, but without their referrals you would be in trouble. You need these people as well. Their referrals translate into income.

▶ *Service Markets:* These are the people that you serve. Think about how many different markets are represented here: each different program you provide multiplied by each different age, socio-economic, and gender cohort you provide those services to. For example, if you provide family planning services, the way you provide them to married couples is a great deal different than the way you provide them to single teenage boys and girls. You have many different service markets.

▶ *Internal Markets:* These are two different markets: *staff* and *board*. The brutal truth is that you need good, solid staff more than they need you. The same is true for your board. They are, in the truest sense, essential markets, ones that you have to attend to if you want to do any mission at all.

Each of these many markets warrants special attention. You need your payer markets: no money–no mission. If you accept the payer markets as your customer (whether you like it or not) then you need to figure out how to keep them as your customer. You need your service markets to be happy and satisfied, otherwise you are not doing good, high-quality mission. If you run out of service markets, you've just run out of a reason for existing.

You need your board and staff as resources to plan and execute your mission. You are also *competing* for each and every one of these markets, just the way Ford competes with Toyota, or Delta competes with United. The payers, the service recipients, staff, and board all have choices, and those choices are only going to increase in the coming years. Without your paying constant attention to those markets, the choice they make may very well not have anything to do with your organization.

☞ **HANDS ON:** To get a handle on your organization's many markets, do this: Sit down with a chart that looks something like the one below, and put all of your markets into it. The key here is to try to distinguish (segment) markets to assure that you give each the attention that it deserves. The chart shown here is an example only. Do you own, showing your own markets and their wants.

CATEGORY	MARKET	WANTS
PAYERS		
	Special Education Districts	Low Cost, accountability
	State Dept of Rehabilitation	Good Bookeeping, Timely Filing
	Private Payers	Low Cost, Prompt Billing
STAFF		
	Speech Therapists	Career growth
	Physical Therapists	Varied patients
	Teachers	Continuing ed.
	Administrators	Stability, retirement
SERVICE		
	Children 0-3 with perceived disabilities	Happy, loving Staff
	Children 3-5 who need physical or cognitive testing	Happy, fun place
	Parents of Children 0-3 in the above programs	Safe place that helps their child.
REFERRAL		
	Special Ed. Administrators	High quality services
	Pediatricians and Family Practitioners	Highly educated staff
	Disability-Specific Parent support groups	Inclusion

Note that I have only included one or two "wants" for each market. In reality there will be many. You need to ask. Also, note that there are different wants for the Special Ed *Districts* (payers) and the Special Ed *Administrators* (referrers). This is not unusual. The paying side wants one thing and the program side another.

Before we go further, I want to give you one overriding caution about markets and market segmentation. Do not fall into what I call the "census" trap, saying that your market is the 590,400 people that live in your county. It's not. Your market is never *everyone*. It's the people between ages 12 and 90 who enjoy live classical music and have the ability to pay and attend concerts if you are a symphony orchestra. It's women between 12 and 50 who are sexually active if you are a family planning organization. But it's *not* everyone. We were trained to think of our "markets" in this way as a result of capitation funding, where an organization's government grant each year is based on the service area's population. This is poor training, but you can begin to relearn if you develop this chart. And, if you do this for your organization, I guarantee that you will be stunned as to how many markets and market segments you have. Don't panic. At least now you know who your markets *really* are, and now you can decide which merit the most immediate attention.

2. ASSESS THE MARKET WANTS

Note that I said "wants", not "needs". Professionals tell people what they need. People buy what they want.

> ● **FOR EXAMPLE:** Statistics tell us that one in eight American adults is in need of substance abuse treatment, mostly for alcohol, but some for harder drugs. If we assumed 1/3 of those people need inpatient care, that's still over 8.3 million adults in need of treatment. There are not 1/10 that many treatment beds available in the country and many of them are empty. Why? Because, as anyone who has an addiction will tell you, people won't seek services until they *want* it. Do they all need it? Sure, and we can prove it to them medically. But until they *want* treatment, there is no point in even trying.

With this background, we now need to establish ways to find out what all of these markets we've identified *want*. There are a variety of ways to do this and they all start with a basic discipline that has just three letters:

ASK

It's really very simple. You ask people what they want, why they came to you, what made them happy or not so happy about your services, whether they will return, if so, why, if not why not, and how you can improve services to meet their wants. By developing a discipline of asking, by getting everyone in the organization in the habit of market research through asking, you will learn extremely important things, many of which will completely astound you.

How do you ask? You can ask formally, through surveys or focus groups. Also, you can ask informally every chance you get. You should, at the very least, establish some kind of baseline of employee and consumer satisfaction through a formal survey. You can then re-measure that satisfaction every 12 to18 months. You should also ask everyone that seeks or utilizes your services in any way how they came to you: was it a referral from a friend, did they see the ad in the paper, did they hear about you from their doctor (minister, art teacher)? You need to know these things, and evaluate trends over time.

There are a variety of ways of asking. Surveys and focus groups often sound very technical, complex, and expensive. Not always so. They are essential tools for you as you develop your asking skills, so let's look at them in some detail.

a. Surveys

Many organizations wrongly assume that establishing baseline survey data is very expensive and the purview of only expensive marketing firms like Harris or Gallup. And certainly, polls and surveys *can* be expensive, sometimes prohibitively so. But let's focus on the important components of a good survey, and then you can decide how you are able to provide or find the expertise in-house, locally, or out-of-town.

First, surveys need to be *focused* around a central theme. Don't ask a referral source the same things you would ask an employee, and also don't ask the employee ten questions about job satisfaction if your main survey goal is to find out what staff want in terms of non-cash compensation.

Second, your survey needs to *ask the right questions*; ones that will generate the information you need. In deciding what questions to ask, be frugal. What do you really want to know? Is it about customer satisfaction in general or about their satisfaction with a particular program? Target your questions.

Third, you need to *ask the questions right*. There is a great deal of difference in the responses you will get depending on how you ask the question. I can generate a huge difference in responses about a particular program if I ask the question "On a scale of 1 to 5 how much did you like the program?" as opposed to asking "Did the program appeal to you or not?"

Fourth, surveys need to be *short enough* to have people fill them in. As a rule, if it *looks like* it will take more than 5 minutes and the respondent is filling out the survey only out of kindness, it won't happen.(You can have longer surveys filled in if you are compensating them: giving them money, a lunch, a free coupon for a pizza, etc.)

Fifth, to make the whole exercise worth it, you have to survey enough people to have a *representative sample.* If you are a church, and you want to survey your congregation's attitude toward a new church building, asking three people out of a congregation of 600 will not tell you what you need to know. On the other hand, not making a move until you have surveyed 597 of the 600 members is foolish.

As you can see, many of these issues are technical, and thus most organizations get some help in setting up their survey. There are some excellent written resources on surveying. A second source is the marketing or social sciences department of your local university, where you might get adopted as a student project. Also, the marketing professor might be willing to help you pro bono, or for a much lower fee than a proprietary marketing firm. Finally, this is another instance of a good spot for a "targeted volunteer", the kind that was discussed in the chapter on Controls.

Surveys are excellent information gathering tools, but get some help with your first one, and don't do just one. Do them regularly, and compare and analyze the data you receive.

b. Focus Groups

Focus groups are great. While they do not generate the kind of objective data that surveys do, the subjective information gathered on feelings, reactions, impressions, and opinions is invaluable. At their core, focus groups are sessions of one to two hours with a *focused* set of questions posed to 10 to 15 people who represent a market or homogenous group. A focus group is almost always run by an outside facilitator, and I urge you to find a local facilitator who is experienced with focus groups, because the quality of the facilitator makes or breaks these sessions. The great benefit of a focus group is that a talented facilitator can follow up on ideas and answers generated by the group, investigating leads that you could never expand on in a formal survey. For instance, a facilitator might ask a question about: "What kind of service improvements could we make for kids?" and a participant might give an excellent idea. Right then and there, the facilitator can pose the new idea to the rest of the group, gathering on-the-spot reactions and modifications that can lead to earlier and more successful implementation. When looking for a facilitator, look for the talent in group facilitation first, and the knowledge of your program second. Once you retain the facilitator, he or she needs to get up to speed on all aspects of the issues your focus group will be discussing, including jargon, and potentially controversial issues.

You also need to hold separate groups for separate issues, even though it is more time consuming and costly. Don't expect a group of lower income service recipients to be as forthcoming if they are mixed in with affluent donors. And, you do need to focus your questions. You just can't ask everyone everything you might want to know. People wear down after about 2 hours, so don't wring them dry.

c. The Discipline of Asking and Listening

Asking people what they want is in itself an image enhancer for your organization. I have facilitated over 100 focus groups in the past ten years, and our firm has surveyed at least 15,000 people. During those activities, one of the comments we hear most often is "Thanks for asking! No one ever has before." By asking, you get valuable information *and* make people feel better about your organization, all in one action. What a deal!

However, there are a couple of other important points to keep in mind about asking. If you ask, you *must* listen. And you may not hear things that make you happy, especially at first. You'll almost certainly hear criticisms of your programs, your management style, your philosophy of service. Take them as opportunities to improve, not as personal assaults on your capabilities and character. And, if you listen, you need to respond, both orally and in writing. Thank people for offering their insights, perhaps in a memo to all who participated in a survey, or in a personal note to anyone who took the time to offer their reactions in a focus group. In that correspondence, close the loop with them and let them in on what you are doing with their ideas. You can put the main ideas that came out of the survey/focus groups into four categories:

1. *Things that you'll be able to do right away.*
2. *Things that you'll have to work on over the near term.*
3. *Things you will need to defer to future years.*
4. *Suggestions that are inappropriate or impossible.*

Tell people all of those things. If the ideas are going into a strategic plan, say so. If they are being passed on to your main funding source, let that be known. If they are going to be used to plan a major capital campaign, a new program for a specific group, an additional site, or any tangible outcome, let people know. Be forthright, don't promise what you can't deliver on, but *do* get back to people.

What can you learn by asking? Wonderful things.

● **FOR EXAMPLE:** A few years ago, our firm helped a rural primary care health center with a community perception survey and focus groups. We facilitated a number of focus groups: two of current patients, one of former patients, and one of community officials. We found a number of common complaints/suggestions during these sessions. These are listed below, with the actions that the health center took to respond.

"Your center looks run down, inside and out." The center found that the grounds maintenance service was not doing the job. Slowly, over time the appearance of the facility had declined, and the staff had not noticed. But the patients, who only came in once or twice a year noticed the difference.The clinic changed maintenance contractors with an emphasis on trash removal and neatness. Inside, a new coat of paint, and more staff emphasis on picking up and neat workspaces, resulted in a much higher satisfaction rating in this area the following year: Total cost: $500 in painting.

"Your receptionist is rude." This feeling was very prevalent among *former* patients, but a fact that the administrator had never noticed—because when he was treated, he didn't enter through the normal patient reception lines. The receptionist was given sensitivity training. That didn't help much, so she was transferred to a different clerical job. Total cost: $100 for the training.

"Your toys are dirty—I worry about the kids catching a bug when they play with them." In fact, the toys were cleaned every night, they were just old. The center bought new toys each year and had the staff clean them in *front of the patients* every day. Total cost: $200 per year.

After these items and a few others were resolved, the center got back to all those interviewed, with particular emphasis on the former patients, noting the changes—new toys, new receptionist, better main- tenance that had resulted from the information gathered at the focus groups. *Every single former patient returned* within the next six months for an office visit. The patients liked the practitioners, and the practition- ers hadn't thought that they cared about these non-medical, but still important issues.   The center never would have known why patients were leaving if they hadn't asked.

Ask, listen, act, respond! It works.

3. DEVELOP THE SERVICE

Only now that you know who your markets are and what your markets want, can you, to varying extents, modify your service array, or develop a new service. Some readers will be hamstrung by service definitions dictated by their funding source: "you must provide inpatient 28-day residential rehabilitation", or "you must have each child tested in an approved setting every 18 months", or whatever guideline you must follow. But you need to try to match your services to your markets and their wants as closely as possible, noting that those wants will change over time.

This is an excellent place to note the conflict represented in the paragraph above: the funder wants you to provide a service in a particular way, whether or not the recipient wants it that way. Look carefully at what is going on—to meet a payer's want (service provided within specific guidelines) you may have to give the service market's wants a lower priority. This is an excellent example of the conflicts that you need to try to resolve, and the balance that you need to try to achieve. It's tough, and no one should misunderstand that. Often, a program that is wildly successful in one community catches the eye of a funder who wants to have it replicated elsewhere. Too often the success was a result of a confluence of events in that initial community, a key staff person or volunteer, a community event that precipitated demand for the program, and not because of the fundamental attractiveness of the program itself. In his book *Reinventing Government*, David Osborne recounts the story of a woman in the Bronx who has organized a tenants group to run their low income housing unit and has turned it around. The group worked out all sorts of ideas and methods to reduce crime, increase occupancy, improve tenants' lives. But Osborne, who advocates similar empowerment programs elsewhere in the country, also found that without the key leader, all of the other items, no matter how admirable, were not used.

In marketing terms, if people don't *want* it to happen enough to *work* for it, it won't happen, and in many cases your organization will try to replicate a program before there is a demand for it. That is hard, hard work. In these cases you also need to ask, and ask regularly, to see if you can refit the program to meet the wants that exist in your community now, rather than in some other community three years ago.

You must also be sure that you have *listened*, and that *all of the staff* is on board and prepared for the changes the market wants.

● **FOR EXAMPLE:** A few years ago, our firm was asked to assist a number of community substance abuse rehabilitation providers with broadening their markets. In discussing this project with the providers, it was clear that they wanted to move beyond the Medicaid-eligible client to, as they put it, "serve the executive covered by Blue Cross". The reasons for this market shift were understandable and valid: the providers could recoup $120 per day from Blue Cross for a service they were then getting $65 per day for from Medicaid. But were they ready to provide the services? They said they were, and many had, in fact, upgraded their physical plant markedly.

I asked them if their staff were also ready to serve this different clientele: noting that business executives, even ones with substance abuse problems, have significantly different expectations than their traditional clientele: those eligible for Medicaid. I was assured that the staffs were ready for this change. I doubted it.

So we checked. We had a woman on our staff call each of the agencies in question and ask for help for her husband, who was portrayed as an alcoholic who worked for a large firm and had Blue Cross coverage. She also called the community hospitals who had competing substance abuse programs in each community. In every single case, the community rehab center staff blew it. The receptionist didn't have any knowledge of Blue Cross. She referred the "patient" to a staff person who was either equally limited in knowledge or never called back. There was never any follow-up to the call in writing or by phone. On the other hand, every single hospital had its act together. The caller talked with a knowledgeable and sympathetic nurse immediately in each case. The nurse followed up by phone and with solid marketing material in the mail.

I returned to a meeting of the community providers armed with this information, and they, frankly, didn't accept it as valid. So I asked them to exchange business cards with another provider, and take a break, and go call in and pretend to be a person seeking care. They returned 15 minutes later and reported their experiences which were uniformly awful.

They and their staff were not yet ready to serve the market that they had targeted. They were not ready to meet the market wants, because they had not asked the market what they wanted: they had *assumed* that they knew, and in marketing, assuming that you know what the market wants is not only egotistical and arrogant, it is suicide.

Ask, but *listen* to the answers.

4. PRICE THE SERVICE

There are so many variables in pricing, most of which you don't control, that I won't take a lot of space discussing pricing here. Also, there are many excellent resources in pricing strategy. Suffice it to say that most not-for-profits underprice their services either because of the training they have gotten from funders (funders don't want to reimburse all of your costs), naivete, or both. However, learning how to price, to say nothing of knowing what an individual unit of service *actually costs* to provide, is a critical skill to develop in any organization. Knowing what your costs are and which programs are making money, which are losing money, and which are breaking even is a key component of any plan for financial empowerment (see Chapters 11 and 12).

I do, however, need to cover these key points. Pricing is both an art and a science. Price development is fluid, not static. It is affected by many dynamics. Pricing is comprised of four components:

a. Fixed Costs: These are the costs that you normally think of as "overhead". Technically, they are the costs that are fixed whether "sales" rise or fall. So, for example, in a school, the administrative costs and building and maintenance are fixed costs, because they won't change if the enrollment (the sales) goes from 70 to 90 (or 70 to 50). The crux of charging a fixed cost component is the issue of how quickly you want to recover these costs—over how many sales. For example, if you tried to recover the entire fixed cost of a Chrysler factory in one auto, the price would be a little steep. Chrysler tries to recover that cost over millions of cars. But if they add too low a charge for the fixed cost component in each car's price, and don't sell enough, they lose money on their fixed costs.

b. Variable Costs: These are the costs that vary as the sales vary. In manufacturing they include the raw materials for the product, the unit costs of labor, and the energy to produce the product. In my school example, there would be the costs directly associated with each student: food, supplies, linens, and differing energy costs (for a residential school). As the enrollment increases these costs increase.

c. Profit: Yes, this is OK. A not-for-profit can have a profit, and nowhere in any regulation or law does it say that you can't. It's just your funding sources that say you shouldn't. The profit you make will help you pay off debt, and put money aside. More about this critical issue in the financial empowerment chapters, but for our purposes here, let's just note that you need a profit. The component of price attributable to the profit will depend on how quickly you want to recover your initial investment and how much the market will bear. Usually the profit margin will be some small percentage (probably 3 to 8%) of the price.

d. Competition and Market Conditions: The competition has much to do with what your price is. If you price out your item (for example, tuition at our hypothetical school) and find, in comparing your tuition to the competition's, that yours is 20% higher, what will that mean? It may mean that you will lose students to the lower-priced school. Conversely, it may mean that you will gain students who want to go to only the "elite" (read: expensive) school.

Obviously this is a very fluid situation. In the case of the school, let's imagine a teacher's union arriving, and a contract signed guaranteeing increases in salary for the next five years. What just happened to fixed costs? They went up. Or what if three graduates get full scholarships to Harvard, or if the test scores for seniors are top in the state, or if the football team is nationally ranked? Demand for enrollment will increase. In one case your price (tuition) *needs* to go up due to cost increases. In the other, the price (and the profit) *can* go up due to market conditions.

Don't fall into the trap of assuming that you can just underprice everyone and that will make people come to your organization. First, it's just plain dumb (which is not to say that people don't do it all the time). If you just keep cutting prices, and have prices less than your costs, you will soon be out of business unless you have very, very deep pockets and can outlast your competition. All one has to do is look at the suicidal price wars that the major airlines have engaged in over the past decade to see that. The second good example is auto rebates. They do encourage sales, but at a loss to the automakers. I can think of a dozen examples of our not-for-profit clients in business development coming to us and saying that they planned to compete on price—without knowing whether or not they could do so and still make money. As I noted earlier, there are a great number of good resources on pricing, and your accountant may also have ideas on this.

5. PROMOTE THE SERVICE

There are dozens of ways to promote your services: word of mouth, referrals, advertising, personal contact, presentations to community groups, flyers put under windshield wipers, and of course, brochures. How you promote your service will depend on your budget, your service, and the people you are trying to inform that you are there. But no matter what your status, think about this: with all of the different *payer* markets and all of the different *referral* markets you have, to say nothing of all of the different *service* markets you are trying to attract and retain, does one brochure with a short history of your organization and a picture of your building really get your point across? Of course it doesn't. Yet that's what most not-for-profits have: a brochure that talks about the organization's genesis, lists its services, often in jargon, and sometimes doesn't even include a phone number.

My question is: Who really cares about a picture of your building? Probably no one but the architect and the builder. Who cares about your history? Hardly anyone, except those who were there at the time. Can one short brochure really attract people with all sorts of different wants to your organization? Can it really explain how your organization can meet the wants of funders, donors, referrers, service recipients? Of course not.

Promotion, whether in person, or written, must *never sell the program*. Rather, it must *attempt to solve the customers' problem*. If I am the parent of a developmentally disabled child, do I care how long you've been in business? No. I want good evaluation and educational opportunities for my son or daughter. I want you to recognize me as a customer. I want to feel that you are sympathetic to my feelings and that you will provide only the best services on the planet to my child. I want to know how much it is going to cost me. So your marketing material must say those things, clearly and in straightforward prose. Show me the benefit that I will receive by sending my child to your organization.

Remember the number one rule of sales: *Don't sell the product— solve the customer's problem.* You need to let the potential users of your service, the potential funders, staff, and board (in other words, all of your markets) know what benefit they will gain from using your services, or donating money to you, etc. Don't just tell them who you are, or what you do, make the connection between what you do and how it will help them. Wording such as "XYZ agency provides substance abuse rehabilitation services" is much less compelling than: "If you or a loved one have a problem with substance abuse, the staff at XYZ can help put them on the road to a more productive, less dependent life." The first talks about services (in jargon), the second promises benefits.

The other major flaw in most not-for-profit promotion comes from falling into the "census trap" I discussed earlier in this chapter. Organizations that wrongly assume that their market is the entire population often also assume that the entire population needs to know about their organization and waste a great deal of time and money trying to achieve that goal.

● **FOR EXAMPLE:** A client of mine, a rehabilitation facility specializing in head injury patients, recently bemoaned the fact that they had done a public awareness survey and only 6% of the area's population recognized the organization's name and knew what general services were provided. Both the Executive Director and the board were adamant about spending money (a great deal of money) on a public awareness campaign that would, in their words, "solve this problem".

"What problem?" I asked.

"Not enough people know about us!" was their startled answer.
"So? Do patients self refer?"

"No," they replied.

"Do you get 5% or more of your money in small donations from the general public?"

"No," they replied.

"Where do your referrals come from?"

"From area neurologists and surgeons," they said.

"What percentage of those physicians know about your programs in detail?"

"We don't know," was their answer.

"Find out, and forget about the public. They don't need to know about you (nor do they want to, for that matter). You need to focus your efforts on your referral sources."

This example is a classic one of misunderstanding the target market, as well as the market wants.

6. PROVIDE (DISTRIBUTE) THE SERVICE

Once you have developed the service you need to provide it. Here you have lots of choices, and are probably doing an excellent job in being flexible, but let's review the options. Just like solving a mystery, writing a story, or preparing a book report, the key parameters of service provision to meet market wants are WHO, WHAT, WHEN, WHERE, and WHY.

▶ **WHO** provides the service. You can't just have someone who is knowledgeable in the service area, you need someone who can "connect" with the service recipient. Someone who doesn't speak Spanish is not going to be an optimal provider in a largely Hispanic neighborhood. Someone who acts very "square" probably won't be the best with kids in a youth ministry.

▶ **WHAT** service is provided. You've already established this through the previous steps.

▶ **WHERE** the service is provided. Your clientele need easy access to the extent possible. Is the place you provide service convenient, is there adequate parking, sufficient security? In the past few years, more and more hospitals are providing off-site radiology and therapy sites that are closer to where their patients live. This helps the patients avoid having to come to the central hospital where parking is often difficult, security is sometimes inadequate, especially after dark, and where patients must walk long distances from their car to their service site.

▶ **WHEN** the service is provided. A family planning seminar for teenagers is pointless if held at your office during the weekday when the kids are in school. The flexible *when* is a key component of market sensitivity in today's predominantly two-income and/or single-parent families. People seek services at odd hours and value time-saving convenience over many other considerations. Thus Domino's Pizza thrives, Toys 'R' Us is experimenting with around-the-clock stores during the pre-Christmas period, and 24-hour convenience stores are solid franchise investments. Be convenient and you will increase both market share and market satisfaction.

▶ **WHY.** Don't forget the *why*. Why is this particular service being provided? To educate, to prevent, to entertain, to cure, to sooth, to enlighten? The *why* becomes a key component of the provision mix, and should always be close at hand.

7. EVALUATE THE MARKETING EFFORT

As I mentioned earlier, you need to know how you are doing. Getting baseline information is a good start, but steady and consistent asking is essential. Are your staff happier than last year? Are you getting better quorums at board meetings than two years ago? Is attendance or occupancy up or down? Are more people responding to advertising or to referrals? You need to ask, ask regularly, and ask consistently.

Also, be cognizant of the fact that the wants and needs of the markets are constantly changing. Thus you may need to change with them. The only way to accurately assess the changes is by asking and tracking the answers over time.

C. ASKING DOES MAKE A DIFFERENCE

I often am asked to speak to annual meetings of statewide or national not-for-profit trade associations, and I regularly point out to them that their best customers are their biggest funders. There is usually uncomfortable silence. I then ask them: "When was the last time any of you went to your state (federal, county) project officers and asked them 'How can I make your job easier?' " There is either silence or laughter. I then point out that this is basic marketing. After these sessions, I am often asked: "What difference will it make if we ask a bureaucrat how to make their life easier? They have no control over our money."

This is an understandable question, and in response I want to offer two examples of what a difference such a simple, no cost technique *can* make.

● **FOR EXAMPLE:** As I told you in the first chapters, in the early 1980's I was the Executive Director of a Health Systems Agency, a not-for-profit formed as a result of federal law, and almost 100% federally funded. We did health care planning and regulation for a specific geographic area. Our federal contacts were in Chicago, at the Federal Regional Office Building.

Shortly after I became Exec, I had to go to Chicago for a meeting, and I made it a point to meet not only with my Federal Program Officer, who was nominally my key contact, but also with the woman who was our Grants Administration Officer, the person who processed our budget, vouchers, and grant checks. This woman, whose name was Betty, worked in a windowless office in the midst of a vast, drab, government building, but she was warm, personable, and obviously pleased to have been visited. "I rarely get to meet the people at the agencies," she said. "In fact, I think it's been three years since I got face-to-face with someone from the field." I said that I was glad to meet her, and that I hoped that our staff would process all of the forms for her correctly, but if we messed up, I wanted her to call me right away. Betty responded appreciatively, noting that everyone usually denies filling in the forms wrong, or complains about their length, instead of offering to cooperate. I told her I would think of her as my best customer. She laughed and we parted friends. The next time I was in Chicago, and the next and the next, I stuck my head in Betty's office and said hi. That was the total extent of my "marketing" with her.

Two years later, 10 days before our 200-page grant application for federal funds was due, our financial manager quit on three day's notice and left the financial part of the application incomplete. I did my best to fill it out and get it in on time, and beat the deadline by 12 hours.

Three weeks afterwards I found out that I had not done a very good job. Betty called me at work on a Thursday afternoon to let me know that a number of figures were wrong, and that she could not submit our application to Washington the next day at five unless they were redone. My heart went through my shoes. How could I rework all those figures and still get them in to her in 24 hours? Betty said "Stay cool. Just put me on hold, pull out pages 23-27 of the financial section, go make a copy of them and get back on the phone." I obediently did so. Betty said, "OK, see line 27c, column 2? You have $356,798 there now. Change it to $398,558." And so it went. Betty had done my work for me. She had spent the previous evening redoing over 100 calculations and essentially saved my organization. I filled out a new form and overnighted it (this was the era before faxes) to Chicago. We got the grant.

I have always believed that, because I treated Betty like a friend and a customer rather than as a bureaucratic enemy, she went the extra mile for me. There was no serious cost to this, it was just good marketing.

● **FOR EXAMPLE:** A few years ago we did a number of focus groups for a residential school that worked with behavior disordered teens. One of the groups was with a primary referral source: juvenile delinquent officers or JDO's. The session was spent assessing what the school was doing well, not so well, and could do better. At the end of the session I posed the question: "What can the school do to make your job easier?" After a long silence, one JDO said "Interesting question, and one I've never heard before. But one thing does come to mind. You know the admission verification form (J-345A) that you need to fill out after you admit a child that we refer to you? Well, my supervisor is all over me to get those in, 'cause then we get our Federal match. Your people are getting those to me in 45 to 60 days, and they're only one page long. Could you get them to us in 21 days, maybe?" The other five JDO's in that session concurred on the need for these forms to be turned in sooner.

I said, "How would seven days be?" "*Terrific!*" they replied, "Oh and thanks for asking." "Keep letting us know what we can do," I said.

I returned to the school to report on the session and brought up the request. "No problem," said the staff, " we didn't realize they needed the form in a hurry. We'll get them out the same day, as part of the admission protocol." They started implementing the change that day.

The next year, the referrals from those six JDO's were up 15% and at this writing, seven years later, they continue to climb, and those six people constitute the highest referral group for the school.

The lesson here is two-fold. First, by asking, we made a very positive impression. By responding, we made an even bigger one. It was a small thing, a minor question, a no-cost response, but it paid huge long-term rewards.

Don't assume that people who work in a bureaucracy are necessarily mired in it. Choices have to be made: where pilot money goes, or lapse funds, or the most interesting research is run, and so on. If you meet the wants of the funders, the funders will help you meet yours.

RECAP

Marketing is an excellent example of the topic that I broached in Chapter 1; that the business world has a lot to offer the not-for-profit world in terms of techniques and expertise. As a mission-based manager, you want to tap that experience in surveying, market identification, promotion, and pricing, all in an effort to do more mission, more efficiently and effectively.

You market every day. Your staff needs to understand this, and that they are a critical part of the marketing team. If you don't market aggressively, if you don't work to keep your market share, you may have none in ten years.

In this chapter we have covered several issues that are central to the improvement of your organization:

▶ *the fact that everything you do every day is marketing.*
▶ *the fact that your markets are much more numerous and diverse than you may have previously thought.*
▶ *the real process of marketing.*
▶ *the ways to ask what your markets want.*
▶ *the ways to develop a discipline of asking.*
▶ *the methods to assure that your marketing efforts are on track.*
▶ *examples of organizations that have profited by asking and by giving their funders what they want.*

Hopefully, you have found ideas that you can incorporate into your organization as you go about building a culture of marketing, a tradition of asking, and an organizational appreciation for your markets, their diversity, and their changing wants.

Overall, the importance of continuing marketing cannot be overstressed. It needs to become part of your culture, and should also become an integral component of your staff training and continuing education program—for everyone in the organization.

10. A Vision to Make the Future

OVERVIEW

Organizations that succeed, organizations that thrive, organizations that are going to be the providers of services in the next century, all know where they are going. A vision of what you want your organization to be, and a road map of how you want to get from here to there, is absolutely essential if you are to be a good steward of your organization's resources. This chapter will give you some hands-on ideas of how to plan, and how to use both the planning process and the plan itself as a tool for the benefit of your organization.

In the following pages, you will read about the nine phases of the planning process and I will provide some detailed ideas on how to use that process. We'll review the four reasons why you should develop and maintain a plan, examine some varying philosophies of planning, and I will offer recommendations on how often you should plan, how inclusive the planning process should be, and how to go about evaluating the planning process and the plan's implementation status.

After that, we'll look at various types of plans, define some important terms in the planning process, and look at outcomes that you can expect from a good planning process and plan. I will also describe a variety of uses of your plan once you have it completed, we'll look at some barriers to planning, and I will include an outline to help you get started.

By the time you finish with this chapter, you should have a better understanding of the task you need to tackle. If you are new to planning, reading this chapter will help you get acquainted with the need for planning and how to do it. If you are an experienced planner, you will probably pick up a nugget or two on how to make your next plan even better.

A. PHASES OF PLANNING

Good planning occurs in several phases. The list below is fairly complete, and we will review each phase in some detail. However, I want to make several points about the list as a whole. First, the sequence listed is just that: a sequence. While it allows for a great deal of flexibility in how you actually do the planning, I urge you to do your planning in this order. I have helped well over 50 organizations of all types and sizes develop their planning processes and their plans, and this sequence has been tried and tested: it works. While there may be a certain overlap—for example, with Data Gathering starting about the same time as the Retreat and extending into the time of Drafting Goals and Objectives—the basic sequence should be preserved.

The phases of planning that I suggest are:

1. *Preparedness*
2. *The Retreat*
3. *Data Gathering*
4. *Drafting Goals and Objectives*
5. *Outside Comment*
6. *Final Draft and Adoption*
7. *Implementation*
8. *Evaluation*
9. *Go Back to 1.*

As I have noted, in a few pages we will go through each phase in some detail, but first we need to discuss some philosophies, decide on which type of plan you intend to develop, provide some definitions, and look at the outcomes that you can expect.

B. WHY PLAN?

Too few organizations that I consult with have a strategic plan. The excuses are many, and we'll discuss them in more detail near the end of this chapter, but the most prevalent concern is "with rapidly changing circumstances I don't want to be stuck with some plan that is totally out of date." I agree. But the planning horizons that we will talk about are not overly long (three to five years) and the key to strategic planning is one of strategy, not of tactics. The issues that you should be considering in a strategic plan both need to be planned for and should not be greatly changed within the planning cycle. Also, your planning process should be ongoing, so that if some major change is initiated in your field, you can adapt the plan to it. I would also argue that few if any major changes in service delivery or funding patterns occur overnight. Usually major changes are researched, discussed, rumored, and debated for months or even years before they are enacted. Thus, in the part of the planning process where you look at the environment, you will be able to predict most of these changes in advance.

Good plans actually help you remain flexible because, like good marketing, they keep you and your organization focused on what is important, and assist you in not wasting resources, not getting tied down in fruitless or out-of-date services, and keeping your staff and board up-to-date on the realities of the world that you are working in. Also, the well-run planning process is often a wake-up call for board and staff members who still think they are working in 1980, and this enlightenment makes later change less difficult for them.

With that in mind, let's examine the four reasons that you should expend the time, money, energy, and political capital to develop a plan.

1. WITHOUT A PLAN, THE ONLY WAY YOU GET WHERE YOU ARE GOING IS BY ACCIDENT

What your organization does is too important to occur by accident. Yogi Berra said it even better: *"If you don't know where you are going, you will wind up somewhere else."*

● **FOR EXAMPLE:** Let's look at the planning process through the metaphor of a family vacation. If you and your family are getting ready to go on vacation, once you know you have the time off and want to go together (Preparedness), you will certainly get together as a family and decide where you are going (the Retreat). Let's assume that you decide to drive to San Francisco and stay for a week. You have to first set the long-term goal of getting there. Your strategy is to go by car. To achieve your goal you buy a road map, check your money and the condition of you car (Data Gathering), and plan your route and your itinerary (Set Goals and Objectives). You will check the conditions enroute and in San Francisco—things like the weather, roads, tolls, fuel, and hotel costs (Assess the Environment), and probably call some friends who have been to San Francisco recently for ideas and feedback (Gather Outside Comment). You then finalize your plans, get packed, and leave (Implement). If between home and San Francisco, you find that a road is under construction, or that there is a place you had not heard about that you want to see, you may vary either your route or your timetable.

Congratulations. You have just done strategic planning. The important thing to remember here, however, is what you didn't do. You didn't just pack up, drive to the first corner and say "Where are we going?" And then go to the next intersection and say "Which way?" and the next and the next. But in your organization, when you don't have a plan, when you act only in reaction to events, when you go from only one funded program to the next or one community need to the next, you wind up in some very strange, and sometimes dangerous places, just the way you would on your vacation if you chose each turn at random. Planning allows you to see where you are going and to transmit that information to the people who are going with you: your staff, board, funders, community, and most important, your clientele.

2. A STRATEGIC PLAN ALLOWS ALL OTHER PLANNING (BUDGETS, STAFFING, FUNDRAISING) TO BE COORDINATED

When you have a good, current strategic plan, you can coordinate the activities of your organization better by using the strategic plan and its overall goals as a basis for decisions. You can discuss management, program, and policy choices in light of the priority goals of your plan. You can ask questions about whether or not a particular item in the budget supports the long-range plan. For example, if, in your strategic plan you have a five-year goal to build a new building and you need to have 30% of the cost of the building put aside, you probably need to show that set-aside in this year's financial plan. And if, as part of that building program, you intend to have 40% of the cost paid for by a capital fund drive starting in two years, your marketing and development staff had better be laying the groundwork for that fund drive this year.

Without your strategic plan, you cannot accomplish this type of coordination.

3. PLANS ALLOW YOU TO DELEGATE MORE EFFECTIVELY

Successful managers know how to delegate well, and how to push the line staff to make as many decisions as possible. Giving up responsibility and authority is very difficult for some people. Having the framework of the strategic plan can make that action easier. The manager who is delegating has a work plan based on the strategic plan for the subordinate to follow. Also, if the subordinate was involved in the planning process, his or her understanding and commitment will be much higher and the likelihood of effective delegation will increase.

4. PLANS ARE GOOD BUSINESS

By now you know that I consider your not-for-profit a mission-oriented business. Good businesses of all types know where they are going. They know their markets and their resources. They have planned how to use the resources to satisfy their markets. They may differ in their products or services, and often differ in their internal philosophies, but they all have one thing: a strategic plan that frames the rest of their activities and provides a benchmark for evaluating their success or failure.

C. PLANNING OPTIONS

There are a variety of ways to do planning. These options include how often plans should be updated, how inclusive the planning process should be, and whether or not to regularly evaluate the implementation of the plan. I have tried to summarize these choices below to point out some of the advantages and disadvantages of each. I then provide my recommendation for each area.

1. FREQUENCY

While there are an infinite number of permutations of the combination of planning horizon (how long the plan is to be in effect) and planning update (how soon should the plan be redone), the options I list below are the most common.

▶ *A five-year plan updated every five years.*
This is obviously the long-term view, and the advantage is that you only have to think about the plan twice each decade. The problem is that it assumes that everything will go as planned, both inside the organization and outside it, for the full five years, and that is naive, to say the least. Imagine a five-year plan written in 1979. It could not have foreseen the Reagan Revolution and the huge effects that it would have on the nation's not-for-profits. Now imagine a five-year plan written in 1991 that assumed that George Bush would win reelection in a walk and that there would be no such thing as national health care reform. You get the point. The second problem with this approach is that as you get to the end of five years, you lose the momentum from the planning process. People (both on the board and the staff) will have left and there may be only a few of the core planning team remaining. Thus the lessons learned and the ownership gained will be lost.

▶ *A one-year plan updated each year.*

This sounds and acts an awful lot like an annual budget and work plan document. It is the most capable of reacting swiftly to changing circumstances, but you lose the big picture, and tend to be shaped by events rather than shaping them. We criticize the government (at all levels) for not thinking beyond the current fiscal year. Don't fall into the same trap. Strategic planning needs to be that: strategic.

▶ *A five-year plan with one-year components.*

This is a combination of the first two, but one that works fairly well. It allows for the long-term strategic vision to guide the flexible annual plan developed each year. The problem with this is that the overall big document is not done often enough, at least in my experience.

▶ ▶ *Recommendation: five-year plan redone every three years, with annual budgets/work plans.*

I feel that the best way to approach the strategic planning cycle is on a basis of a five-year plan, redone completely every three years, but with annual work plans done every year. Let me explain. A five-year horizon forces the staff and board that create the goals and objectives of the plan to step back from the day-to-day concerns of the organization and look at the big picture. This is essential. By reworking the full plan every three years you accomplish three important things: you keep the planning process fresh in the organization, you can react to environmental changes, and you can have each board member take part in the creation of a strategic plan once in his or her three-year term, which is the term that I recommend in Chapter 5. By having an annual plan of action that supports the strategic plan, you have the staff pull out the highest priority items for each year's work plan, and the board is kept apprised of the implementation status of the plan.

2. PROCESS

Once you decide what planning horizon and update schedule you will use, you then need to decide what process of planning you will have. Here, you have what I think is a golden opportunity to maximize the use of the planning process itself as a tool for organizational growth, improving staff and board morale and marketing your organization. However, your realization of that goal is dependent on which type of process you choose. Some choices are:

▶ *Keep It Small*

The idea here is to have the fewest possible number of people involved in the planning process so that you get it done and done quickly. Thus, staff and board might go on a short retreat to set the goals and priorities, then the senior staff, or even just the executive director, would draft the plan and bring it to the board for review and approval. The problem with this process is that it short-circuits one of the best parts of planning: bringing people in for their ideas and their ownership.

▶ *Highly Inclusive*

Speaking of ideas and ownership, that is what the inclusive process is all about. Inclusion in the planning process is designed to get input from all of your staff, board, funders, community representatives, clientele or their families or representatives, and any other group that you may need or want such as referral sources or alumni. You don't need to put all of these people on one giant planning committee. They can be involved in three ways: having a Planning Committee that is more broadly representative than just board members; asking a large number of people for input through surveys and focus groups during the data gathering phase; and encouraging a broad review and comment on the draft plan during that phase. In this way, you offer the opportunity for input to a much larger group, they in turn now have a feeling of pride in being asked and ownership in the final product that would not have been possible in the "keep it small" philosophy. Inclusion obviously takes longer, and is somewhat more expensive, but I am a strong advocate for using this method.

▶ *Planning Committee Generated*

This model has the board appoint a strong planning committee, made up of all board members, or board and staff combined, who generate the plan on their own, and bring it to the board for review and comment. Although not entirely exclusive of the method above, this process usually does not include a data gathering phase that looks at more than hard data. It almost never includes outside review and comment before the board sees it. It is a variant of "keep it small", and the one that organizations with strong committee structures tend to fall into. This process is fast and controlled, but it also does not include the entire board in the retreat setting, which is a mistake.

▶ *Staff Generated/Board Reviewed*

In a strong staff model of organization, there is the tendency to allow the staff to lead the board, and this sometimes includes the development of the long-range plan. Here, a group of senior staff would develop a draft plan and have it reviewed (and usually adopted with few changes) by the board. This model leaves the board—an essential resource—out of the loop, and also usually forgoes the inclusion that we have been discussing. It is fast, and it is controllable, but I feel that it has more drawbacks than benefits.

▶▶ *Recommendation: Inclusive as Possible*

My recommendation is easy to predict here: include as many people as time and money will allow. Start with a retreat of all board and senior staff. Then give the primary responsibility for coming up with a draft plan to a planning committee made up of board, senior staff, line staff, clientele, and community members. Ask lots of people for their input. Circulate the draft plan and listen to the comments. Publish and distribute the plan widely. This method is a lot of work, but it is the best method for maximizing the value of the planning process, in addition to getting the best plan.

3. EVALUATION

Unfortunately most people don't evaluate their plan at all, or hold off doing the evaluation until it is time to do the next plan. If you are going to use the plan as a management tool, you need to constantly be reviewing where you are in relation to where you wanted to be (your deadlines for your goals and objectives).

You need to review your progress toward your goals regularly. Otherwise you will get to the end of the planning cycle (three to five years) look back and discover that you have only achieved 15% of your goals because you got distracted.

▶▶ *Recommendation:*

Use the plan as a management tool. Once a month review it in senior staff meetings, asking: Are we on schedule for this goal? If not, why not? Have conditions changed? Are the resources that we thought would be available not there? The same holds for board meetings, but this should only be done quarterly.

Also, when the plan is complete, your planning committee needs to make written recommendations to the board about how to do the planning better the next time. These can be used by the next planning committee. If you don't write it down now, you will forget, and the experience of this committee will not benefit the next one.

138

D. TYPES OF PLANS

There are several categories that I put plans into. All of the plans that fit into these categories are intended to be strategic plans, and the people who wrote them intended them to be useful and flexible. But something happened along the way, and the results are:

▶ *Tomes*

These are documents that rival a New York City phone directory in size, take a professional football lineman to lift, and that nobody reads. They include everything you ever wanted to know, plus a lot more, and are too imposing and all-encompassing to be flexible and useful.

▶ *Work Plans*

These are just work assignments for the staff, often put together to submit to a major government funder. They cover the "what" in minute detail, but don't relate it at all to the all-important "why", the mission. They also ignore the larger strategic issues, such as overall strategies of service.

▶ *Public Relations Documents*

These documents purport to be plans, but spend most of their time selling the organization. They focus on the need for the organization in the community and the wonderful things it has done in the past. This leads to a lack of objectivity and an inability to see the organization "warts and all" which is crucial to good planning. Also, a strategic plan is not an appropriate place for you to do your marketing. It is not supposed to be a sales brochure or a "feelgood" document.

▶ *History Text*

These plans make up for their lack of forward thinking with a heavy emphasis on past accomplishments and how the organization was formed and grew. They are often produced by organizations that have grown rapidly and are so caught up in looking back at how far they have come that they forget to look ahead and see where they are going. This kind of plan is a great document for a student of your discipline who wants to know your history, but it usually only pays superficial attention to the changes in your community and where you want to be in five years.

▶ *Doctoral Dissertation*

This is a highly technical document, full of jargon and acronyms.

These types of papers are written by staff people who use the technical veil to hide a lack of understanding of some of the fundamental issues such as "What is our mission?" They cannot see the forest for the technical trees, and such a document is useless to non-professionals in your field, such as your board, some staff, the community, and the people you serve.

▶ *Working Document*

This is a document that provides strategic vision, but also practical application. A document that attends to the mission. A document that is written in lay language. One that is true to the wants of your clientele and expresses the best of what your board and staff have to offer.

▶▶ *Recommendation*

Do your best to get a working document as the product of your planning process. But, be wary of the traps that others have fallen into and try to avoid the other types of plans listed above.

E. PLANNING DEFINITIONS

Now it is time to define what I mean in the planning process. There are lots of different definitions and many misuses of the terms listed here. But, for purposes of our discussion, here are my definitions.

▶ *Strategic Plan.* A working document that discusses the organization's mission, the environment that it will work in over the planning period (three to five years), and the goals and objectives to realize the mission over that period. This is not a work plan, but it should be written with enough specificity that it is usable on a monthly basis by staff.

▶ *Goal.* A statement of desired long-term outcome. A goal may or may not be *quantified*, but usually does have a *deadline*.

▶ *Objective.* A much more specific statement that supports the goal. All objectives must have a *deadline*, be *quantified,* and have an *assigned responsible agent*—the person, group, or organization that is responsible for implementing the objective on time. There can be many objectives to implement a goal. Sometimes they will be sequential, sometimes simultaneous.

▶ *Action Statement.* The most specific item on the list, action statements support the implementation of an objective. They too need to be *quantified*, have a *deadline*, and an *assignment of responsibility*. For most organizations, these statements will be included only for high-priority goals or in the one-year plan that flows out of the five-year plan.

F. OUTCOMES OF PLANNING

What can you expect from the planning process? If you use my recommendations and renew your plan every three years, use an inclusive model, and evaluate the plan regularly, you can expect at least the following benefits:

▶ *Better and More Effective Services.* By evaluating during the plan development process what is needed and wanted and what is not; by asking people instead of assuming you know; by bringing customers, clients, patients, students, or parishioners into the planning loop, your plan will result in better and more effective services. You may find that you need to reduce or eliminate services that no longer make sense in terms of mission or in terms of markets, and you may find that services that you are sure are needed are not wanted and that certain services that you never even considered are in high demand. You will also hear a lot about current services: what works, what doesn't, small ways to make big improvements, practical (and sometimes impractical) methods of being more effective. The planning process helps you focus your resources on what is important, and that means better and more effective services.

▶ *Higher Ownership and Morale.* If you follow the inclusive model recommended here, you will have a higher overall morale of staff, board, funders, community, and clientele. Just asking people their opinion, just including them in the loop flatters them. If you then follow through and actually use some of their suggestions, and get back to them, and let them know that they were listened to, all of those who participated now have a stake in what you do and who you are. Additionally, if you are like most organizations who do not have an organizational strategic plan or have developed it a long time ago with only a few people, most of your staff as well as many of your board may never have been given the opportunity to see the big picture, to step back and look at the organization as a whole. Being part of an inclusive strategic planning effort allows that to happen.

▶ *Lower Levels of Conflict.* Planning, and the planning process I recommend, facilitates a forum for healthy debate over resources, discussions over direction, airing disagreements over policy and the shape of the organization in the future. By providing a positive structure for healthy conflict to emerge, and for unhealthy conflict to be vented, you allow those who harbor a grudge, who have not had their say in the past, who have felt "muzzled", to get on their soapbox and have their say. While not a preventative for all conflict in the organization, planning does provide the forum for discussion of policy and resource allocation. It also lets people have a clearer view, in writing, of what the organization stands for. This will confront some board, some staff, and perhaps some funders with the choice of staying or leaving. The clarity of purpose and the focus on the future of the organization make actions more predictable. It is often when people are surprised by actions that they are most upset.

G. THE PLANNING PROCESS

Now for the planning process itself. As I said earlier, I hope that you will adopt a process that meets your own organization's needs and capabilities, but still holds to this basic sequence. There is a lot of room for customization in this outline. For example, there is the time set aside for each activity. You may want the entire process to take three months (which is very, very fast) or allow it to take 18 months. You may want to only do focus groups in your Data Gathering phase, and not do primary research or surveys. You may decide to have the planning committee meet monthly, or just three times during the process. You may decide to minimize the Preparedness phase or take three months to have everyone in the organization trained in goal setting.

All of these variations are fine, as long as you don't skip any of the phases altogether. I know it is tempting to go straight to the fun part: the drafting of goals and objectives. But, if you do, you miss an opportunity for your organization. Take the time to do this right.

1. PREPAREDNESS

There is no point in starting this until you are ready. To get prepared, make sure that a number of things are in place. First, that your senior staff and key board members agree that planning is important and that they are willing to commit the time and the money necessary to see the process through. Second, develop a planning process and get your board to agree to it. Third, using the draft planning process, develop a planning budget, both of time and cash, that will be committed to the plan. Cash costs could include a retreat facility, meals and travel, data gathering costs such as surveys, focus groups, and possibly a consultant. I always recommend that organizations get a facilitator for their retreats, and, if this is the first time you have planned, you may also want to hire a planning consultant to help you lay out the process and advise you. Never hire a consultant to write the plan. That is your job.

2. THE RETREAT

The best way to get started is by getting away. I strongly suggest that all board members and senior staff go away for a day to cover at least the following things:

▶ *A review of your mission.*
▶ *An agreement on the planning process itself.*
▶ *A discussion of the environmental conditions under which you will be operating.*
▶ *The development of preliminary goals and a prioritization of those goals.*
▶ *The appointment of a planning committee.*

Have such a retreat at the start of each revision of the plan (every three years in my model).

☞ **HANDS ON:** Having facilitated over 60 retreats, I strongly prefer the evening-morning model over any other. Get your group together for dinner, let them review your planning process, review the mission, and consider what kind of world they will be operating in. Then quit and socialize. In the morning, the retreat participants will return fresh and ready to set goals and put them into a priority order for you. This model produces better results because it gives people a break, and also allows the staff present to socialize with the board—a key extra benefit.

At the retreat you need to do at least the following:

▶ *Review and agree on the planning process.*
▶ *Review and update your mission statement as necessary.*
▶ *Discuss your predictions for the world that your plan will be implemented in. What trends or activities are going to affect you and how?*
▶ *Walk through a SWOT analysis. (SWOT stands for Strengths, Weaknesses, Opportunities, and Threats.) These should be identified for your organization.*

▶ *Set preliminary long-term goals.*
▶ *Discuss the goals and do an initial prioritization of them.*

3. DATA GATHERING

Once you have the key goals, you can begin the job of data gathering. You can do this through hard data research and gathering from your own internal data, or at the library. Additionally, you can run focus groups and surveys of such people as staff, clientele, funders, alumni, and the like. For more information on surveys and focus groups, see the section on them in Chapter 9.

The data that you gather now will be used to help the planning committee and its subcommittees make the most knowledgeable decisions about the issues that confront you. Some data gathering will go on throughout the planning process, and you do not need to wait to begin drafting fuller goals and objectives until all the data are in.

4. DRAFTING GOALS AND OBJECTIVES

Now comes the fun part, the examination of the goals, and the setting of objectives to support them. You can use one of two methods for this. The first is to have your planning committee do all of this work for all of the goals set at the retreat. The second, used by most of the organizations that I assist in planning, is to have specialty subcommittees that examine certain areas in depth. For example, you might have a subcommittee on Administration, one on Finance, one on Programs, one on Marketing, etc. The breakout of the groups will depend on your organization. For example, a school might break the issues out by primary, middle, and secondary programs. A church, on the other hand, might have subcommittees on Finance, church-based Programs, Outreach Ministries, and Buildings & Grounds.

The benefits of using the subcommittee model are that each subcommittee can go into its subject in great detail, and you can add people to the planning subcommittees who are experts in the area. More inclusion.

Whoever is setting the goals and objectives needs to look first at the goals that came out of the retreat. Can they be consolidated? Improved? Are there important issues that were overlooked in a one-day retreat? Once the goals are established, then each goal in turn should have objectives added to it. This will happen before, during, and after the data are gathered. In fact, the setting of preliminary objectives will help you identify additional data that you need to go after.

Remember that the goals are long-term statements of desired outcomes, but the objectives need to have a deadline, be quantified, and have someone or some organization responsible for their implementation.

5. OUTSIDE COMMENT

Once the goals and objectives have been fully drafted it is time to get outside opinion. Let as many people as you have time for offer their comments. I usually suggest that major funders, your banker, key referrers, community leaders, representatives of your clientele, and all of your staff get a chance to review and comment on the plan. They should be given a deadline for getting their comments to you of about two weeks. Bring all of the comments to the planning committee.

6. FINAL DRAFT AND ADOPTION

When the planning committee has reviewed the comments and any late arriving data, the final draft can be written. At this time a second prioritization should be done, and the highest priority goals should be tackled in the one-year plan for the first year of the planning cycle. The one-year plan is really a work plan for staff and board.

This one-year plan should be developed by staff and should include Action Steps to accomplish high priority goals and objectives. The staff should run the one-year plan by the planning committee, but it needs only a cursory review.

Once the board adopts the strategic plan, get it printed and distribute it widely.

7. IMPLEMENTATION

As noted earlier, the plan should be a working document. Its use as a tool will be discussed in a page or two, but the point of the product is to do what the plan says. You've invested a great deal of time and effort getting the plan together, and, while the process has been useful, you still need to do what you've committed to. Implement!

8. EVALUATION

I've already told you how I think you should evaluate the plan's implementation, but you also need to evaluate the planning process. Write down any things you would change or improve and file it away for the benefit of the next planning committee.

9. GO BACK TO 1.

In three years, start again. By then, you will have had three one-year plans, conditions will have changed, you will have accomplished a great deal, but probably not all of your goals, and it will be time to develop a new five-year plan.

H. USING THE PLAN AS A TOOL

Once you have the plan completed, printed, and distributed, you now need to use it. There are a number of uses for your plan, some of which people neglect or never even consider.

1. A MANAGEMENT TOOL

The plan should be written in a format that allows you to use it as a management tool. Too few organizations do this. The plan tends to collect dust until it is time to update it, and, as a result, there is little interest in doing the update.

The progress in achieving the goals, objectives, and action statements in the *One-Year Plan* should be reviewed at least monthly in staff meetings, and, in some cases, every two weeks to make sure that you are still on track, that situations have not changed, or resources have not been reduced to make it more difficult to implement the plan. The senior staff as well as the line staff need to stay on top of anticipated deadlines and work toward meeting them.

The *Strategic Plan* implementation should be reviewed monthly at staff meetings, and quarterly at board meetings as a formal part of the session. Staff can report on progress or the planning committee can.

As new issues develop during the year, staff and board need to consider their impact on the plan. How will this effect our ability to complete the goals and objectives? If it will interfere, is this a higher priority? Which is more in line with our mission and our strategies? Use the plan as a guide, but don't be constrained by it.

2. A MARKETING TOOL

An organization that has a plan has a marketing tool. I know that I said that marketing and sales material belong in a marketing or sales piece, and that is still my position: the plan should be written as a plan, not as a sales brochure. But the very fact of your having a plan puts you ahead of many organizations, for-profit and not-for-profit. It's like having a mission statement: it helps people to know who you are and where you are going. This is excellent marketing to funders, potential donors, and elected officials.

3. A POLICY TOOL

A plan will help you do good policy, because the strategies included will remind you, and help new staff and board who join you to see what the belief of the organization is. For example, if you are a school for hearing impaired children, your organization may have adopted a communications policy that calls for the use of ASL (American Sign Language—the language preferred by most deaf people as opposed to signed English) on the campus. This policy will be reflected in your goals ("Within two years the school will have 100% of faculty and 90% of non-teaching staff fluent in ASL") and objectives ("The Director of Instruction will provide four ASL courses each year for staff", "The Director of Instruction will offer three off-campus ASL courses for parents per year", "The Director of Instruction will offer ASL to the general community three times next year"). All of these push the communications policy further and actualize it with a speed that would have only happened haphazardly otherwise. If you don't agree with the policy of ASL implementation, the plan tells you right up front, and if you are an ASL advocate, you also know that the school is in agreement immediately upon reading the plan.

4. A RECRUITMENT TOOL

As with the use of the plan as a marketing tool, the plan becomes an excellent recruitment tool to attract the board and staff that you want. You can show people the plan, and they will know before they decide to come on board what kind of organization you are and where you are going. If they like what they see, they are more likely to stay. Also, the better potential candidates (both staff and board) will be impressed with the simple fact that you have a plan, and are more likely to choose your organization over a competitor to give their time or services.

I hope that you recognize that your plan is valuable in a number of ways beyond the process and the document. You have spent a lot of time, effort, and money to develop the plan. Now, as a good steward, it is your responsibility to use this new resource as fully as possible.

I. BARRIERS TO PLANNING

Of course, there are barriers to planning. If there were none, everyone would have a great and up-to-date strategic plan in use, and you could have skipped this chapter altogether. There are many reasons not to plan, none of them really all that valid, but many good enough so that organizations never get to plan. Here is a starting list. Perhaps you can add a few from your own experience.

1. NO TIME

This is my personal favorite, since it is so widely used and so obviously false to anyone who really thinks about it. We all have the same twenty-four hours in the day. We may or may not choose to do a particular activity (such as planning) because other things are (or seem) more pressing, but we all have the time. What people really mean when they say this is "I choose not to plan because I am too busy fighting fires". For more on this, see "Poor Management" below.

2. STAFF RESISTANCE

Planning, especially when done for the first time in an organization, is a very unsettling experience for many employees. Some staff may try to dissuade the executive director from going ahead with a planning process because they are concerned that a plan will force major change on the organization—and eliminate programs or jobs, such as theirs. Planning, and asking the community for its opinion, is very threatening to many people, and you, as a planner and change facilitator, need to be aware of that perspective. You need to reassure the staff that planning is good mission, good business, good for the clientele, good for them, and that they will have significant impact on and input into the planning process.

3. BOARD RESISTANCE

What seems to happen here is that an executive director suggests to the board that the organization go through a planning process, and one or more of the board members object to the allocation of time and money to a process that does not directly and immediately affect clientele or the community. These board members have often been on the board since the inception of the agency and have the attitude: "We've come this far without a plan; why do we need one now?" or "That's just a lot of bureaucratic paper-pushing." Since the board is in control of policy and budget, this can be a significant barrier to overcome. Two suggestions for those readers faced with this issue: go over the conditions that your organization will be encountering (See Chapter 2) and the Characteristics of a Successful Organization (See Chapter 3) with your board. If that doesn't do the trick, go to Chapters 5 and 6 and the section on getting the board you need!

4. PLANNING IS A NON-PRODUCTIVE USE OF TIME

This is the excuse of the "fire-fighter" or the organization with a fee-for-services structure of reimbursement. It means that the organization is living by the skin of its teeth from payday to payday. Good planning requires contemplation, sitting back and thinking of options and circumstances well into the future. People and organizations that are totally crisis-oriented have a great and understandable difficulty in planning, especially the first time. This barrier also surfaces as staff or board resistance in a different guise.

You need to assure the board and staff that the time and money spent on planning is good stewardship, good management, good mission, and that they will see a benefit. Only the hard-core crisis junkies really want to go from fire to fire.

5. PREVIOUS BAD PLANNING EXPERIENCE

I often hear from people who say they tried a plan once and "It was a waste of time and effort" or "We never used the document", and just don't want to try again. Perhaps someone wrote a "tome", perhaps too few people were involved, perhaps unrealizable expectations were raised. Getting people re-motivated after a bad experience is tough. I suggest that you find out what went wrong the previous time (assuming that you were not there) and ask those who were involved how the process could be made better this time. Assure them that you will do everything in your power to have the product be a useful and meaningful document.

6. DOCUMENT PHOBIA

Some people don't like to wear seat belts: "They're too restrictive and besides, in a crash I might be stuck in the car." This belief survives, despite all the hard data that contradicts it. Some people don't like plans for the same reason: "They restrict flexibility, they make us into robots. We can't be creative if we're under a plan. If a crisis develops, we're stuck." Of course, nothing could be further from the truth. Plans should be flexible guidance, not a harness to which you are inextricably tied. Many times, the people who give these excuses simply don't want to be publicly account-able for their actions.

7. POOR MANAGEMENT

Put simply, a place that is poorly managed will "not have the time" to plan. Additionally, an executive director who sees poor management skills in his or her subordinates will often assume that the plan, no matter how good, will not be utilized. In both cases, the organization makes a mistake and its clientele ultimately lose. Planning is part of good management and a necessary skill, like delegation, supervision, and communications, for all managers to learn. Living and working with a plan is also an essential skill and the executive director who doesn't let subordinates take part in such activities is hindering their professional development.

J. SAMPLE STRATEGIC PLAN FORMAT

This sample format is just that; a sample from which you can create your own, unique plan. It is provided here to get you going, and is not necessarily the best format for you. The suggested maximum lengths of certain sections are offered to remind you to keep it short in these sections so that people will read the really important parts.

1. Executive Summary (Key areas of action, priority goals: *2-4 pages*)

2. Introduction to the Plan (Why you developed the plan: *2 pages*)

3. The Planning Process (*2 pages*)

4. The History of Your Organization (*2 pages*)

5. The Agency Today (descriptions of services, clientele, and funding: *3-5 pages*)

6. The World We Will Work In (a listing of the environmental assumptions that you first developed at your retreat, and how you think they will affect the agency: *5 pages*)

7. Goals and Objectives (19__ -____ : *five years*)

8. One-Year Plan (the highest priority goals, objectives, and action statements that will be addressed this year.)

9. Time Line (a graphic depiction of the implementation of the goals and objectives. This is very helpful to allow the reader to see the goals and objectives collected onto one chart, and for the staff and board to visualize the work load resulting from the plan: *2-3 pages*)

10. *Evaluation and Update Methodology* (How you will evaluate the implementation of the plan, and when the updates of the one year and strategic plans are scheduled: *3-4 pages*)

11. *Appendices*

RECAP

In the first pages of this chapter I said that "Without a plan the only way you get anywhere is by accident. What you do is much too important to be accidental." Too many people depend on your organization and its services to let your management and policy setting be one long ad lib. You need to have a plan to focus you, to help you set priorities, to guide you in the most stressful times that you will face.

In this chapter we have covered the key parts of planning, the five reasons why it is critical, both in the process and the product, for your organization to have a consensus on where it is going. I have urged you to use an inclusive process. That will help your implementation of the plan, improve the ownership in your organization, the morale of your staff, and the positive impression of your funders.

We have seen a planning process that has worked well for many of my consulting clients. Finally, I have reviewed for you the outcomes and uses of planning, how to get the most out of the document that you put so much into.

Planning is good management, and thus good mission. It is a way to get everyone involved in having your organization meet its mission commitments more efficiently and effectively. You have the time to plan. Go ahead and do it.

11. Seeking Financial Empowerment

OVERVIEW

There is a rule that I like to use whenever I am confronted with a staff or board member who wants to provide a new service, or an expanded one, and is taking the attitude "We're here to provide the service; if we do that, the money will take care of itself." When I hear this, I say:

NO MONEY, NO MISSION.

If mission is important, so is money. This does not mean to suggest that money is paramount. You are not a *for-profit*: you should always be most concerned about mission. But being most concerned about one thing does not mean that you should be unconcerned about everything else. In your zeal to provide more and better mission you must accept the reality that there is only so much money to work with.

The purpose of these chapters on Financial Empowerment and Social Entrepreneurship is to show you how to make and keep more money so that you can do more mission, and most importantly, more mission that you want to do, not the mission that your traditional funders limit you to.

Imagine having funds that you can both depend on, and spend without approval from anyone other than your own board of directors. Imagine having a great idea, or noting a terrible problem in your community, and being able to attack it head on, this year, this *month* without having to go to your state capital or to Washington, D.C., for a lengthy review and then denial. Sound great? You bet. This is the reality for many not-for-profits today, the ones that have worked toward financial empowerment, and away from the traditional dependency (and thus subservience) model that I discussed at length in Chapter 2. Successful not-for-profits, those that will flourish in the 21st century rather than wither, will be those who are financially empowered.

Here's the hard truth: if you want to be around doing good service in ten years, you had better work toward financially empowering your organization, starting today.

Here's the good news: you don't have to be big to be financially empowered. Small not-for-profits can be just as empowered as large ones, and often remain more flexible, a key trait we'll discuss in Chapter 14. Also, you don't have to have been around since 1932. Many start-ups are positioning themselves for financial empowerment from day one.

Here's the bad news: if you are like the vast majority of not-for-profits, you are anything but empowered, you are regularly teetering on the brink of financial disaster, you have little or no operating reserves, and your cash flow is too often a trickle in and a river out. For you (and this includes most not-for-profit managers) the road to financial empowerment will not be short or smooth. But, you *can* do it, in fact you must, if you are to do your job at all.

There is too much material on financial empowerment to share with you in just one chapter, so we will use two. In this first chapter we will cover the issues that will allow you to start becoming a financially-empowered organization. For those readers who are already working in an organization that is financially stable, these discussions will reinforce your good habits, and perhaps provide an insight or two to help you improve further. In the following pages, you'll learn about the five characteristics that exist in financially-empowered organizations, how best to use your financial statements, how to communicate about finances inside your organization, and how to estimate the capital needs that your expansion in the next decade will require.

Then in Chapter 12, we'll concentrate on how to keep what you've earned, how to find and work with a lender, how to seek an endowment, the truth about the Unrelated Business Income tax, and how to use your empowerment to benefit your mission, your clientele, and your community. At the end of that chapter, I've provided a sample empowerment plan for your review.

By the time you finish these chapters, you will know what you need to do to become and remain financially empowered.

A. WHAT MAKES A FINANCIALLY-EMPOWERED NOT-FOR-PROFIT

I define a financially-empowered not-for-profit organization by the following five characteristics:

1. It makes money in at least seven out of ten years.

Nowhere in any state or federal law or regulation does it say that just because you are a not-for-profit that you must lose money. No one in Congress ever said you had to lose money or just break even to qualify for your 501(c)(3). In fact, in the IRS code it says "that the profits of the [501(c)] organization shall not inure to the benefit of....", proving that profits are legal in the IRS's eyes.

On a practical level, we all know that an organization that loses money each year will eventually fold. It's just a question of how long it will take. I contend, however, that each of you should have a goal of making money nearly every year to allow you to continue to provide high-quality services in the years to come. Why? For many of the reasons we discussed in Chapter 2: there will be little new government funding, there will be higher demand for services, and there will be more competition for everything. You need a profit—yes, a profit—to give you some maneuvering room.

2. It has outside sources of income.

More and more not-for-profits are developing a business that supports mission without drawing revenues from traditional sources. This means risk, and we'll discuss business development at length in the next chapter, but suffice it to say that organizations who meet this test have done one of the things we need to do: They have expanded their universe of income streams. Don't assume for a moment that these entrepreneurial organizations are swimming in cash and are now independent of their traditional funders; they aren't and never will be. But they do have a source of funds that is no longer as dependent on bureaucratic or political whims, and that is a strength in and of itself.

3. It gets at least 5% of its annual operating income from its endowment.

Endowment? Yes, endowment. They are not just for the big organizations, the ones that have been around for decades. I have a client organization that is only five years old, grosses only $250,000 a year, but annually gets between $10,000 and $13,000 from its $125,000 restricted fund.

Endowments for not-for-profits are the best way you can get and maintain a source of income that is steady and inviolate. You cannot, like a for-profit, sell stock or issue debt (although that is changing). You can, however, use your 501(c)(3) designation to secure long-term funds in a restricted account or subsidiary corporation. More about this later.

4. It has a "comfort" level from at least 90 days' operating reserve.

So many not-for-profits go from financial crisis to crisis, and I see organization after organization struggling to make rent and pay-roll every month. Why? The most common answer is that "we just never seem to be able to get ahead". Trust me, "getting ahead" never just happens. It is planned. It is the result of careful discipline. And, a comfort reserve is not only stress reducing on senior management. It is also a turnover reducer and a morale booster for both staff and board. As you become financially empowered you should strive to have funds in an accessible interest-bearing account equal to *at least* 90 days of your operating budget. Some funders don't allow you to keep more, but we'll get to how to circumvent that in a few pages.

5. It is mission-responsive through its "Mission Reserves".

More reserves, you ask? Where does all this extra money come from?

First, it's not extra. You need all your money, but putting aside a mission reserve allows you the ability to respond to local needs as they occur, not when someone far away with control of the dollars finally recognizes the problem. This is the ultimate result of financial empowerment.

As we move through the rest of the chapter, we'll examine some techniques to become empowered, some of which are basic good financial management, some of which are a bit more entrepreneurial. At the end of the chapter we'll review one agency's five-year plan to head toward empowerment.

I should emphasize here and now that becoming empowered is not easy. It is not the result of a single action in a single year. It is a long-term objective that combines a commitment to financial well-being by all members of the board and staff, a setting of reasonable goals in each year, savings, reexamining the budgeting process, fundraising, and usually some corporate restructuring. It is a multi-year (and in some cases decade-long) task. But it can happen in almost any organization with the will to make it happen. So let's get started.

B. EXPANDING THE UNIVERSE OF INCOME STREAMS

You must begin by learning to look beyond your traditional sources of income. For most not-for-profits, these sources are: grants (from government or foundations), contracts (from government or private industry), and donations (from individuals, corporations, or United Way). These three sources, in some combination, make up the income side of most not-for-profits', ledger sheets. Hopefully, through better staff and board management (Chapters 4-6), tighter controls (Chapter 8), and a more focused marketing program (Chapter 9), you will get more mission out of your current income as well as glean additional income from each of these traditional sources. But there are other sources as well, sources that can let you do more mission than you do now.

Look at the figure below. It shows a flow from your mission to a plan (whether that be a work plan, marketing plan, or strategic plan). The plan's implementation will use resources from four areas: cash, personnel, equipment, and property. These become the expense side of your budget for the plan. It is at this point that reality imposes itself on the plan. If you dream big mission, and develop big plans, you are always limited by the sources of income necessary to at least balance the budget (and remember, I want you to make money seven out of ten years). If you only seek funds from the traditional sources (grants, contracts, and donations), you necessarily limit your ability to do your mission. The other sources at least need to be considered: Business Profits, Debt, and Net Worth.

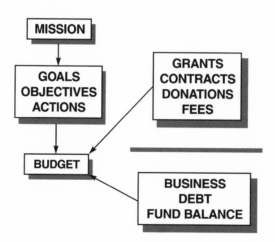

1. BUSINESS INCOME is legal for a not-for-profit. You do not lose your 501(c)(3) if you have a business, even if it is unrelated to your mission. If you do something that is unrelated to your mission statement, you pay tax at the normal business rates on the profit. (We'll cover the Unrelated Business Income Tax in detail in Chapter 12.) Thousands of not-for-profits have started and continue to run businesses, ones that supplement their mission and/or supplement their income. Are there risks? Sure. Does it happen overnight? Never. Will it make you independent of government funding? No way. Are there tricks to doing it right? You bet, and we'll talk at length about them in Chapter 13. But I want you to start thinking about your own business as a potential new funding stream now.

2. DEBT is not the source of cash to turn to in every crisis. That's like running up all your credit cards to the maximum with no way to pay the bill. But prudent debt is a tool, like many others, that can leverage your organization to do more and better service today. For more on debt, see Chapter 13.

3. NET WORTH only comes from profits (net revenues over expenses). As a not-for-profit, you cannot raise money by selling stock, so the only way to gain net worth is to make money. Additionally, if most of your net worth is tied up in fixed assets (your building(s)) it's tough to get at it to use for today's mission-related needs. However, the mission reserve I referred to earlier can, over time, be a source to use to meet today's mission needs, to match foundation grants, to reallocate resources within your community. It is a source, but only if you make money and put aside some cash.

You need to think beyond your traditional sources of income—there will always be more need for your services than you can meet with those income streams. Isn't it time to branch out? By doing so, your total income becomes more stable, more reliable, less dependent on one or two funders.

C. NUMBERS THAT MEAN SOMETHING (AND THOSE THAT DON'T)

While it is important to have more and more diverse income, and to spend less through bottoms-up budgeting, it is also a staff responsibility to manage what you have well. This means knowing where your money comes from, where it goes, what causes income and expenses to go up or down, and, in general, to understand the finances of the organization. Many managers think they do know their organization when they really don't. For example, I know of ten large organizations where the exec wants to know the cash flow, cash in over cash out, for the day, but never asks to see a cash projection. So what if cash flow is positive or negative today? For a senior manager it's the *trend*, the projection into the future, the analysis of a long period of the past that is important, not so much the present. These execs think that they are in control because they know how much money is in their organization's wallet. They aren't.

On the other hand, Robert Crandall, the CEO of American Airlines, runs a multi-billion dollar corporation with hundreds of thousands of employees, billions in assets, and operations in 40 countries. Is it possible for him to know what is going on everywhere? Of course not. But Crandall does need to know what's important, the numbers that mean something, and every day, seven days a week, he gets a sheet with ten numbers on it: the ten key numbers that help him run the airline. What are they? He won't tell, but in a recent interview, he noted that the ten numbers have changed over the years as the priorities of the airline have changed. Why just ten numbers and not 12 or 20? Crandall says that's all anyone can really handle and use, and he sets the number as a discipline for himself. If there is a deviation from the goal or standard in a particular number, he investigates, pursues, prods, and demands answers. If not, he leaves it alone.

Crandall also sees monthly statements in great detail, but it's the daily numbers I want to focus on. Since he won't divulge his secrets, I will hazard some guesses as to what they are. First, knowing Crandall's management philosophy, there is bound to be cash flow and cash balance. Second, the percentage of seats full upon takeoff versus a day, week, or year ago. Third, cost per passenger mile. Fourth, on-time departure and arrival percentages. Fifth, the percentage of aircraft down for non-routine maintenance. Sixth, some sort of income projection into the future based on reservations. Seventh, some numbers on the competition, including fares, on-time arrivals, etc. Eighth, probably some number on a focus of his, such as the profitability of a regional hub, or the profitability of his reservations network.

While these are just conjecture, I hope that they illustrate a number of points. First, Crandall realizes that his job is too complex to spend all his time with a calculator, but just because it is doesn't mean he should *ignore the numbers*. Ignoring the numbers is a key mistake that managers who were not initially trained in business, (which includes nearly every reader of this book) make. "I'll leave those to others who really like to deal with numbers." This is a big mistake and one that can be fatal. Remember, while the subject of the chapter is financial empowerment, the point of the exercise is *mission*. If you, as a mission-based manager, do not take the time to learn how to most effectively use your financial resources, you are short-changing your organization and your clientele. Second, Crandall realizes that he will lose the big picture if he drowns in detail (pardon the mixed metaphor). Therefore, he limits his daily (and, I assume, weekly and monthly) numbers to a critical few. Finally, those numbers, by his own admission, change with time. I would imagine, for example, that the on-time departure and arrival numbers were not on his list five years ago, until they became a competitive advantage.

So, what numbers do you need to know? The choice will, obviously, depend on your organization. Most, if not all, readers will be in organizations that cannot produce daily numbers of any great accuracy. But that does not mean that they cannot produce numbers at all, or on a regular basis. Again, what you need to know depends on your organization, but let me at least propose some general areas that you need to have information on. You will see that most of these numbers are either trends, or are numbers weighed against a goal or an industry norm. This is important to give you perspective. Also, in a few pages, we'll discuss internal reporting and there will be some actual sample forms for you to consider.

1. CASH

Cash is like blood or water to an organization: you die without it. You need to have reasonably accurate cash flow *projections* for six months in advance, and you need to see these every two weeks (have them updated after each payroll). This can be done most efficiently on a computer spreadsheet such as Lotus 1-2-3 or Microsoft Excel, and it is essential to your organizational well-being that you know when you will be cash-rich and when cash-poor. Daily cash in and out is fine, but it is the trends and future projections that you need to focus on most.

2. INCOME

If you have income-sensitive numbers that you can see, read them regularly.

For example, if you are a museum and your income is heavily dependent on the number of visitors each day or week, take a look at that number, and compare it to a month ago, a year ago, and any goals that you may have. If you are a school and get reimbursed for a student-day, what was your attendance last week? If you are a hospital, you probably want to know how many beds are full. If you are a church, what was your count of parishioners this week and what was in the collection plate?

3. PAYABLES

Payables are the amounts that you owe people in the short term. Particularly if you don't write the checks yourself, you need to know the trend in this area. What is the amount of payables that you have (usually recorded monthly), versus a month ago or compared to average monthly expenditures? For example, if your average expenditures per month are $100,000 and your payables are $150,000, you are not paying your bills in 30 days. Worse, if that payables number is climbing while your expenditures are staying the same, you are falling further and further behind, something you *really* want to avoid. Keep on top of your payables, and ask questions to make sure you are keeping current and not incurring late fees. You should also see a monthly listing of any and all accounts that are late: usually past thirty days due. Find out why these are late and do your best to get them paid. If they are going to be very late, call the person you owe and explain why.

4. RECEIVABLES

This is the other side of the coin. Particularly in organizations where primary customers (government, foundations, insurance) often play such a huge part in your income stream, you need to stay on top of what you are owed. It is very easy for organizations to pay late if you let them. You need to be on top of the system, know how it works, and be a pleasant bug in their ear to get paid sooner rather than later. You need to know how "old" your receivables are, and have a policy for when you personally get involved to collect a late receivable. Again, if your income is $100,000 per month, and your receivables are $140,000 month after month, or are growing in relation to income, you are getting paid late and it's getting later. Watch this number as a trend and take action as needed.

5. EXPENSES

Usually, expenses are recorded and fully accounted for once a month in a monthly statement. I assume that you see the statement the minute it comes out, but do not be content with just the overall statement. You should see the income and expense statement compared to your budget for the month, and your year-to-date statement compared with the budget for the year-to-date. Only by having these comparisons can you ask reasonable questions about expenditures, make staff justify any changes in the budget and, in general, stay on top of this key area. Again, this is a once-a-month set of numbers, but many managers just look at the bottom line, and don't examine the statement against their budgeted goal.

It should also be noted that your highest expense, unless you are very unusual, is your payroll. You want to keep a handle on how much your people are costing, because cutting people is the most painful thing you will ever have to do as a manager.

6. BALANCE SHEET AND RATIOS

Balance sheets are snapshots of your organization at the end of a period, usually each month. They show your Assets (what you own or what you are owed), your Liabilities (what you owe or are obligated to pay over the short- and long-term), and your Fund Balance (Assets minus Liabilities). For many non-financial managers, balance sheets are confusing. However, balance sheets can be used to generate important numbers that help you manage: financial ratios. Ratios are, like so many other tools, often misused, and too often misunderstood.

A financial ratio is a comparison of two factors in your balance sheet (or in your balance sheet and your income and expense statement) that allows you to get a better viewpoint of your organization's financial position.

There are literally hundreds of such ratios, but you do not need to deal with more than a few key ones. Like everything else, which ratios you need will depend on your organization: talk to your CPA or a financial expert on your board about which ones are most important to you and how to use them. Some examples would be:

▶ **Profit Margin:** Net Revenue divided by Total Income. Is the percentage of profit high enough?

▶ **Current Ratio:** Current Assets divided by Current Liabilities: this is a measure of how much liquidity you have—can you pay off your current obligations with cash and current receivables? The number should always be higher than 1.0 and probably your goal should be between 1.5 and 3.0 (not including your endowment). Much higher means that you are probably sitting on too much cash.

▶ **Debt to Fund Balance:** The Total Debt divided by your Fund Balance. This number measures the ability of your organization to take on more debt if you need to and monitors your debt against your net worth. You don't want this ratio too high. A high ratio indicates over-leveraging.When this occurs, interest costs will begin to eat you up.

As I noted, there are more of these than can be discussed here, since the specific ones that will help you may be obscure. See your CPA and your banker. Talk with them about which ratios will give you the best help in monitoring your finances.

7. NON-FINANCIAL INDICATORS

Not all of the numbers you need to see have to do with money. There are other items that bear regular scrutiny that are indicative of whether or not you are succeeding with your mission, your people, and your stewardship. For example, the number of units of service provided per full-time-equivalent staff person, the number of people on waiting lists for service, the average turnover of staff per quarter or per year, the number of people seeking service for the first time, or the number of people who return repeatedly, all could be important to you. Now that you understand that even a non-financial manager needs to pay attention to the numbers, don't limit those numbers to the ones with dollar signs in front of them.

8. PROFIT AND LOSS

You need to know what you are earning or losing, and this is so important an area, that I've broken it out separately.

D. KNOWING WHAT YOU EARN (AND LOSE)

As you've read repeatedly in this book, it's OK for a not-for-profit to make money. Not just that, it is essential that you make money seven out of ten years to maintain and improve your ability to help your community. To do that you have to know what programs and what parts of your organization make money and what parts lose money, and, in both cases, how much money is involved. I've also said repeatedly that it is fine to have some programs that are subsidized by others: there are things that not-for-profits do that will never be fully reimbursed. But, you *have* to balance those programs with profitable ones or you will be out of business.

The problem for most not-for-profits, especially those that get government reimbursement, is that they are trained to fudge the numbers, and this training leads them to take shortcuts in actual accounting so that they don't know their real costs of operation for anything.

● **FOR EXAMPLE:** A not-for-profit mental health agency in the South receives federal funds for one of its programs. For the past five years, this particular program has allowed for a 15% overhead charge (for all administrative support) in addition to rent, utilities, and actual documentable costs. Whether the actual time spent on the project by the administration was 9% or 19%, the "charge" was 15%, the allowable maximum. If it was higher, the administrator would just say "That's the most we can get reimbursed". If the actual administrative cost was lower, the administrator would rationalize "We can get the reimbursement, and we need it to cover underpayments elsewhere". In truth, probably no one in the agency ever checked their real costs of administration by watching them for a three- to six-month period. Thus, they never knew the real costs. As time went by, they began an internal accounting method that charged each program a percentage for administrative time. The percentage: 15%, the amount they had all gotten used to as their overhead cost. But was it really 15%? Almost certainly not, and definitely not on every program.

You need to know your real cost of doing business. If you are like most organizations, you are probably pretty good at recording income by program and in doing estimating and accounting of direct costs for an individual program: the costs of the people, supplies, transportation, and equipment used each day, week, or month. But it is in overhead, administration, rent, depreciation, and utilities that many organizations grossly under- or over-estimate their expenses.

☞ **HANDS ON:** Time sheets are a start to teaching your staff where their time is *really* spent. I admit that time sheets are no fun, particularly when staff have never used them before. To make a point with administrative staff about how important accurate accounting is, try this: ask your administrative team to estimate how many hours in the coming week they will spend on different tasks. You should ask them to break their roles out by program where possible, and then by administrative task: budgeting, marketing, evaluation, fundraising, etc. Develop categories that make sense for your organization and then let staff fill in their hour estimates in advance.

Now collect their estimates, and have them do it for real, *in 15-minute intervals,* for that week. Have them carry their timesheet with them all day. If your staff are like most of us, they will find serious differences between their estimates and reality. Use this to underscore the fact that a standard organization-wide percentage is not the best way to account for overhead and administrative costs.

Once you know your real administrative costs, you can begin to examine which programs are profitable and which are not. Why? Are you going to simply cut out the "losers" and keep the "winners"? Of course not. There will always be programs that you need to provide that will lose money, and it is naive to think otherwise. But knowing which programs are making money and which are losing (and how much each year) is part of both the management and policy-setting mix. If, for example, a program that is a high priority in your needs assessment or strategic plan is losing money, you will probably be more willing to subsidize it than a program that has outlived its mission-based usefulness. Alternatively, decisions about where to put your marketing dollars will be a mix of where the most net income can be generated (to subsidize other programs) and how much mission can be accomplished. Thus, the profitability of a program is not, and never should be, the only issue. But it *is* an issue, and one that your management team needs to consider.

E. SPENDING LESS THROUGH BOTTOMS-UP BUDGETING

I will start with the assumption that you have an organizational budget. If you don't, *STOP READING AND GO DEVELOP ONE.* Now let's discuss why bottoms-up budgeting saves money, because, if it is appropriately implemented, it *always* does, even in the best-run organizations.

The term *bottoms-up budgeting* comes from the idea that people nearest the provision of service make the best decisions about resource needs and use. Now, in my ideal organization, these people would be nearest the top of the chart, just below the recipients of service. The people that need to develop and then monitor your budget are the people who are as close to the provision of service as possible. These people know more than you ever can about what their real needs are, how to spend money the most effectively, and how to monitor outcomes best. Why? Because it affects their lives on an hourly basis.

1. THE COMPONENTS OF BOTTOMS-UP BUDGETING

Now, you cannot just make a major change in your budgeting process by going to your line managers and staff and saying: "Here, write the budget", and expect it to work. You have to do the whole process, and that includes some things you may not care much for. Bottoms-up budgeting has some important components. They are:

▶ *Training and Orientation.* Many of the staff that will be included in the budgeting process will have never seen the budget much less understand how it is generated. You need to walk them through the budget and help them to understand where your income comes from, its limitations, the history of your expense numbers, and how they have been developed in the past.

▶ *Delegating both Budget Responsibility and Authority.* In using this process of budgeting, the entire point is to pass the responsibility and authority for the budget development and implementation to people other than senior staff. But note I said responsibility *and* authority. If you just ask your staff to help you develop the budget but then micromanage its implementation, you are no better off (and arguably worse) than you are now. What you want is for staff to have ownership and input into the budget development process. Once the budget is reviewed by senior staff and adopted by the board, the line items in the budget should, within programs, be authorized and approved by the line managers within those programs. Thus if your board has authorized a $5,000 line item for supplies for one of your programs, you as an executive should have no real oversight into what supplies are bought, or when, or from whom, as long as the program meets any bidding requirements and stays within its $5,000 per year budget. For some readers, this will require changes in procedure for check writing approval, and rethinking their control systems. That's probably overdue for many organizations, and this is a good time to look at these areas. Remember, give authority with responsibility.

▶ *Risk-Taking and Risk Reward.* This system will not work without the added component of risk and reward. Staff who are monitoring budgets must be at risk for their implementation. Thus their performance evaluation should, in part, incorporate their budget management skills. More importantly, if staff come in under budget on the expense side, or over budget on the income side (for those programs that can impact on their income statements) they should be rewarded. My recommendation is that, when a program beats its budget, it should get to keep half of the "net". In other words, if you are a private school, and your pre-school staff cut their expenses by $40,000 under budget, they get to keep $20,000 (at no penalty on next year's budget) to do with as they see fit to further their mission. This reward system is absolutely essential—otherwise the staff don't have the incentive to look for bargains, cut their costs, etc. Any less than half of the savings, and your incentive levels start to drop. Don't be greedy as an administrator. Remember, you just got some "free" savings. Share the wealth and there will be more. Get greedy now and the source of those savings will dry up.

▶ *Regular Feedback and Reporting.* The only way that your staff can monitor how they are doing is by regular reports from your accounting people. The best format is to have a monthly statement that shows actual vs. budgeted income and expenses for the current month and year-to-date. These should be done for each program. The administrator in charge of overseeing that program should go over the statement with the line staff and manager. Only question items where there are large discrepancies—perhaps 10% in a monthly item and 5% in a year-to-date item. This communications flow will help everyone be more comfortable with the delegation of responsibilities, and assure that no program area staff have concerns or questions that are not answered.

If you do this kind of budgeting, you will see results. These results could be as much as 10 to 15% savings in non-personnel areas and even personnel cuts, in some cases. I would not, however, suggest that you implement this wholesale if you have had a traditional top-down approach. Try this method next year in the one or two programs with the highest likelihood of success, orient all staff to the new approach, and, at the end of the year, publicize the results and expand the program.

Don't expect all staff to welcome this idea. Again, here we have change on the march. Perhaps your biggest surprise will be that those staff who always gripe about not having enough say will resist having control over their budget.

● **FOR EXAMPLE:** A few years ago, a good friend of mine took the job of Headmaster at a large residential school on the East Coast. His predecessor had been at the school for 20 years and had been the penultimate autocrat. For the first full year my friend was there, he listened to staff griping about management making ridiculous decisions, and how the allocation of resources was just plain stupid. In his second year at the school (the first where he was on hand for budget planning) my friend called all the program heads into his office and told them that they were going to make allocations of resources based on the budget amount that had been received from their state funders. He told them that the first year they would only have to allocate the purchases of equipment, books, and classroom supplies. This meant that the managers, who had previously been given these allocations and could just sit back and gripe about not getting enough, now had to come to a consensus on how to divvy up the school's entire allocation for each line item.

They hated the job, and found it was much tougher than they had ever imagined. Four days later they came back to the Headmaster and asked that he do the job. He refused, saying that it was crucial for them to have an understanding of the budget dilemma and the allocation of resources.

Resistance to change aside, this process works. If you can come in under budget the next three years, and have enough discipline to then set the funds aside, you are well on your way to a culture of financial empowerment.

F. REPORTING INSIDE THE ORGANIZATION

One of the key areas where empowered organizations excel is in the area of internal reporting. In external financial reporting, what you do is dictated by your funders, by your auditor, and by, in some cases, tradition. But internally, you can be much more flexible and creative.

Internal reporting means getting the right numbers to the staff and board. All organizations are different, and what you report and who you report it to will vary with your management style, your organizational policies, your organizational history, your size, and whether or not you have a collective bargaining unit (a union). No matter what your shape and size, there is one key tenet of internal financial reporting:

GIVE PEOPLE THE INFORMATION THEY NEED
IN THE WAY THAT THEY WANT TO SEE IT
AS OFTEN AS THEY NEED IT.

Why should you be flexible in your reporting? Why not just give everyone the monthly profit and loss statements and perhaps a cash flow projection? Let's look at the different groups you need to report to. As you review this list, ask yourself: do all these people need the same information on the same schedule?

▶ *BOARD—All*
▶ *BOARD—Finance committee*
▶ *BOARD—Treasurer and Chairperson*
▶ *STAFF—CEO*
▶ *STAFF—Senior Management*
▶ *STAFF—Middle Management*
▶ *STAFF—Service Providers*

Of course they need different numbers in different forms at different times. And with today's accounting and reporting software, giving each of these groups what they need in the way they want it, as often as they need it, is neither time-consuming nor expensive.

In the next few pages we'll review some sample ideas of the kinds of information these different groups might want in your organization, as well as look at some sample formats that transmit this information the most efficiently. Understand that these are starting points for you, not all-inclusive—because they can't be. You will need to find the mix of reports and the types of formats that work best for your organization, and to do what you need to return to our high-tech marketing technique:

ASK!

Ask the people in these groups what information they need, how often they need it, and why they need it. Ask whether they want their reports in numerical form, on a spreadsheet, in graphs, or interpreted in writing. Or, do they want some combination of these? Once you have established what people want and how much they need, remember to ask them regularly if the information is working. If it is, great. If it is not, amend it. Remember, this kind of information targeting is cheap in both time and money, particularly if it gets the information that people need in their hands promptly. If you gave each of 20 people an extra half hour a month by saving them from wading through unnecessary data, that's 120 person-hours per year or *three weeks* of staff time saved. This is not an unusual savings from targeting your information.

There is however, information that is *off-limits*, information that should not be generally shared. Briefly this information includes salaries, perks, retirement, and medical information, as well as information on individual contracts and contractors. Additionally, you should never send out inaccurate, indecipherable, or misleading numbers, reports, charts, or graphs.

With all of that as background, let's examine when you do send information and who gets what. Let's start with some premises:

1. The more your people really understand how your organization's finances run, the better. If your organization is like most, few if any of your staff outside of your central management team understand how your finances work. Most of your staff assume that the money comes from the state (Feds, city, foundation), that you have lots of it, and are just stingy in giving it out. They probably have no real understanding of the length of time it takes you to get paid, the reporting requirements that you have to go through, nor the true nature of your balance sheet. In truth, most of them have probably never seen a balance sheet and wouldn't know how to read one if they saw it—through no fault of their own.

If you are going to include staff in budgeting, give them responsibility for their areas of budgeting, value them as individuals, let them see the numbers that help them do their job. I work with dozens of organizations where no one but the executive director and comptroller/financial manager ever see the complete budget and the monthly financial statements. The staff does not know how much over or under their budget they are. They don't know where they are in relation to their budget or how much they have left to spend in any line item. But, consistently in these organizations, the exec will tell me that his staff are involved in the budget process and have spending authority. How can they when they haven't a clue about where the money came from, is, or will be going?

2. The more people participate in the budget development process and are held accountable for its implementation—the better. We've already discussed how you save money by including staff in the budgeting process. Letting line staff develop and be responsible for the budget in their area saves money, period. But for staff members at any level to be involved meaningfully in the budget development and budget implementation process, they have to have the information they need at the time they need it in a format that they can understand and use.

3. A little knowledge—especially in the financial area—is a very, very dangerous thing. Imagine (and this may not be too much of a stretch for those readers who have had this very thing happen in their organization) a staff member who makes $25,000 per year being given a copy of your organization's balance sheet and reading things like "Total Assets $1,450,000" or "Cash and Securities $767,560". To a person unfamiliar with financial terminology, that could sound as if you have bags of money hidden in your office somewhere. Without the context (that perhaps 90% of your total assets are fixed or that most of the cash and securities are in restricted funds) this person will be justifiably upset with the fact that the staff only got a 2% raise last year, or that needed programs have been cut.

The moral? If you are going to hand out financial information *train* your people in how to use it and what it means. If possible, have an outsider (who will be seen as neutral) come in and go over what a balance sheet is, explain an asset, a liability, a fund balance, a restricted account, a fixed versus liquid asset, and how your cash flow really works. Have the trainer explain how your income streams are set up, how staff can influence them, how growth may actually mean less cash in the organization's hands instead of more, and how an organization should configure itself for financial strength. This training is not only important for the development of the staff, but it is a key preventative against a general uprising over resources.

Now let's look at who needs what:

1. STAFF

The CEO: The CEO of your organization will need a variety of information. Again, what he or she wants is a decision he or she will have to make, but at the least, the CEO should see the following

▶ *Cash Flow Projection:* The cash flow projection should be for the coming six months shown by payroll or by the 1st and 15th of each month. It should have a rolling net cash line to show the total cash situation. This is a *key* piece of information that too few people have.

▶ *Monthly/Annual Statements versus Budget—Overall and by Department Area:* This statement should show the actual income and expense in the previous month and for the fiscal year-to-date versus the budget for the same period. Discrepancies should be investigated.

▶ *Working Capital Projections:* How much is the expansion of the organization going to cost? How much should we set aside for a new program? Working capital projections tell that.

▶ *Receivables (aging):* How long has it been since your major funder paid you? How much are you owed now versus a month ago and a year ago? This item is important for the CEO to know as he or she interacts with your funders.

▶ *Occupancy/Utilization:* If you have a "capacity" number or a census, show it versus a month or a year ago. For example, if you have residential beds, what is the percentage of occupancy in each program? If you have a capacity of ticket sales, what percent were sold? Or, what is your count of patrons last week, or the number of students, or parishioners? Trends are the key.

▶ *Cost of Capital:* How much is the cost of the capital you have? For most readers this will be a calculation of the overall cost of any debt reduced by your cash invested and adjusted for your working capital "losses". Talk to your CPA about how to calculate this, but watch the number carefully from quarter to quarter. You don't want it to rise too steeply.

How often and in what format should you provide this information? Here are some samples of an "Executive Director's Data Sheet" a "Statement of

Income and Expenses" and a "Cash Flow for Six Months". Note the simplicity of the Executive Director's sheet, the combination of numbers and charts. Some people like their information this way. If so, give it to them!

EXECUTIVE DIRECTORS DATA SHEET 04-Nov				
DATA		AS OF	MONTH AGO	YEAR AGO
OCCUPANCY-REHAB	34	31-Oct 95	36	29
OCCUPANCY-DT	120	31-Oct 95	96	145
STAFF FTE	48	31-Oct 95	49	52
DAYS RECEIVABLE	37		31	28
NEW CLIENTS	8	04-Nov 95	4	2
DONATIONS REC/MO	12,450	31-Oct 95	15,460	16,790
COST PER FTE/hour	13.43	31-Oct 95	11.03	14.66

NET CASH ON HAND PROJECTION

STATEMENT OF INCOME AND EXPENSES
31 Oct.

INCOME	ACTUAL 31-Oct	BUDGET 31-Oct	NET	ACTUAL YTD	BUDGET YTD	YTD NET
DONATIONS	11,310	12,500	(1,190)	44,920	50,000	(5,080)
GRANTS	21,123	22,500	(1,377)	92,450	90,000	2,450
INSURANCE	13,350	9,000	4,350	53,400	36,000	17,400
INTEREST	6,206	5,600	706	25,800	22,000	3,800
PER DIEM	3,340	3,560	(220)	9,380	14,240	(4,860)
TITLE XIX	23,890	23,990	(100)	95,800	96,960	(160)
TITLE XX	21,222	23,880	(2,658)	102,280	95,520	6,760
TOTAL INCOME	100,441	100,930	(489)	424,030	403,720	20,310

EXPENDITURES

	ACTUAL 31-Oct	BUDGET 31-Oct	NET	ACTUAL YTD	BUDGET YTD	YTD NET
INTEREST	9,600	9,600	0	38,400	38,400	0
EQUIPMENT	2,480	2,200	280	8,420	8,800	(380)
FOOD	9,403	9,400	3	38,712	37,600	1,112
OCCUPANCY	14,575	14,575	0	58,300	58,300	0
PERSONNEL	25,536	25,790	(254)	98,268	103,160	(4,892)
SUPPLIES	2,590	2,000	590	10,667	8,000	2,667
TELEPHONE	1,145	2,000	(855)	7,653	8,000	(347)
TRAVEL	3,400	800	2,600	3,400	3,200	200
UTILITIES	1,946	2,756	(811)	6,268	11,024	(4,756)
TOTAL EXPENDITURE	70,674	69,121	1,553	270,088	276,484	(6,396)
NET INCOME (LOSS)	29,767	31,809	(2,042)	153,942	127,236	26,706

CASHFLOW FOR SIX MONTHS
01-Nov

RECEIPTS	31-Oct	30-Nov	31-Dec	31-Jan	28-Feb	31-Mar
DONATIONS	12,500	12,500	12,500	25,000	12,500	12,500
GRANTS	65,370	0	0	65,370	0	0
INSURANCE	13,350	9,000	9,000	9,000	9,000	9,000
INTEREST	6,206	6,291	6,528	9,106	1,718	1,509
LOANS RECEIVED	0	0	0	0	0	0
PER DIEM	3,340	3,560	3,000	3,000	3,000	3,000
TITLE XIX	23,890	23,890	23,890	23,890	23,890	23,890
TITLE XX	21,222	24,560	23,880	23,880	23,880	23,880
TOTAL RECEIPTS	145,878	79,801	78,798	159,246	73,988	73,779

DISBURSEMENTS

	31-Oct	30-Nov	31-Dec	31-Jan	28-Feb	31-Mar
DEBT SERVICE	12,500	12,500	12,500	12,500	12,500	12,500
EQUIPMENT	2,480	0	0	0	250,000	12,770
FOOD	9,400	14,100	9,400	9,400	9,400	9,400
OCCUPANCY	14,575	14,575	14,575	14,575	14,575	14,575
PERSONNEL	25,536	25,536	28,090	30,068	25,576	26,136
SUPPLIES	2,590	3,100	2,000	2,000	2,000	2,000
TELEPHONE	1,145	1,577	2,000	2,000	2,000	2,000
TRAVEL	3,400	22-May	0	0	2,450	0
UTILITIES	1,945	2,145	2,356	2,766	1,760	1,367
TOTAL DISBURSED	73,571	76,963	70,921	73,299	320,261	80,748
NET CASHFLOW	72,307	2,838	7,877	85,947	(246,273)	(6,969)
STARTING CASH	134,567	206,874	209,713	217,590	303,537	57,264
CASH FLOW	72,307	2,838	7,877	85,947	(246,273)	(6,969)
ENDING CASH	206,874	209,713	217,590	303,537	57,264	50,295

Senior Managers: What senior managers want and need depends on the areas that they supervise. They will need at least the following:

▶ *Organizational Cash Flow.*
▶ *Overall agency statements of income and expense versus budget.*
▶ *Similar statements for each department they supervise.*
▶ *Budgeting information.*
▶ *Occupancy/Utilization figures for the areas they supervise.*

Service Staff: Service provision staff need information too. If you agree with my philosophies of information being a good thing and of staff becoming involved in the budgeting process, then they need at least these:

▶ *Organizational cash flow.*
▶ *Statements of income and expense versus budget for their area of work.*

2. BOARD OF DIRECTORS

Does the board of directors need the same information as the staff? No, most of the board should focus on policy, and have no need to see the nitty-gritty. They are, however, fiduciaries, and responsible for supervising the appropriate utilization of your financial resources. The board needs:

▶ *Information that they can use efficiently.*
▶ *Information that makes sense.*
▶ *Information without jargon.*
▶ *Information that is not out-of-date.*

Let's look at the differing needs of different parts of the board, from the people that need the most detailed information to those that need just the overview.

Board Treasurer and Chairperson: These two people need to *understand* how the money flows in your organization, how it is earned and spent. They need to be able to articulately advocate for your financial needs in front of a funder, as well as give the other board members some peace of mind that someone understands your finances.

Thus they need to see at least the following:

▶ *Organizational cash flows.*
▶ *Statements of income and expense versus budget.*

▶ *Critical information about new or crisis programs.*
▶ *Early information on major changes in funding streams (a rate change, a foundation award).*

They also need to be involved early in the budget development process.

Board Finance Committee: The finance committee is the key oversight group of the board, and should have at least the following information:

▶ *Organizational cash flows.*
▶ *Occupancy/utilization figures.*
▶ *Statements of income and expense versus budget each month.*
▶ *Budget projections.*
▶ *Working capital projections.*

This group should be closely involved in budgeting prior to the budget going to the board.

Board (General): These people can be the least involved in the financial oversight, if there is a strong finance committee, and if the treasurer really understands how the numbers run. They need:

▶ *Summary information on cash and income and expenses.*
▶ *Audited statements from your CPA.*
▶ *Management letter from your CPA.*
▶ *Organizational Cashflows.*

See the example of a Board of Directors Cash Flow Report below.

Again, the key to all of this is to give people what they want in the format they can best use, and to train them in the information's use and meaning. Good information is critical to financial empowerment in your organization. Don't force your people's needs to fit one format. Scrimping on the time and software to make flexible reports will only cost you in both the near- and long-term.

Finally, remember to ask, at least annually, whether the information is still working. People's needs and wants change, as does the key information the organization produces. For example, a particular program that was running in the black last year may be a loss center this year and need more senior level attention. Or, you may have received some kind of accreditation and need to monitor a new data set. Ask and amend as necessary, but no less than once a year.

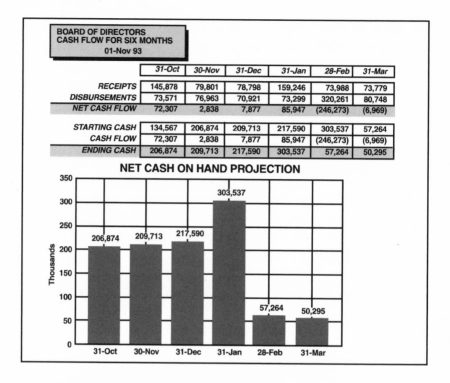

	31-Oct	30-Nov	31-Dec	31-Jan	28-Feb	31-Mar
BOARD OF DIRECTORS CASH FLOW FOR SIX MONTHS 01-Nov 93						
RECEIPTS	145,878	79,801	78,798	159,246	73,988	73,779
DISBURSEMENTS	73,571	76,963	70,921	73,299	320,261	80,748
NET CASH FLOW	72,307	2,838	7,877	85,947	(246,273)	(6,969)
STARTING CASH	134,567	206,874	209,713	217,590	303,537	57,264
CASH FLOW	72,307	2,838	7,877	85,947	(246,273)	(6,969)
ENDING CASH	206,874	209,713	217,590	303,537	57,264	50,295

G. PLANNING FOR YOUR FUTURE CASH AND CAPITAL NEEDS

One last part of constructing a financially-empowered organization is planning for your future cash and capital needs. This is an area where many organizations (for-profit and not-for-profit) fall flat on their faces, because they forget that growth costs money. You need cash for new programs and cash for growth. Unfortunately it is not just cash to spend on equipment or on a new building or on people. It is the cash that will be lost in the mail: working capital.

Working capital is the money you need to operate on between the time you create a product or provide a service and the time you get paid. The more business you do, the more working capital you need. The longer it takes people to pay you, the more working capital you need. A simple example is this: If one of your programs is currently reimbursed at cost for $120,000 per year, and if the funder of that program pays you in 60 days, you need two month's working capital ($20,000) just to carry that program. Now suppose the program doubles in size—presto—you need $40,000. Or perhaps the funder now decides to pay in 90 days—your working capital needs just went up by 50%. This is why so many rapidly-growing organizations are starved for cash—it all gets sucked up into their working capital.

The Working Capital Needs worksheet follows. Take a look at the section labeled "For Growth".

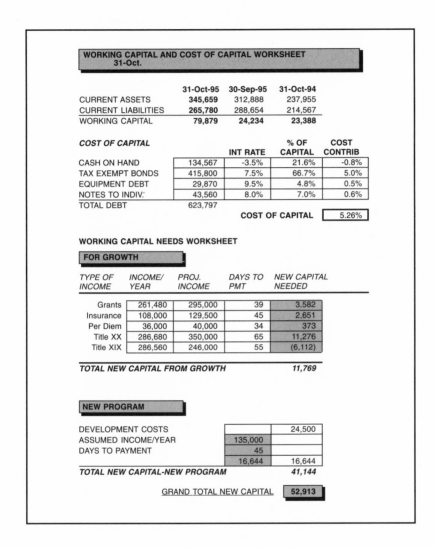

You'll see a format for estimating your working capital needs that I recommend you use every year. The first column shows the current income per year, the second column shows the projected income, and the third column shows the days to get paid. If you subtract the projected income from the current income and multiply that times the days to get paid and then divide by 365, you'll get the new cash needed next year for the growth in that program. If, as in this example, you do it for all your programs, you'll get a better idea of your working capital needs for the entire organization. If the number is very large, you may need to start working with your banker to borrow funds to cover the cash shortfall.

The second part of the format has to do with New Program working capital needs. Here you have the development costs (the "up-front" costs) and the working capital costs which are the income per year times the days to payment divided by 365. Here you see the agency needs $41,144 just to open the new program that will only bring in $135,000 per year!

Do these same calculations for your organization. They are part of a better understanding of how your organization works, how the cash really flows, and how to do business in an enlightened and empowered manner.

RECAP

We've covered a lot of ground in this chapter, and have started you on the road to empowering your organization financially. Now you know the five characteristics of financial empowerment, you know how to use numbers to your benefit, and how to pick those numbers that mean something to you and those that don't. You have been exposed to methods of using financial and non-financial indicators to tell how your organization is doing, and how to give different people in your organization the numbers that they want and need to do their job.

Finally, I've shown you some ways to predict future financial needs so that you can plan well in advance and not get caught short. In the next chapter we will look at ways to maintain the financial empowerment that you have built.

12. Maintaining Your Financial Empowerment

OVERVIEW

Now that you have started on your path to empowerment, you need to know how to stay there. In this chapter, I will help you do that. Unfortunately, a not-for-profit with money in the bank has many detractors. So how do you keep your hard-won reputation, make sure that funders don't penalize you for doing well while you are doing good, and consolidate your financial position so that in 10 years you are no longer worrying about financial stability?

You do the following things:

▶ *Keep what you earn.*
▶ *Develop a long-term relationship with a lender.*
▶ *Understand the Unrelated Business Income Tax.*
▶ *Create an endowment.*

These will be covered in the following pages.

And finally, once you have attained a degree of financial empowerment, and worked to protect that status, what do you do? You *use* the empowerment to the benefit of your clientele and your community. I'll show you how.

A. KEEPING WHAT YOU EARN

I wish I had a magic potion to give you to avoid what is still a major problem for many not-for-profits in this country: punishment for being financially responsible. However, many funders still feel that if you don't use the money you said you were going to spend, then they deserve the money back. Worse, some funders still feel that if you have any money, you don't need theirs.

So, if you do become empowered, and you have reserves for mission, or for simple financial stability, how do you keep it? How can you make money seven out of ten years and not get punished? There are a number of ways, and these work singly or in some combination for most of our clients. But I must caution you, in some states the government is *extremely* aggressive about coming after "excess funds". They have an overdose of what I discussed in Chapter 2, "What is Yours is Ours". Thus, for some readers, there may be little protection. You may need to start now to lobby for some common sense regulation that allows you to set aside your earnings in the future.

Here are some techniques that have worked:

1. AVOID "USE IT OR LOSE IT": CONTRACT RATHER THAN GRANT.

When negotiating with a funder, contract for a specific set of services rather than accepting a cash grant. Negotiate into the contract wording that says that you will provide X services for Y dollars at Z level of quality, and that any excess is yours to keep, not theirs to recapture. Of course, this means that if you don't keep your budget under control and you spend more than $Y, *you eat the losses*: you can't go back to the funder to ask for an increased contract unless they change the scope of services that they want.

2. PUT INCOME-PRODUCING VENTURES AND/OR PROPERTY INTO SEPARATE CORPORATIONS.

In the next chapter on Social Entrepreneurism, we'll discuss earned income ventures. If you start having large enough net revenue from these ventures, it may be beneficial to place them in a new not-for-profit subsidiary to harbor their assets. Many not-for-profits have their property (buildings, vehicles, equipment) in a secondary corporation and lease it at fair market rates to the primary corporation. Funders will reimburse rent but not depreciation or interest on debts.

Corporate restructuring is a tool, not a panacea. You will probably need to have a related but uncontrolled corporation to hold your assets to qualify for reimbursement, and thus, technically will lose control of your assets. Check your funder's regulations on related party transactions before setting up a second corporation to house assets (other than a foundation).

3. HAVE RESTRICTED ACCOUNTS.

Set up accounts that are restricted in use for specific items—such as a depreciation account, a capital fund account, etc. Funders are more likely to attempt to go after general revenue than targeted, restricted funds. Have a board resolution to restrict the funds and have your accountant show them that way in the audit.

4. SET UP A FOUNDATION.

In a few pages we'll examine the need for an endowment. The most common method to house this money is in a second 501(c)(3) that is loosely termed a foundation.

*NOTE: You do **not** want to be a foundation in the technical sense with the IRS. If you file your own paperwork for your new 501(c)(3), do not check the line that says "Private Foundation".*

A "foundation" corporation will allow you to keep the money that you raise "off the books" of your current 501(c)(3) and will be a marketing tool for donors, some of whom will be concerned that their donation will just get eaten up in operating expenses.

5. WORK WITH YOUR FUNDERS.

Try to work with your funders to help them see the cost of growth (in working capital), the cost of future capital expenditures, the need for financial stability, and a quick-reaction fund for your mission. Explain to them that you aren't just hoarding the money, you are managing your resources to the best mission outcome possible.

You can't be financially empowered if you lose everything you have gained. Try these ideas to retain your earnings.

B. WORKING WITH LENDERS

As a CEO or CFO, you may think that your most important working relationship is with your board president, or with your primary governmental or foundation funding source, or with another key staff person.

But, sooner or later, your most important business relationship is going to be with your banker.

The problem is that, if you are like most not-for-profit staff, you have little or no relationship with a bank, other than having a checking account and perhaps a CD or money market account .

Why is this a problem? There are a number of reasons, the most important of which are :

▶ *At some point, you will need to borrow.*
▶ *The lending decision process excludes you.*
▶ *Most bankers don't understand not-for-profit finances, and all bankers fear what they don't understand.*

Let's look at each of these in more detail.

1. YOU WILL NEED TO BORROW

Sooner or later, you will almost certainly need a loan, either to cover cash flow (when your major governmental funding check is late and you have to make payroll) or to cover the advance costs on a new contract.

Nearly all organizations need some form of debt at some point, and your credit rating (how the local lenders look at you) is influenced in no small part by how well those lenders know you and how promptly you have repaid any past debt. But commercial banking is, oddly enough, a personal business, and your personal relationship with a single person in a single bank will go a long way toward improving your "credit-worthiness".

Nothing, of course, can help you like a solid balance sheet and profitable (net revenue over expenses) operations, but you will find that even with good numbers, no one will want to take a risk on your organization until they know you and understand your organization. More on this later.

2. THE BORROWING PROCESS EXCLUDES YOU

Second, when you go in for that debt, you will (let us hope) have prepared your numbers, showing the need for the debt, the term (length) of the loan you need, and how you plan to pay it back (where the funds will come from, over and above your normal day-to-day expenses). You will give this information to your banker, and the banker will ask you a number of questions and then say, "Thanks for coming. I'll get you the answer in a week."

What happens now? The banker prepares whatever forms and applications are necessary and takes the application before a loan committee made up of people who probably don't know you, who have only a superficial understanding of your organization, and whose job it is to minimize the bank's risk (in other words, figure out all the reasons they can to turn your loan down).

Your only advocate, aside from the material you prepared, is your banker. If you have not kept your banker up-to-date on your organization, your activities, and your plans, the odds are that the bank will not take a risk on you, and your loan may be reduced, be made very expensive (a high interest rate or loan fee), or denied altogether. So, you need your banker solidly in your corner, and later I'll show you how to do so.

3. BANKS DON'T UNDERSTAND NOT-FOR-PROFITS

The third issue is one that makes the first and second tougher to resolve: banks don't understand how not-for-profits work. To a banker, not knowing about something is risky, and risk to a banker is like acid rain to an industrialist—something they'd rather avoid thinking about.

Look at it from the banker's point of view:

"You get most of your money from one source—government—and everyone 'knows' that this source is, at best, unpredictable and, in any event, only guaranteed for one year at a time. You (the executive director) are probably not a trained manager, and your organization prides itself on giving services away and doesn't collect very well from those who are supposed to pay. You are overseen by a citizens' committee of well-wishers and do-gooders, staffed by a bunch of program zealots. Who's watching the store, and why should I lend my bank's money? I mean, you are a NOT-for-profit, and loans are only repaid from profits!"

Sound exaggerated? It's not. I've heard every single one of these arguments from well-educated, well-meaning bankers, referring to not-for-profit organizations that were (despite the banker's prejudice) very well-run. The problem is one of education as much as it is internal operations, but you do have an uphill battle with most lending institutions, no matter how much they love what you do and no matter how much they have given you in donations or staff time in the past.

There are a number of things that you can do to beat these problems and to develop or improve your relationships with your lenders. Here are the steps to take:

a. Fix up your finances. No business, for-profit or not-for-profit, is going to be given a loan if its finances are in disarray. Make sure things are in order before you go to the bank. Regular statements, an annual audit, good cash and receivable controls are all essential. So are many of the things we've talked about: making money, knowing which programs make money and which lose, tracking your productivity, being aware of trends in your field. In short, be businesslike, while pursuing your mission.

b. Seek a banker, get to know him or her. Once your house is cleaned up, if you don't already have one, go down and meet a real commercial banker. As noted earlier, banking is, at its heart, a personal business. The banker will want to know lots of information about your organization and will also be keenly interested in *you*—your background, your attitude, your management skills.

Meet with this person regularly, every six months (one good time to go in is just after your annual audit comes back, then on a six-month basis). Talk business—your industry, your past six months of operations, your high and low points. Let the banker see that you know your organization from a business point of view.

c. Give the banker lots of information. Give your banker lots of information. As we said before, what people don't understand, they fear. This information should include at least the following: your monthly statements, your audit, your newsletter, copies of all major grant awards, certifications, etc., all news releases and newspaper articles on your organization *and* your field. Keep your name regularly on your banker's desk. The more they know, the better off you are.

Invite the banker to visit your program site(s) once a year. If you have multiple programs at many locations, pick a different one each time. Invite the banker to a board meeting, particularly the one which includes discussion of your budget. Let them see you in action. If you have an open house, or ribbon-cutting, or press conference, send the banker an invitation.

When you are developing your strategic plan, invite your banker to sit in on the financial parts of the discussion or at least review the numbers. The same for a business plan, a capital spending plan, etc. Such a consultation will have lots of benefits. First, you'll receive excellent advice and ideas. Second, you'll know what to expect from your banker if any part of the plan requires debt. Equally important, your banker will be forewarned about your requests, and you'll give the banker more "ownership" in your organization.

The idea is to develop a long-term relationship that benefits your organization and the bank. It is an ongoing process, a discipline, but one that will pay off enormously when you need it most. Remember, the banks want "good" business. You want to be a good business that does good things. By working together, you can both accomplish your goals.

C. DOES YOUR BOARD PROHIBIT DEBT?

As I work with not-for-profit organizations around the country, I regularly see organizations that have board-generated policies prohibiting the organization from taking on any debt. Often these policies are many years old, and may have resulted from abuses by former staff, from former board members' concerns about major funding cuts in the early 1980's, or from a feeling that this policy reduces the board's risk and exposure.

When I ask each organization's board about the policy, the conversation usually goes something like this:

Board: "We cannot take on debt because our funding is only approved annually. If our funding were cut, we would be unable to pay a loan back."

Peter: "How many of you have lifetime guarantees of employment?" (No hands go up.) "How many of you live in a house that you paid cash for?" (No hands go up.) "OK, so you took on a debt, a risk, even though your major source of income (your salary) may be ended at any time?"

Board: "But that's different. We are individuals. Our board job entails responsibility for an entire organization, and we must be prudent."

True. But not-for-profit organizations are also businesses, and business is risk. The real issue here is how much risk your organization is willing to take on behalf of your clientele. Understand that I am not talking about highly-leveraged, pyramiding craziness. This is not the "Buy Real Estate With No Money Down" commercial you see on your cable channel.

What is important to understand is that, in some instances, taking on debt to expand a service, build a building, or purchase equipment may be a *good* risk to take on behalf of your clientele. Each organization is different, as is each situation, but I strongly recommend that you consider *all* your options in planning your future; and carrying a prudent amount of debt is one avenue many highly successful businesses (both for-profit and not-for profit) use to grow and serve their customers better.

D. FINDING THE RIGHT BANK

Now you know why a good relationship with a banker is so important to your organization. But there's more to it than that. The banker with whom you work will only rarely be the owner. Bankers are employees of the bank and must abide by its policies, processes, priorities, and, of course, its prejudices. These may very well affect your banker's ability to meet your needs and thus may preclude your wanting to invest a whole lot of time fostering a relationship that, as far as you are concerned, is a one-way street running the wrong way.

So what should you do? Well, first, let's get our perspectives straight. You are the *customer.* I know that's hard to believe, given the way some banks treat you, but it's the truth. Remember, the bank is *selling* you money. In fact, the bank is almost certainly selling *your* money (your checking deposits) to *other* people for short periods of time. Unfortunately, some bankers tend to forget this with small businesses or with not-for-profits, and it is up to you to remind them politely of the fact.

Still, you want to find the bank with the best set of services and the best possible attitude toward your organization. Just as with anything you buy, it is prudent to shop around for a bank, even if you have been using one to your satisfaction for some time (some would say, *particularly* if you have been with one bank for a long time). But what is the best way to compare? Here are the steps to take.

1. START AT THE TOP

Find someone who knows the CEO of each of the three or four (or more) banks that you wish to check out. Have that person (let's call him Mike) phone the CEO (let's call her Jan) and inform her of your interest (let's call you Joe). Have Mike say, "Jan? This is Mike. I heard that Joe's organization is looking around for a new bank, and I thought you might want to give him a call, since I know you're always looking for some new customers. He's got an annual budget of around $1.5 million. Just thought you'd like to know."

Now what has Mike done? He's done his friend Jan a favor, and he has not taken any risk by declaring you a good risk. Proving that is your job.

Now you wait and see how far down the organizational chart you dribble. If Jan or her first vice president calls you back and invites you to lunch at the bank to explain their services, you know the bank is interested and will probably treat you pretty well (assuming their prices are competitive). If, on the other hand, you are never called back, or your call is returned by a junior loan officer with $2,500 in personal loan approval authorization, then you have a good idea about what that bank thinks of not-for-profits in general, and of yours in particular.

2. REMEMBER THAT YOU ARE THE CUSTOMER

For the banks that call back, you need to take the next step: shop prices and services. Always ask what services are available for a commercial account. Are there checking fees? What minimum balance waives such fees? Do balances in checking over a minimum earn interest? How much? Are investment services (CDs, money market accounts) available? What types of loans does the bank make? What collateral do they want? Who makes the decisions?

Also ask for comparative interest rates and terms on lines of credit, equipment loans, and receivable loans.

☞ **HANDS ON:** Banks will often tell you that your loan is "two over prime". The question to ask is, "Whose prime, and what is it today?" Some banks use New York prime, and some use their own (often inflated over New York by one or two percent). You need to know the rate so that you can make a valid comparison.

Ask the bank for small-business references, as well as references of other social service clients. (Be prepared for a shocked look. Bankers are hardly *ever* asked to give references.) Then check the references out. Ask the reference person at least the following questions:

▶ Who is your contact in the bank? How is your relationship with that person? Do you think your contact person values your business with the bank?

▶ How long have you been a customer? Why did you choose this bank? What services of the bank do you use? Are they of high quality? Were loans easy to apply for or a major hassle?

▶ If there were periods during which you had a downturn, did the bank stand by you or get nervous? How did your banker act toward you in hard times?

▶ Do you feel that your banker understands your business? What has your banker done to show interest in your organization?

▶ (Explain a little about your organization.) Would you recommend your bank (and banker) to me? Any advice on how to deal with your banker?

Weigh the financial information along with the references and then make your move. If you are bringing a major account to the bank (over $1,000,000 in payroll in most towns, less with smaller banks), negotiate for the waiving of fees. Then stick with your bank. You should build a long-term business relationship with the bank and the banker. Jumping from bank to bank is bad business, unless you are poorly treated over a period of time.

Note, however, that many banks are being bought and sold these days. If your bank is acquired by a new owner, this should lead to a reevaluation of whether the bank still sees you as a priority customer. You should also reevaluate whenever you are assigned to a new loan officer.

Finding a good bank, one that values you for your economic contribution to the community as well as for your mission, is one of the best management moves you can make. It takes some time, but you will reap the benefits over and over in the coming years.

E. THE UNRELATED BUSINESS INCOME TAX

Now we need to turn to another issue that is essential if you are to keep your empowerment: payment of taxes on income from outside sources. There are few parts of not-for-profit business that are more misunderstood than the Unrelated Business Income Tax (UBIT). People so often assume (or are told in error) that if they have any income not related to their mission they will lose their 501(c)(3) status. This is NOT, repeat NOT true.

While the UBIT part of the IRS code is complex let me try to cover the highlights.

NOTE: UBIT regulation is changing. Check with your accountant and attorney about current exemptions and conditions. The technical aspects contained in the following pages may no longer be in effect when you read this.

Why do we have a UBIT law? Because the federal government wanted the not-for-profit community to pay taxes on income not related to its mission. This legislative action grew out of the fact that in the 1950's large academic organizations owned property, stock, etc., and did large transactions that were very profitable and hid behind their "charitable" status to not pay taxes on the profits. Congress, I think justifiably, said that if you make money doing your mission, you are exempt from tax. If you make money from things not associated with your mission, you pay tax on the profits, like everyone else.

Two key points to remember. First, making money is OK, and even if the money is earned in an activity unrelated to your mission you will not lose your tax-exempt status. Second, you only pay taxes on *profits*, not on *income*. In other words, you have to make more money than you spend before you pay part of the profits to the government. This is not an income tax like the one we pay as individuals. This is a business tax, and businesses only pay taxes on profits.

Let's look at some definitions:

▶ *A RELATED (nontaxable) BUSINESS* is one that makes important contributions to the charitable purpose of your organization, regardless of how large or small that business venture is.

▶ *An UNRELATED (taxable) BUSINESS* does not contribute to your organization's charitable purpose.

Having listed those, there is a lot of room for subjective interpretation. What are "important" contributions? To attempt to answer these kinds of questions, the IRS has developed the following questions:

1. *Is the activity in question a trade or business?*

2. *Is it regularly carried out with the frequency of a like commercial venture?*

3. *Is it unrelated to the tax-exempt organization's mission and purpose?*

If your answer is "yes" to these questions, the venture is probably an *unrelated* business. It is probably *related* if you can answer "yes" to the following questions:

1. *Does it significantly contribute to the organization's mission?*

2. *Is the scope of the activity appropriate? Is this business operating within the geographic boundaries stated in the bylaws? Is the size of the business activity appropriate?*

3. *Are the beneficiaries of the organization appropriate?*

Be sure to consult your articles of incorporation, bylaws, or constitution to determine what your charitable purpose is and in what areas you operate.

There are, of course, exceptions to the rule. There are a number listed below. As with the caution noted above, remember, these change over time, so before you rest easy on any of them, check with your financial advisor.

▶ *Those businesses primarily staffed by volunteers (85:15 ratio) are exceptions to the test, and pay no tax on net income. An example of this would be a thrift store or gift shop that is staffed by volunteers.*

▶ *If the goods sold by your not-for-profit are donated, paid staff can be involved in the business venture without paying taxes on net income. The Salvation Army's sale of donated items is an excellent example in this case.*

▶ *Passive income from the following sources is usually considered related for not-for-profit organizations: dividends, interest, most rent, capital gains and losses, and other similar items.*

NOTE: All _net_ income from advertising is considered unrelated taxable income!

If you determine that an activity is unrelated to your organization's charitable purpose and the business earns a profit, *pay the taxes!*

If a not-for-profit earns over $1,000 a year in profit from an unrelated venture, the organization must file a separate IRS tax return called a 990T Business Tax Return *and* pay taxes based on the current corporate rates.

It is better to pay the tax than to risk a penalty from the IRS. It makes no sense to scrap a business venture that can earn additional income for a struggling agency because the agency may have to pay tax on the profits. Look at this in another way. If a venture earns a net profit (after expenses) of $25,000 and the tax is paid at the present corporate rate of 15%, a not-for-profit will earn $21,250 in additional income!

Again, for up-to-date advice on related or unrelated income issues, be sure to consult an attorney or a certified public accountant, or request a private letter ruling from the Internal Revenue Service. However, a private letter ruling can be expensive and may take a great deal of time. It is better to make the activity clearly related, or simply to pay the taxes on profits, which may be significantly less than the thousands of dollars it will cost you in legal fees to get a private letter ruling issued.

One final note on UBIT. It should not be ignored. The IRS is justifiably targeting not-for-profits who are not paying the taxes that they owe under the UBIT—and there are a lot of them. File your 990T, pay your tax, and stay out of trouble.

F. CREATING AN ENDOWMENT

Wouldn't it be nice to have a cash machine, one that churns out money every year—whether or not the government funds you or donors give to you, one that you could depend on, not have to advocate or beg for? There is such a cash machine: it's called an endowment, and lots of your peer organizations have one—even organizations that are very new and very small.

My rule for endowments is this: You need a large enough endowment to have *at least* 5% of your total annual income come from the endowment's earnings. That means if your endowment earns 5% return each year it needs to be the same size as your annual budget. If it earns 10% it needs to be half the size of your annual budget.

Why do you need to do this? For a number of reasons. First, it's good fundraising marketing: you need a steady source of income and sophisticated donors know this. If you just ask for money with no endowment, you can only ask for operating or special funds. If you create an endowment (usually in a separate 501(c)(3) "foundation" corporation) you can attract larger funds from people who know that their gift will keep on giving. Second, you need the steady income, income that is free of the need to lobby, the need to beg. And don't stop at 5%. That's the *minimum.* If you can have 20% of your income per year from the endowment, great! Just think of all the additional things you could do. Third, you have the resource of your 501(c)(3) status which allows you to take financial contributions. Use it, and not just for current operations. Show some long-term vision and save for the future.

I am not an expert in development and fundraising. Thus I will not even attempt to tell you how to go about this. There are, however, a number of excellent texts on the subject. Make it part of your long-term planning to put aside money in a restricted fund or in a foundation established so that you get the income, but do not touch the principal. This is the toughest part: the discipline of not touching sources of funds when you have done without for so long. Learn how, and your organization will really benefit.

G. USING YOUR EMPOWERMENT

Getting to the point where you feel you are financially empowered will continue to be a tough, long-haul job. So why do it? Why raise the expectations of your staff, board, and, yes, yourself to do this work now for the benefit of others in five, ten, or even 15 years? For a number of reasons. First, it's your job. You are not just a senior staff person for this year's work, you are also building a better organization for the long term. I hope you buy property for the long haul, with an eye to minimal maintenance and appreciating resale value. I hope that you buy computers and software with the capability to upgrade easily and inexpensively, and that you buy vehicles based on utilization and on repair and resale records. If you are doing this, you are investing in the future. When you spend money and time on a strategic plan, you are investing in the future. And, when you train staff, or start a marketing plan, you are counting on a future reward for your investment.

Imagine if you or your predecessor had started financial empowerment planning for the organization 10 years ago. Just think what you could do with that money now! The second reason to become financially empowered is that it is good mission. Only by becoming less dependent on your key funders will you and your organization be able to meet the needs of your community quickly and with the skill and knowledge that you alone possess. Your ability to do good mission, and thus the value that your community places on your organization, will both rise. If the mission is the reason for your existence, financially empowering your organization is a key component, and one that you need to start on—today.

One other caution. It is key in empowerment planning that you bring all the staff, board, and funders in on the plans early, if possible. You need to educate your staff and funders to the fact that having money is OK—and that just because you have some funds now and are putting other funds aside, is not an indication that you have given up on the mission and are hoarding. You need to let them know that these funds that you are setting aside are targeted for mission, for long-term income, and for financial stability. As I noted above when we discussed keeping what you earn, work with your funders and staff on the front end to let them have input, and it will pay off.

H. ONE AGENCY'S EMPOWERMENT PLAN

I've said repeatedly in this chapter that financial empowerment is not a one-year goal. It is a major, long-term commitment for you, your staff, your volunteers and, yes, your funders. But how do you get there? What follows is one organization's plan. It extends over five years, and at the end of that time they plan to reassess for the next five. Five years may not be enough for some organizations. But get on with it. Time is a'wasting.

ORGANIZATION AGE: 12 years
CURRENT ANNUAL BUDGET: $1,240,000
**FIVE-YEAR PROJECTED BUDGET: $1,997,000 (10% growth
  per year)**

FIVE-YEAR EMPOWERMENT GOALS:

1. *Endowment:* Have an endowment of $1,000,000 in an outside
   foundation.
2. *Reserves:* Have a 60-day operating reserve or $300,000.
3. *Outside Income:* Have at least one new business venture that nets
   at least $30,000 per year after taxes.
4. *Mission Reserve:* Have at least $100,000 reserved for mission
   uses (this to come from our new business venture).
5. *Net Income:* In at least four of the next five years have a net revenue of at least 5% of total income—not including our outside
   income and endowment income.

YEAR ONE:
   Establish a business plan for outside income.
   Establish the Foundation corporation and board.
   Find fundraiser and start marketing for future requests for
      endowment.
   Begin bottoms-up budgeting for two existing programs.
   Establish limits of revenue reserves, establish restricted funds.

YEAR TWO:
   Start subsidiary business—lose less than $10,000.
   Begin to market endowment.
   Estimate capital needs for five years.
   Transfer property and equipment to related uncontrolled subsidiary—
      increase reimbursement.
   Place 1% of all income for the year in operating reserve.

YEAR THREE:
   Put 3% of all income in operating reserve.
   Have business break even.
   Attract $200,000 to endowment.
   Increase net revenue to organization to 4% of income—place all net
      revenue in mission reserve.

YEAR FOUR:

Earn 6% on income. Place all net income in operating reserve.

Outside business earns $25,000. All net after tax is put into mission reserve.

Attract $300,000 to endowment. Reinvest earnings in endowment.

Develop business plan for second business.

YEAR FIVE:

Earn 6% on income. Place all net income in operating reserve.

Attract $400,000 to endowment. Reinvest all earnings in endowment.

Start second business—lose less than $15,000.

First business nets $30,000—place all income into mission reserve.

RECAP

In this chapter we've focused on how to keep your empowerment. You don't want to work hard, increase income, reduce expenses, and then have some funder take it all away. Nor do you want to have a funding source reduce and leave you short. You need to keep what you earn, develop an endowment, pay your taxes, and put your empowerment to good use. In this chapter we've examined these issues.

We've taken a look at aspects of the Unrelated Business Income Tax, and showed you how to seek a bank and work with lenders over the long term. I've given you some guidance in the need for an endowment, and discussed why it is essential that you have one. I've shown you one agency's empowerment plan which details their commitment to increasing their financial strength over the long haul.

Again, no money, no mission. Financial empowerment will take your organization from being a creature of the 1970's to being a thriving, contributing member of your community in the 21st century.

13. Creating a Social Entrepreneur

OVERVIEW

All of us know the common wisdom that small business entrepreneurs are the hands-on people that generate jobs, develop new products and services, and are the engine of the economy. In truth, so are many not-for-profits today. I must add: all not-for-profits were entrepreneurs in their start-up phase. But how about now? How about your organization? Have you been around long enough that you are no longer flexible, no longer willing to embrace and shape change, no longer willing to take chances with your organization's resources?

I want you to become (or get back to being) a social entrepreneur; an organization that is constantly on the lookout for how to do more, how to do it better, and willing to take prudent risk on behalf of its clientele. This means that you will fail occasionally. But more often you will succeed in both satisfying and mission-oriented ways that serve your community much, much better.

In this chapter we'll go over ways to help your organization get comfortable with the idea of social entrepreneuring. We'll talk about how and how not to set up new ventures (the outside businesses that I discussed in the last chapter). I'll show you how to decide how much return on investment is enough, and the ten biggest mistakes people make in developing their business plan financials. We'll go over how to and how not to seek debt, which can be one of the sources of capital that you may need to expand and prosper. We'll look at ways that your organization can become a culture of new ideas, constantly seeking new thoughts from staff and board, evaluating them, and trying the best out. We'll review ways to get comfortable with *prudent* risk.

I hope that by the time you are finished with this chapter, you will be excited about the possibilities open to you if you become a social entrepreneur. I don't want you to become reckless. *Prudent* risk is what it's all about.

A. UNDERSTANDING AND ACCEPTING RISK

If you and I and eight other people were to be given $20,000 today, we would do ten different things with it. Some would buy Certificates of Deposit, some would pay down the mortgage, or buy a car, or pay off other debt. Some would go on a vacation, or try to win big at a casino. Why the variety? Because we all have a different willingness to take risks with money. We are raised differently (some of us are children of the depression, some self-indulgent baby boomers), we are in different places in our lives (some of us have kids to put through college or big medical costs staring us in the face), and we have different financial situations (to some $10 is a lot of money, to some $250 is pocket change). And, some of us are very meticulous and some are just plain reckless.

But all of us take risks. It's a risk to get in your car and drive to the store. It's a risk to get married, to have a child, to take a job, to buy a house, to buy stock, to fly on a commercial airliner. Some risks are so small that we just accept them as part of life and stop even calling them risks. Some are so big that we don't take them. Some of the risks that we took as youths we no longer have the stomach for. Some things we never would have ventured as a child we now do without thinking.

Risk is relative, and our willingness to take it depends on a combination of many things. In not-for-profit organizations, our willingness to take risk—or be reckless—-depends on the makeup of the people in charge of the organization, as well as on the organization's history and its financial condition. If, for example, there has been a history of recklessness resulting in big failures (even with another executive director), the board of your organization may be less willing to take on a risk than if you have a record of success. Also, the board's willingness to take a financial gamble will be influenced by how much money is at stake, and how financially secure you are. If you are already financially empowered, it is more likely that your board will be willing to use that empowerment for the good of the community.

Your willingness as an organization to take risk also depends on your view of yourself as an organization. On the next page is a graphic depiction of the way many not-for-profits view themselves.

You will see that not-for-profits view themselves in four ways. These descriptions are not what not-for-profits actually *are*; rather, they are how they perceive themselves.

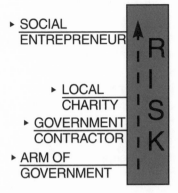

▸ *RISK LEVEL OF A*
  NOT-FOR-PROFIT

▸ SOCIAL
  ENTREPRENEUR
      ▸ LOCAL
        CHARITY
      ▸ GOVERNMENT
        CONTRACTOR
▸ ARM OF
  GOVERNMENT

R I S K

1. Arm Of Government. These organizations see themselves as virtually an extension of the government agency that funds them. Basically their view is: if the government tells us to do service X, we'll do that. If they tell us not to do service Y, we won't. These people are the least empowered and the most dependent upon their funders, both financially and psychologically.

2. Government Contractor. These organizations are only slightly less dependent on the government than the *Arm of Government* agencies. They view the government as their major market, and, like a defense contractor, their fortunes rise and fall with the funding from the government. They may do things outside of the government's direct payment stream, but the bulk of their time is spent on government-driven programs.

3. Local Charity. These organizations view themselves as a tool of their community as *evidenced by its giving.* Thus, in their view "If people come to us with money for a certain project, fine, we'll do it. If not, we won't." These organizations are centered on their local community's needs.

4. Social Entrepreneur. These organizations are focused on their mission. They say "We are here to provide service X and whatever it takes to do that is OK. If it means expanding into new areas, fine. If it means investing in new ventures, fine. If it means starting up an unrelated business and using the profits to do more mission, fine." These organizations are comfortable with the idea of taking risk that will result in more mission.

All of these viewpoints are valid, and I've consulted for organizations that expound all four. There are some of those to whom I would have been crazy to suggest taking any substantive risk—they just weren't able to comprehend the idea. Others were already taking risks on new ideas. They were ready to go with a venture or a new method of providing service, even at some financial or political risk.

As you can see, however, the further up the chart you go toward social entrepreneurism, the higher your willingness to take risk is. I would like you to be willing to take prudent risk on behalf of your clientele, but you must understand that you can't do it alone. The most dangerous situation in this area occurs when you feel that your organization should be a social entrepreneur and your board and staff feel that your are an arm of government or government contractor. Then you and they cannot address the issue of a new business, or a new service in the same manner.

> ☞ **HANDS ON:** Talk with your board and senior staff about this chart. Ask them what they feel is reasonable. Should you take financial risk on behalf of your mission? If so, how much and how often? You won't come to any consensus about this issue the first few times you put it on the table, but you will get a reading on the board's and staff's willingness to even consider the issue, and you will get them comfortable with the idea and with sharing their views on it.

Risk is here, risk is now, and prudent risk is part of your job as a service provider in your community.

B. BUSINESS VENTURES

Nationally, thousands of not-for-profits are turning to outside businesses to supplement and broaden their income streams. Since 1982, I have helped hundreds of not-for-profits throughout the country examine their capabilities in this area and have assisted them in developing their business plans.

The development of good business plans by a not-for-profit is a complex enough issue to merit an entire book. Here, I want to review the steps of business plan development, focus on the preparation of financials, and review the big mistakes people make in preparing their financials. Hopefully, this advice will help you avoid the big pitfalls in business development and will excite you sufficiently so that you will take the time to seek out other resources.

First, a reality check: no business is going to make you independently wealthy as an organization, nor is it going to make you independent of your current major source of funding. Nearly all of our clients come to us and state that one of their main reasons for wanting a new business is to "become financially independent of the state (feds, county, foundation, United Way)." Sorry, this is not going to happen. The services that your major funders will pay for may not be provided by anyone else, and, in all likelihood, the funders will continue to be a major part of your income stream far into the future. But you can, by expanding your income sources, become *less* dependent on the major funders. But independent? Not likely.

Second, remember that business income is OK and will not result in a threat to your 501(c)(3) status unless it grows to dwarf your charitable functions. Also, most of you will start new ventures that are related to your mission anyway. Why? Because it's what you know, and if you are a professional in education or in the arts or in substance abuse treatment, you are not going to start a Wal-Mart or an engineering firm. People take what they know and find new markets for it. You will too, and so, in most cases (about 90% of our clients), the business that you start will result in more services being provided.

Finally the idea of a business is to maximize profits, and for you this is only slightly diluted (and I'll address the issue in a few pages). Suffice it to say here that any profits that you make will have a social use: either to fund your mission reserves, or subsidize a money-losing program. You aren't just starting this to make a ton of money: there is a social purpose.

Let's start the examination of the business planning process by looking at the steps listed below. Note that most people start with number four, "Idea Generation", and that this is a big mistake. If you don't do these in order you are going to get yourself in trouble. Take them one at a time and you will do fine.

1. THE STEPS OF THE BUSINESS PLANNING PROCESS

a. Establish (reestablish) your mission. We've already talked at length in Chapter 4 about your mission statement and the need for it to be up-to-date and reflective of the organization that you want to become, rather than the organization that you were in the past twenty years. If you have not already reviewed your mission with your board and staff, now is a good time. Make sure that your mission statement does not conflict with the idea of your business venture, and that you all agree that a new service fits into the parameters of the mission statement.

b. Establish the "risk level" of your organization. Using the figure on risk level, go over your organization's willingness to take on risk with your board and senior staff. How much income do you need from this venture, how much social outcome? Talk this through in great detail and with frankness. If you don't, you may wind up leading the charge and turn around to find that there is no one behind you: they thought it was too risky.

c. Establish uses of profit. Of all the steps that people miss, this is the most important. You simply have to specify what you want to do with the money you will earn. If you do, people will be able to rally around the extra work (and risk) involved in the business development process. If you don't, they won't be able to focus on the outcome—they will just question why they have all the extra work.

> ● **FOR EXAMPLE:** A number of years ago, I was asked by a large provider of services to the developmentally disabled in the Southwest to come and facilitate a session with board and staff on the development of a new business. The Executive Director was totally committed to starting a new venture, but it quickly became obvious that the board and staff was anything but excited about the prospect. Questions such as "Why should we try to be in business? We're not IBM." abounded. After about 45 minutes of this, I asked the group to imagine what they would do with unrestricted funds of $100,000. After a brief pause the ideas started flying around the room. To make a long evening's discussion short, the focus came to rest on the idea of buying a small residence for three people with mild developmental disability that the state would not fund.
>
> I then asked the group "Where are you going to get the money for that?" and they immediately chastised me with comments like "We can't get it, and you said just to imagine what we would do," etc. I said "OK, but what if a business, one that employed people with disabilities in the community, was able to NET $100,000 in two or three years, and then its ongoing profits were used to support the home? Would you support the idea of a new business then?"
>
> "YES!" was the answer, with great enthusiasm. The group had gone from staunch resistance to avid support simply because they could now get their hands on a tangible social outcome.
>
> *POSTSCRIPT:* The organization started a swimming pool cleaning service three months later, with developmentally disabled persons on the crews. Three years later it had broken even, profited almost $90,000 which was used to buy the house, and contributed over $30,000 in annual profits to subsidize the facility.

Establish the uses of your profit—specifically. For example, name the program that will be subsidized by the profit, and list the amount you need per year and by when to accomplish your social goal. Then, when you finish your business plan, you can look back and see if your business meets your goals for social outcome.

d. Idea generation. Only once you have done steps a. through c. should you seriously consider what it is that you and your organization can do to earn extra income and provide new services. In developing ideas, use your staff and volunteers. They almost certainly have thought about what the needs are in the community, and how you could meet them. They just may, however, never have had the forum in which to voice them.

☞ **HANDS ON:** Get your staff together for a brainstorming session with a facilitator. Explain the need for a business and the social outcome that the business will meet. Then ask for ideas. Remember, in brainstorming every idea is a good one. In a minute or two the ideas will start to flow. If there are problems in getting the group started, use the questions below.

1. What is your organization's primary purpose as a not-for-profit?

2. What needs exist in your agency's area or locale?

3. In which of these areas would your organization like to direct its efforts?

4. What kind of tangible assets, skills, and areas of expertise exist within your organization?

5. How much time and energy can your organization devote to planning and developing a new business venture?

6. Can a group of experts be mobilized for assistance?

7. Is there a market for the product/service you select?

When you have your list, develop some criteria against which to weigh each idea. For example, you might want to prioritize businesses that can be started up in less than six months, with no more than $10,000 invested, and have a direct social impact. The combination of criteria will be up to you, but by establishing what is important now, you can fairly weigh all your potential business ideas, and not get the people whose ideas don't get used mad at you.

e. Feasibility study. There are two steps to establishing feasibility: draft and final. In the draft stage you use about three to five pages and review the business, its markets in general, and what kind of services are being provided in this market. In the final feasibility study, you go into much greater detail about the market you want to serve, a definition of the service you want to provide, why the market wants this service, how you will provide it, the barriers to success and how you will overcome them, and preliminary financials.

The emphasis in the feasibility study phase is "Can we do this?" "Do we have (or can we get) the resources to accomplish this?" and "Does it meet our social outcome goals?" If you do your homework and complete the feasibility study well, the majority of the work in your business plan will be done.

Do not, however, automatically proceed to the next stage without considering the key question: "Is this business feasible?" In some cases it will not be, and then your choice is to rework the idea or wait for conditions to improve. For example, if you are considering a recycling business, you might have to wait until the market for recycled goods rebounds to a certain level. Or, if you are in a highly-leveraged business (buying, renovating, and reselling low-income housing for example) you perhaps could not afford to start the business if mortgage interest rates were high.

Remember my maxim of "prudent risk". The idea of a feasibility study is twofold: to focus you on what the business is, and to see if it is feasible. Some businesses will not be and that's OK! Whatever you do, however, don't throw out the idea or the work that you have done. Even the biggest "failure" in today's market may be tomorrow's success.

● **FOR EXAMPLE:** By now, almost everyone has heard the story of the development of Post-Its, the restickable notes from 3-M, and how the developer had to battle against the odds to get his case heard, and how the product is the single most successful product 3-M has ever launched. What you may not know is the part of the story about the glue that is used on Post-its. It is a glue that "failed" all the tests that the chemists put it through. Prior to Post-Its, 3M's criteria for adhesives was that they stick to something and hold things together.

This glue failed that test, but was not discarded, and thus was available when the new product idea was presented. The chemists simply kept the formula in case an unanticipated condition developed, which it certainly did.

It may for you too. Don't discard your work.

f. Marketing plan. The marketing plan portion of a business plan is crucial. Here, all the questions that need to be asked are the same as those we went over in detail in Chapter 9: Who are the markets? What do they want? How do we know? How do we let them know we are here? You want your business to be market-driven, not service-driven. You will probably have to change the method of service delivery a number of times from your original concept through the business planning process as you ask the market what it wants.

g. Business plan. Now that you have done all the preliminary work, and found that your business is feasible, why go on? For three reasons:

▶ *Writing a business plan forces you to take an objective, critical, unemotional look at your business project in its entirety.*

▶ *The finished business plan is an operating tool that, if properly used, will help you manage your business and work toward its success.*

▶ *The completed business plan is your means of communicating your ideas to others and provides the basis for your financing proposal.*

Over half of all new businesses fail within the first two years of operation and over 90% fail within the first ten years. A major reason for these failures is the lack of planning. If you have a well-written business plan that takes into account all the variables involved in starting a new business and is based on reality, you can move your venture on the road to success.

C. WHAT SHOULD A BUSINESS PLAN COMMUNICATE?

1. A business plan is a formal document, but not a tome. Verbiage does not substitute for solid ideas, careful research, and clear expression.

2. The plan should be persuasive, but objective. The document needs to acknowledge problems with the business venture that may or will exist.

3. A business plan need not be fancy, but should be well done.

4. Readers expect to see the following components in a business plan:

> ▶ *evidence of customer acceptance.*
> ▶ *appreciation of all of the investor's needs.*
> ▶ *evidence of focus on a product or service.*
> ▶ *recognition of the target market's desire for the product or service.*
> ▶ *financial projections that are consistent with the rest of the industry.*
> ▶ *realistic growth projections, including high, low, and expected growth.*
> ▶ *marketing information that determines market boundaries, analyzes the market share, shows the results of surveys and tests of potential customers, includes a sales technique, and pricing that is responsive to costs and the markets in question.*

D. WHAT DOES A BUSINESS PLAN INCLUDE?

1. PARTS OF THE PLAN

A business plan consists of several parts. The most important components are:

1. *A cover letter identifying the business plan as the property of your organization.* This cover letter includes your name, address, and telephone number, and the month and the year that the plan is written or revised. One paragraph states in simple terms who the business plan belongs to and the limitations on its distribution. (1 page)

2. *A table of contents.* (1 page)

3. *A summary of the plan with a brief paragraph about your organization.* A four- line description of the product or service; a four-line description of the market; a brief paragraph on production

and one on distribution, if needed; and, a short paragraph on the financing requirements. (2-4 pages)

4. *A description of your organization and the business with the following subheadings.* (4-6 pages):

▶ *The organization.*
▶ *The product or service.*
▶ *The target consumer.*
▶ *The consumer's desire for the product or service.*
▶ *The sales strategy.*

5. *A description of the market for your product or service.* Include information on the competition and cost-price comparisons between competitors and your organization. (4-8 pages)

6. *A marketing plan that includes information on:*

▶ *the markets.*
▶ *customers.*
▶ *competitors.*
▶ *the macroenvironment:*
  *demography.
  *economy.
  *technology.
  *government.
  *culture.
▶ *how each of these areas affects the marketing and selling of your product or service.*
▶ *evaluation of potential pitfalls. (10 pages)*

7. *The financial plan with sources and applications of cash and capital.* This should include:

▶ *an equipment list.*
▶ *a balance sheet.*
▶ *break-even analysis.*
▶ *cash flow estimates by month for the first year, by the quarter for the second and third years, projected income and expenses for the first three years, and notes of explanation for each of the estimates. (10-15 pages)*

Other reports and statements that can be included in this section (but are not appropriate for all plans) are:

▶ *historical financial reports for your organization, such as balance sheets and income statements for the past three years.*
▶ *a current audit report.*
▶ *an annual report if one is available.*

8. An appendix with:

▶ *management resumes.*
▶ *your organizational brochure and newsletter.*
▶ *other pertinent material about your organization and its work.*
▶ *letters of endorsement.*
▶ *copies of signed contracts for business.*

2. IMPLEMENTATION

Once the plan is written, reviewed, and adopted, the final step—and certainly not the easiest—is to go and set up and run the business. Obviously, only through the implementation of the plan can you hope to achieve the social outcomes you desire, as well as the new income streams that are so important to your financial empowerment.

Remember, the most successful entrepreneurs often fail the first few times before they hit it big. I *don't* want you to be like them. I want you to develop a sound business plan based on good research and valid marketing and succeed the first time out. With a solid business plan, you should only be taking prudent risks, not the "leap off the cliff" that so many small businesspeople refer to.

E. HOW MUCH "RETURN ON INVESTMENT" DO YOU NEED?

So now that you have a business plan (or are considering developing one) your board and you need to consider a key issue: how much return should we get on our investment, our risk? The answer? It depends.

● **FOR EXAMPLE:** A not-for-profit organization in Colorado was developing a business plan for a janitorial service that would employ some of its clients—people with developmental disabilities. In completing the plan, the staff and board found that they could go two ways. First, they could clean upscale offices with crews made up of both workers with disabilities and those without. If they proceeded this way, they would make about 25% return on their investment due to high prices and high profits. Or they could clean factory and warehouse space using crews with a much higher proportion of people with disabilities. If they did this, however, they would make less money. The quandary: Should they earn more dollars and employ fewer people with disabilities, or employ more and make less?

● **FOR EXAMPLE:** A performing arts not-for-profit in Connecticut decided to offer children's theater classes to utilize staff and volunteer talents and to take advantage of the theater building in late afternoon when it was empty. They knew from their financial projections that they could make some money, but their dilemma was whether to charge a high fee—say, $120—for the lessons, turning a larger profit, or charge less—$40—thus making the class affordable to more youngsters but receiving lower returns on the investment.

What should these organizations do? How much return on investment is enough for an organization that is going into a new venture? Are there any benchmarks or ratios that should be followed? Is there such a thing as making too much money? How can you assure that the staff and board of your organization are getting the most from your limited resources?

These questions are among the most commonly asked by not-for-profit staff and board members as they examine the feasibility of new ventures, and rightly so.

Analyzing return on investment (ROI) is not as simple for a not-for-profit as it is for a for-profit organization. This is a good time and place to discuss the issues and options open to you.

First, though, some assumptions and definitions. For purposes of this discussion, ROI means the aggregate of the financial and social results of a new venture weighed against the time, cash, and political capital invested. If we make $5,000 a year in profit and receive 100 units of service, the combination of those two is our return on investment. Also, I assume that we are discussing ventures designed to make money *and* provide service; thus, we must consider both these factors as we weigh the options surrounding any venture. Finally, the term "service unit" will be used. This term describes one of whatever an organization does. For a museum, it might be one visitor; for a hospital, a patient-day; for a detoxification unit, one outpatient visit. Many not-for-profits have more than one type of service unit, all of which can be used in analyzing return on investment.

Instead of looking just at the financial return on its investment, a not-for-profit must look at the social return of its activities as well. Thus, the two organizations in the examples above had to consider not only their earnings but also the social impact of their new venture: jobs for people with disabilities, or arts for kids. Having more of one meant having less of the other (although that is not true in all cases).

The two kinds of return make this analysis more complicated, though still fairly straightforward. Let's look at the way the performing arts organization described in the second example analyzed its return on investment.

Before starting the theater classes, the organization staff and board discussed the purposes of the venture. They set goals for the classes and made sure that these goals supported their mission (either financially or in service units).

Suppose, for example, that their main goal was to expand appreciation for the theater throughout the community, starting with its youngest members, while, at the same time, not losing money. To accomplish this goal, it would be of the greatest importance to keep tuition low so that the most possible children could attend. If, however, their main goal was to contribute $15,000 a year in related profits to a fund for renovating the theater in three years, the profits become paramount, and tuition may need to be higher (although not so high that no one comes to the classes). In this case, cash return is a higher priority than social return.

It's important to note that putting a higher priority on cash than social return is not only OK in certain cases, it is often essential, even for the most compassionate not-for-profit staff or board member. As we've noted repeatedly up to now, don't associate profits with bad things; making money in one area can help subsidize another area of service that will never pay for itself.

Next, the staff and board developed feasibility studies and a business plan. These documents gave them a good handle on their total investment, including cash, staff time, board time, and volunteer time. They were thus able to make a true comparison of the cost and benefit of various outcomes.

As in any investment decision (and that is exactly what this is), there are options. Our theater group, for example, could start the class with a high price and profit, start with a lower price and profit, try a different tack altogether, or do nothing. Let's examine how they might view each option.

Assume a cash cost of $25,000 to start the class and staff and an investment of staff volunteer time equivalent to $5,000. Look below to see the results of three options.

Option One—High Tuition

Start-up cost—CASH	$25,000
Start-up cost—TIME	$ 5,000
TOTAL COST	$30,000

Profit per year $ 2,500

Students per year   100 (service units)

Cash return on investment in year one: $2,500/$30,000 or 8.3%.
Invested cost per service unit $30,000/100 or $300 each.

Option Two—Lower Tuition
    Start-up cost—CASH $25,000
    Start-up cost—TIME $ 5,000
         TOTAL COST $30,000

Profit per year $ 500
Students per year   225 (service units)

Cash return on investment in year one: $500/$30,000 or 1.6%.
Investment cost per service unit: $30,000/225 or $133.33 each.

Option Three—Leave Funds in Bank at 7%
    Start-up cost—CASH $25,000
    Start-up cost—TIME $ 0
         TOTAL $25,000

Net income: $ 1,750 ($25,000 at 7%)
Students per year   0 (service units)

Obviously, the last option—leaving the money in the bank—is the least risky, but it also offers no return in service units and in visibility. The decision between the first two options (high or low tuition) is tougher, and will depend on the goals the board and staff set earlier; do they want cash or service? And if their goal is to have $15,000 a year in profit for the capital fund, are the outcomes of any of the options good enough? Probably not.

One flaw in this analysis is that we can't consistently quantify the risk associated with the business. Is the risk of failure (and of losing some or all of your investment) high or low? You will need to make some estimates of risk, include these estimates in your analysis, and weigh them in your decision-making process.

The other intangible to consider is the benefit to your organization from exposure. For example, if your museum is offering classes, a low fee will bring more people into the museum and, therefore, provide more exposure for the museum. Greater exposure may translate into more potential contributions, visibility, public awareness, and overall goodwill.

Good management is basically resource allocation—making the best use of what you have and committing resources where they will do the most good. By setting and sticking to your goals, carefully accounting for all your costs, and reviewing your options fairly, you and your board can make the best decision possible with the information available regarding your new business. No manager can ask for more than that.

F. PREPARING YOUR BUSINESS FINANCIALS

Now let's turn to the issue of how to prepare your financials. Too many of our clients focus on the markets, on the service or product, and forget the key parts of the financials.

There are a number of steps to go through in developing your financial information. They are listed below:

1. ASSEMBLE YOUR FINANCIAL DATA

In the early stages of product or service selection and feasibility analysis, you should have gathered most of the information you need to prepare your business plan. Your work now is to refine and organize that information, check the accuracy of your estimates, and to replace as many estimates as you can with firm figures. For example, for the purpose of your feasibility study, you may have estimated that your rent payment would be $600 per month. In your actual business plan, you may state that you are leasing property for $675 per month.

The following is a description and listing of the information you need:

a. Sales Targets. In order to make reasonable financial projections, you need to predict as accurately as possible what your volume of business will be. There are two major constraints here: the market and the assets (like money, skill, and time) that can be put into the enterprise. One way to approach these constraints is to estimate, based on your market research, what the potential market for your product or service is if you have restraints on money, skills, or time. The next factor is your internal constraints. This information allows you to estimate with some confidence what your potential sales will be. You should project sales for at least a three-year period.

Be careful not to project growth that cannot be sustained by the market. For example, if you are selling janitorial services in a community of 10,000 people with only 25 business establishments, there are only a limited number of the businesses that may be willing to buy your services. This is true even if you provide top quality service and beat the price of all the competition. You simply cannot sell any more. Conversely, in a big city, there is a much broader market for janitorial service at the quality and price you offer. But if your potential work force is limited to ten employees, it makes it difficult for you to reach your entire potential market.

Finally, remember that there is a relationship between price and sales. In general, lower prices mean more sales, *but only to a point*. There is a point at which no matter how low you price your service, no one will buy it. For example, if you clean swimming pools, you can only have as many customers as there are pools: even if you give services away, you will have no additional customers. So, in your sales projections, remember to consider the impact of price, and of competition.

Speaking of competition, remember that your competitors are out there. They will react to your entry into the market, and changes in your pricing or service structure. Thus, you must constantly be on top of what your competitors are doing. Too often I see business plans or talk to not-for-profit managers who say they want to do a certain service because there are no competitors. My reaction is twofold: First, why is there no competition? Is it because there is no real business opportunity? Second, if you do start a service and have success, competition will quickly appear.

Remember, competition is a good thing. It makes for better products and services, and more efficient production and delivery systems. Competition is something that you will be dealing with in all areas of your service array, not just in your entrepreneurial services. You need to learn how to work within a competitive environment. Your pricing, your marketing, and your management must all reflect a willingness and an ability to compete.

b. Pricing Information. Pricing is the art of finding the price that will maximize your return on investment. This price may be high or low. By using the information you gathered in your market research, you can determine the going price *or price range* for products or services that are similar to yours. Next, set a target for the amount of profit you wish to make during the first three years of operation. This information is used to set the price after you analyze the various costs involved in your operation.

As I have said repeatedly, nearly all not-for-profits are trained to *underprice* their services and thus they do. Do not assume that you will compete solely on price. Perhaps you can do what your competition does better, faster, or with less turnaround time.

Consider both the fixed costs and the variable costs in your pricing mix, as well as your profit and your competition. I touched on these briefly in Chapter 10 and they are so critical that they deserve an entire text. Remember, you will have the tendency to underprice: fight it!

NOTE: This is a very important subject, and if you have not already read it, see the more extensive discussion of pricing in Chapter 9.

c. Start-up Costs.

Capital items: These are the one-time items that you need to purchase to operate your business. This category includes the purchase of land, buildings, equipment, and furniture. These are the assets that continue to benefit your business operation. Items like inventory or supplies that are *used up* in the course of conducting business are expenses. With the exception of land, you depreciate your capital assets. Depreciation is simply an accounting method of distributing capital costs to the expense of the business operation over time. Some not-for-profits don't bother with depreciation because they don't pay taxes and can't take dvantage of depreciation as a business expense deduction. However, depreciation gives you a more accurate picture of the cost of running your business. Large ticket items should routinely be depreciated even if the business is a not-for-profit; otherwise, you never recover your full costs.

For your larger expenses, review one or two financing options even if you plan at this point to pay cash. Borrowing or leasing might be more advantageous and you need this information to test the financing options.

Other initial costs: In addition to capital items, you have other costs related to getting your business started which are not reflected in your operating expenses. Items such as legal fees, costs incurred to set up an accounting system, licenses, and introductory advertising are included in this section.

d. Operating Expenses

Fixed costs: These are the expenses that you pay whether or not you sell any product or service. They are sometimes called indirect costs or overhead. These expenses include items like rent, heat, electricity, and support salaries. Most of your fixed or indirect costs change at different levels of sales or production. For example, if you operate a mail order nursery, you produce a certain limited number of plants to sell from one greenhouse. If you wish to sell more, you need two greenhouses. This action increases your capital costs and fixed costs. If you anticipate growth during the first three years of operation, you need to estimate your fixed costs at various sales levels and identify the levels where your fixed and capital costs increase.

Variable Costs: These are expenses that vary directly with the number of items or services you sell. Variable costs are also called direct costs. These costs vary depending on the type of business. If you manufacture a product, then all of the costs of material are considered variable costs. If your product is made by workers who are paid only for contracted work, then their wages are part of the variable costs. If, however, your workers are salaried, you must pay them, whether or not there is work to do. This makes salary expense a fixed cost.

2. ANALYZE THE FINANCIAL DATA YOU GATHER

After you organize the critical financial data, you are in a position to analyze the information to help you make decisions about financing and pricing your product or service. There are specific types of analysis you need to perform. Each of these is described below:

a. Start-up costs and working capital needs.

Start-up costs are those costs you incur to get the business up and running. Licensing, land, building, equipment, raw materials, and training are all start-up costs.

Working capital is the money you need to operate your business both during its start-up phase and then, when the business is operational, this money becomes what you run the business on between the time you deliver a service or manufacture a product and the time you get paid. Your working capital needs are not fixed. For instance, if you make 1,000 widgets a month and you get paid in 30 days for those widgets, you need to have enough working capital to pay for the direct costs of the widgets plus your fixed costs (overhead) for the same period. But what if your customer suddenly decides to pay you in 45 days? Now your working capital needs go up by 50%. As I've noted before, more businesses fail making profits than making losses, because they forget that fast growth starves businesses of working capital—of cash. *(For more on working capital and some hands-on estimation forms, see Chapter 11.)*

b. Break-even Analysis. Break-even analysis provides you with a

sales objective which is expressed in either the number of dollars or units of production at which your business is neither making a profit nor losing money. The break-even point is the point where sales income is equal to fixed costs plus variable costs for a certain period of time. Break-even analysis is a technique used to analyze your cost information. The technique helps you to decide how much you have to charge at various levels of sales or how much you have to sell at various prices in order to get a return equal to your expenses. Break-even is calculated by the formula:

$$\frac{Fixed\ Costs}{Unit\ Selling\ Price - Variable\ Costs\ Per\ Unit} = Total\ Units\ Sold$$

You may find that to charge a competitive unit selling price, you have to sell an unrealistic number of units to achieve a profit. In this case, you need to reexamine your cost assumptions to see if expenses can be reduced.

How important is break-even? It is on my list of the ten biggest mistakes people make on their financials.

c. Pro forma profit and loss statement. This statement is a projection of your income and expenses. Like the break-even analysis, it provides a further check on the soundness of your venture. Most business plans project income and expense statements for at least three years. I recommend that you project income and expenses for a three-year period, the first year by month, and the next two quarterly. However, the further you move from present day, the less meaningful your numbers become. To develop your profit and loss statement, simply use the figures from your operating expenses form. Subtract your expenses from your income to show your pre-tax profit, add taxes if you anticipate operating your business as a for-profit enterprise, and subtract any profit-sharing or bonuses. The final figure is your retained earnings or fund balance.

d. Pro forma cash flow analysis. Your cash flow is probably the most important analysis for internal management of your new business, just as it is for your not-for-profit. It is the document that banks are most interested in because it indicates your ability to pay back your debt. The cash flow analysis shows how much cash is needed, when it is needed, and where it comes from. After you develop the cash flow analysis, use it as a check on how your business is doing. If you spend more or take in less cash than you anticipate, you may run into trouble. Variation from your cash flow projection helps you see early on if you are likely to run into cash problems. This analysis gives you a chance to take action and correct the flow of cash before you run into a serious shortage. Do your cash flow by month for the first year and quarterly for the next two. This will give you the most realistic view of your cash situation and then you can design a credit policy to get you over temporary short-falls, but *only* if they are temporary.

Working with these financials will give you a much better idea of how your business will operate, let you have a clearer idea of the risks you will run, and make the policy decisions for the senior management and board much more prudent.

G. THE TEN BIGGEST MISTAKES PEOPLE MAKE ON THEIR FINANCIAL PROJECTIONS

Now that we have looked at how to prepare your business plan financials, let's see what not to do. In working with hundreds of not-for-profits developing plans to start or acquire businesses since 1982, I have seen a lot of great plans and a bunch of so-so ones. It seems to me that not-for-profits are quicker to "get" the marketing concept, to understand the idea of meeting market wants, than they are to do really good, indeed, useful, financial statements.

I have a week's worth of theories as to why this is, but perhaps the most salient is that all of us in the not-for-profit sector have been trained (by our funders), since we were right out of school, how to do financials that *don't* cover all of our costs, how to rationalize expenditures that may or may not be related to the program, how to double up, maximize match, make something out of nothing. This accounting alchemy is difficult to overcome in developing a business plan and it leads to serious business planning problems that I see repeated over and over again.

In order to help you avoid some of those common and often fatal (to the business) mistakes, I've developed the top ten list.

10. MANY PEOPLE DON'T READ FINANCIAL PROJECTIONS AFTER THEY ARE PREPARED.

Now why would you spend the time putting together financials and not read them? Well, lots of people do. The financial manager develops the numbers and then the management and board ignore them or only give them a cursory glance. This often leads to a fundamental misunderstanding of how the business will perform. For example, the "bottom line" on an accrual-based profit and loss projection may be "in the black" starting in six months, but the cash flow may be negative for a year or longer. If the decision-makers don't thoroughly read and digest *all* of the financials, the organization is in for trouble.

9. FINANCIAL PROJECTIONS DON'T SUPPORT THE STATED GOALS OF THE BUSINESS.

As I have said repeatedly the point of your not-for-profit going into business is to (a): do more mission by having the business be part of the mission; (b): earn money from an unrelated business to then use to buy more mission by supporting another program; or (c): a combination of the two. The trouble with financials for a new business is that too often decision makers get so excited about the business that they forget about the point—the overall mission. If, for example, the new business' financial projections show a profit of $15,000 per year for the 2nd through the 4th year, that may be great. But if the point of the entire exercise is to get a $30,000 per year boost to support a key program, the numbers aren't meeting the goals. We've already talked about this, but it bears repeating.

8. NUMBERS IN THE PROFIT AND LOSS STATEMENT, CASH FLOW ANALYSIS, AND BALANCE SHEET DON'T JIBE.

This is, yet again, a surprisingly common problem. People put together different financials at different times, the sources and applications one week, the P&L the next, the cash flow after that. They then revise each one a number of times, but don't remember to cross-check the numbers, and wind up with a lot of mistakes. For example, if in revising and fine-tuning your numbers, you merely change the interest rate on a loan from 8.0% to 7.75%, that changes the interest rate shown in the P&Ls, the debt service shown in the cash flow, any calculation that you may do of the cost of capital, and the display of liabilities in the opening balance sheet. If you change one or two and not the others, your numbers no longer jibe, and someone reviewing your plan—particularly a banker who may be considering lending you money—may rethink your business acumen.

In my experience the numbers are not usually off by just a quarter of a percent. I see things like the Sources and Applications noting the purchase of $250,000 of factory equipment and *NO* depreciation in the P&L, or a loan for $300,000 in the balance sheet and the appropriate interest line in the P&L, but no debt service payments shown in the cash flow. Little things like that. Little things that can sneak up and bite you. The solution? Have an objective outsider look at your numbers and make sure that they agree with each other.

7. PEOPLE DON'T DO A CASH FLOW ANALYSIS OR CREATE JUST ONE CASH FLOW ANALYSIS EACH YEAR.

P&Ls are nice, balance sheets are "cool," breaking even is important; but you live and die by cash flow. And yet, agencies repeatedly don't do them, or only do them on an annual basis. Particularly in a business start-up, doing a yearly cash flow analysis instead of a monthly one is a recipe for disaster. In truth, it would be better to not have one, as a yearly projection too often provides dangerously out-of-touch information. An annual cash flow predicts the cash at beginning and end of the year only, with nothing about the status in the middle. It would be comparable to assuming that temperatures are cold year 'round if you only measured the temperature on January 1 and December 31.

Do cash flow projections and do them monthly.

6. PEOPLE DON'T ALLOW AN ADEQUATE NUMBER OF DAYS FOR ACCOUNTS RECEIVABLE.

Unless you are a retail business, always assume that people are going to pay you as late as possible and then add 15 days for the mail. Then add 15 more for bureaucratic mess-ups and an extra 21 days if you get your funds from the Feds. If you assume you will get paid too soon, you won't set aside enough working capital to get you through. Receivables are part of your cash flow estimation process. Remember to always assume that your expenses go in the category "Sooner" and that your income goes in the category "Later".

5. PEOPLE DON'T UNDERSTAND THE CONCEPT OF BREAK-EVEN ANALYSIS.

Breaking even is *so* important to good business planning for not-for-profits and yet, so few managers and board members really understand how to compute it and—more importantly—what the numbers really mean. First, break-even is computed by the following formula:

$$\frac{Fixed\ Costs}{Unit\ Selling\ Price - Variable\ Costs\ Per\ Unit} = Total\ Units\ Sold$$

This calculates the units of service or number of widgets you need to sell to break even *in a particular time frame*. For instance, if you were selling widgets for $10 that had a variable cost of $4 and you needed to pay off a fixed cost of $3,000 per month, you would need to sell 500 widgets [$3,000/($10-$4)] *per month* to not lose money *that month*. The value of this projection is to allow you to see how much sales volume is needed to stop losing money, and then to calculate how many months it will take for you to get up to that sales volume. Unfortunately, many people take breakeven to mean the volume of sales that will let you start to make money for the *life of the business*, and it is anything but that. Thus, they make incorrect and overly optimistic assumptions about the business, and assume that the money will start to roll in long before it really will.

4. PEOPLE DON'T UNDERSTAND MURPHY'S LAW.

Here's a news flash. Stuff breaks, people get sick, machines get stuck, storms occur, airline flights get cancelled, customers change their minds, or get fired, or lose their income stream. If you don't allow for many things to go wrong, you will be very, very unhappy. In terms of your financials, that means not cutting your working capital so close and your cash so thin that any one of a hundred things could put you under. I recently saw a business plan that had projections of $250,000 income per year and a net profit of just $34 each year. And on the basis of these projections they were prepared to borrow $200,000 over ten years. I did my best to talk them out of it.

3. PEOPLE DON'T START NEW BUSINESSES WITH ENOUGH CASH RESERVES.

This mistake is a combination of nearly all the items that have preceded it.

People don't do or understand break-even, so they don't reserve enough cash. They don't do a cash flow analysis, so they don't know how much cash they really need. They don't allow for a lengthy enough receivable time, so they don't reserve enough cash. They forget Murphy's Law and don't give themselves a cash cushion. Sounds like I'm repeating myself.

If you doubt me, remember this. More businesses fail making profits than making losses. How? They get starved for cash and close down.

2. PEOPLE PRICE THEIR PRODUCT OR SERVICE TOO LOW.

This is a major mistake, and easy to understand given not-for-profits' training in getting paid for work at less than costs. In a new business, you must (a): charge enough to pay all your expenses or (b): have very deep pockets. I have heard people tell me in their business plans on more than one occasion that they will compete based on price, *before* they know what their costs are!

If you think you can compete on price, great—but read on before you think you can.

1. PEOPLE DON'T TAKE INTO ACCOUNT *ALL* COSTS WHEN PREPARING FINANCIAL PROJECTIONS.

This is so common it must be a communicable disease. I've lost track of the number of not-for-profit execs who don't add their time into the overhead of the new business even though they will be spending 25% of their time on it for the first six months. Or those who leave out rent as an expense "since our building is paid for". Well, let me put it this way; if your competition is charging for it, you should be. Or, let me put it another way; if you are not accounting for all your costs, you are probably losing money on each sale, and you will *not* make it up in volume.

Be brutal in this area. Compare your business P&Ls to your own organizational books. Are all the same line items there? If not, why? Are the additional things that are different accounted for? Is there a realistic number for depreciation, administration, rent, utilities, support services, accounting, and bad debts? If you are manufacturing, is there a contingency for wasted raw materials? Put everything in, or you don't have a realistic view of what's really going on.

So there they are. The ten big mistakes that you can avoid if you try. They are easier to make than you might imagine.

E. CREATING A CLIMATE OF NEW IDEAS

One of the most important things that you need to do if you want to develop or enhance your social entrepreneurism, is to develop a climate of endless new ideas, one where suggestions are encouraged, ideas are fairly weighed, and the best ones implemented.

In line with our theory of the inverted pyramid of management, this means *everyone's* ideas, board, management, and line staff. You need these ideas to stay fresh, to see new methods of providing service, to keep in step with the changes in your many markets' wants.

To create this climate of ideas you must constantly be asking. Do at least these things:

1. Talk to all staff—particularly managers—about the need to use people's ideas. Let all staff know that ideas are welcome, valued, and will be evaluated fairly and objectively. Let them know that no idea is too small, and that all suggestions—even those that are not used—are appreciated.

2. Create a number of ways for people to offer ideas. Have something such as a suggestion box. Ask for ideas at staff meetings. Make a new idea or process a reward item on people's evaluations, and make time during the evaluation for discussion of new ideas. The freer people feel, and the more opportunities they have to offer their thoughts, the better.

3. Develop an objective review system. People need to know that their ideas will be reviewed impartially. For small suggestions, the managers can probably do this; for larger ideas, you perhaps can adopt the criteria you developed in your business development process to use to weigh varying suggestions.

4. Close the loop—get back to people. Let anyone who puts forth a suggestion know what happened to their idea—it was implemented, it will be implemented, it cannot be implemented and why. And *always* thank people for their ideas.

5. Consider a reward/recognition system. If someone makes a suggestion, or does a great deal of work on a particular idea, at least recognize them publicly, and consider rewarding them financially. If you feel the need to systematize this, fine—just make sure the reward is a reward, not a punishment. (For more on rewards systems, see Chapter 7.)

You need your staff to use all their synapses and neurons on your organization's behalf all the time. Creating a climate where new ideas are valued, recognized, and encouraged will not only make you able to be more entrepreneurial, it will also keep you flexible, the subject of our next chapter.

I. DEBT

In Chapter 12 I told you the ways to find and work with lenders, and in that discussion, I said that you would inevitably take on debt. Why? If you are a social entrepreneur you are either going to outgrow your cash flow, or you are going to start up something new and need cash for the startup. Both of these will mean debt.

Prudent debt, like prudent risk, is good business. But there are some rules to follow and some sources to consider before you take the plunge. I assume in this section that you have found a good lender and have started developing a long-term relationship with your banker. Let's start by looking at the kinds of debt available:

▶ *Line of credit:* This type of loan is based on seasonal cash needs. A line of credit is used only as you need it and must be "rested" (or zeroed out) at least once a year. Standard interest rates for this form of debt are usually the prime interest rate plus 2 or 2 1/2 percentage points.

▶ *Equipment financing:* This type of loan is made with equipment as collateral. Payments are usually made over the "useful" life of the equipment, which can range from three to ten years depending on the type of equipment used for collateral.

▶ *Working capital financing:* This type of loan helps a new business venture meet its cash needs until retained earnings accumulate. A working capital loan generally runs for two to five years and should first be sought from an economic development agency. The interest rate for this type of debt is prime plus two percent or more. Working capital loans are often difficult to obtain from traditional lenders because of the risk level involved.

▶ *Economic development financing:* This type of loan comes from a variety of sources including the Small Business Administration, your state Commerce Department and city or county development agencies. Interest is usually charged at lower rates. This type of loan is mixed with standard commercial lending and may be a good vehicle for capital if you are creating new jobs, hiring minority employees, or locating your business venture in an enterprise zone. Each locale has different criteria for this type of loan or loan guarantee. Be sure to check with your banker and your mayor's office for information on what is available to you in your location.

Also find out where any "enterprise zones" are in your community. These areas often have attractive financial incentives for businesses that locate in them.

▶ *Mortgages:* This type of debt is available for property and generally extends over a 12 to 30 year period.

▶ *Tax-Exempt Financing:* In recent years there have been a spate of state-sponsored tax-exempt bond "pools" where the risk for the bond purchaser is, in part, guaranteed by the state. These pools have become extremely popular for both the buyer and the seller (your organization) as they offer very low- cost debt. Check with your funder and your state trade association to see if there is a pool available for your organization.

Additionally, now that buyers are used to seeing tax-exempt bonds for not-for-profits, there are more and more organizations that are issuing their own bonds—often for total amounts as low as $1,000,000. Talk to a bond specialist about this—there are numerous rules and regulations, but it is a low-cost way of refinancing existing debt and paying for new property and equipment.

1. WHAT ARE THE RULES FOR SECURING FINANCING?

Some basic rules apply when you weigh various financing options. The first rule is that no investor or lender will consider your organization for a loan unless you plan to make a significant capital investment in it. The reason is simple. If you don't believe in the operation and your ability to be successful and profitable, no one else will believe in it either. Your capital investment is a statement of your belief in your business venture.

When you borrow funds:

▶ *Always borrow for as short a term as possible to save interest.*

● **FOR EXAMPLE:** Look at the difference in monthly payments and total interest on a $100,000 mortgage at 9% with a 15-year repayment as opposed to a 30-year repayment.

PAYMENT SCHEDULE

Principle:	$100,000	
Interest rate:	9%	
	15 years	*30 years*
Monthly payment:	$ 1,014.27	$ 804.62
Total interest:	$82,568.00	$189,664.00

By paying $209.65 more each month or $37,737 over a 15 year period, you can save $107,096 in interest!

▶ *Seek a variable rate, fixed payment loan.* This type of loan usually has lower initial interest rates and allows you to plan your cash flows more accurately. If interest rates rise, your loan lengthens. If interest rates drop, the length of the loan decreases. In either case, your loan payment stays the same.

▶ *Always negotiate for the ability to prepay the loan at no penalty.* Paying a little extra each month on the principal significantly reduces your overall interest costs.

2. WHAT KIND OF LENDERS ARE THERE, AND WHAT DO THEY WANT TO KNOW?

There are a variety of lenders available in the current deregulated market. The list includes:

▶ *commercial banks.*
▶ *savings and loans.*
▶ *credit unions.*
▶ *foundations like Program Related Investments (PRI).*
▶ *retirement funds (particularly unions and government employee funds).*
▶ *insurance funds (usually for loans over $1,000,000).*
▶ *commercial lenders.*
▶ *vendors (trade credit).*
▶ *your not-for-profit organization (as a lender to a new corporation that you own).*

Most loan officers don't just turn down a loan application without explaining what your organization can do to become eligible for funding. No matter what kind of lending institution you choose, your lender must know:

▶ *the purpose and objectives of your business.*
▶ *how much money your organization needs in the first 18 months to start this business venture.*
▶ *how the funds will be used.*
▶ *how the initial investment will be repaid.*
▶ *how much equity your organization has in the venture.*

▶ *the number of investors or lenders and how much each has invested.*
▶ *your organization's track record and significant milestones.*
▶ *who the shareholders are, if any.*
▶ *the debt level of the business venture now, if any.*
▶ *the qualifications of the owners and key employees.*
▶ *the strengths of the management team.*
▶ *the possible liabilities.*
▶ *any litigation, tax, or patent difficulties.*
▶ *events or technology that may affect the business venture.*

Debt is a tool, like any other. Don't overuse it and pyramid your organization into an early death. On the other hand, to preclude your organization from ever taking on any debt is shortsighted and too cautious for a successful organization to afford.

RECAP

Life is full of risk, and all of us learn to accommodate a certain level of risk every day. It is no different for mission-based managers. The skills that you have learned in this book will make it easier for you to take risk on behalf of your clientele. Building a better board, a stronger staff, becoming market-oriented, having strong controls, and becoming financially empowered, all build your ability to evaluate and take risks. Some of these skills increase your strengths, some reduce unnecessary risks, and others build an important financial cushion.

All of which leads us to the skills you have been learning in this chapter: how to be more entrepreneurial for the benefit of your community.

In this chapter I hope that I have given you food for thought on how to become a better risk taker and more entrepreneurial. We have reviewed how to assess and take risk, and how to accept its presence in your organization. We have looked at new sources of income and have reviewed the steps necessary to start an outside business venture.

We studied the need for and the value of prudent debt, reviewed the rules for borrowing, and the types and sources of debt available in today's marketplace. We discussed how much return on investment makes it worth the risk for your board, and how to develop a focus on mission while taking risk on behalf of your community and your clientele.

The next decade is a risky one for you and for your organization. You need to meet those risks with the ability to think and act like an entrepreneur.

14. Changing Flexibly

OVERVIEW

Have you ever watched a small child move forward from a sitting position? They simply lean forward even with their legs in front of them and move out over their feet into a crawl. They are incredibly flexible, and can get through small spaces, change direction, and adapt quickly to new environments. As we get older, we get less flexible, both in our bodies and in our points of view.

As organizations, we need to avoid this loss of flexibility. Change is with us always, and we can let it run over us, or we can work with it. The one common complaint of modern life is that the pace of change is increasing exponentially: things are changing faster and faster. Products that in 1980 had a useful "product life" of years now often have that life measured in months. Choices abound and people's attention span has shrunk. This all translates into a need for doing things the way that *today* necessitates, not the way that you did them yesterday.

Good marketing and staying abreast of your market wants are essential in this activity, and you learned many of the important skills of how to market earlier in the book. With those capabilities in hand, we must now seek to be flexible and adaptive in the face of ever-increasing changes in the markets you serve.

This chapter will help you manage change and at the same time keep your organization from becoming too enamored of the past and too scared of the future to adapt quickly and confidently. We'll cover the ways for you and your organization to become and remain flexible. I'll discuss the ways that you can be a facilitator of change in your organization and how you can shape that change to your benefit.

One problem I see repeatedly is holding on to the central values that make you what you are, while still accommodating to the changing demands of your markets. Is there a way to hold on to values? Yes, but it's not easy. I will give you some situations to allow you and your board and staff to begin the discussion of your core values and how they can be made to help the change process rather than to hinder it.

As you think of withstanding the winds of change, remember the old story of the hurricane at the shore, the huge brittle oak, and the flexible dune grass. Which survived the storm? The flexible grass survived the storm.

A. FIXED FORTIFICATIONS AND OTHER RELICS

General George S. Patton, one of the most successful military commanders in history, was fond of saying " Fixed fortifications are monuments to the stupidity of man." Certainly World War II has shown the necessity and benefit of flexibility. In 1939, at the beginning of the war, when the German army was overrunning much of Europe, the French had scoffed at the idea of a German invasion of France, as they were sitting confidently on their renowned Maginot Line, a series of bunkers and artillery that conventional military wisdom said was "unbreachable". The advancing German army agreed. They simply went around the line, at which point the French discovered that they could not turn their guns around. France fell, the war lasted six more years, and so much for the conventional wisdom.

Later in the war, General Eisenhower turned the tables, practicing the key skills of flexibility and speed, landing in Normandy where the Germans didn't expect it, with more forces than they expected, in bad weather, thus breaching their "Fortress Europe", a line of fixed fortifications. The war in Europe ended in less than a year, and so much for the Germans learning from the French mistake!

The one constant in life is change. Nothing stays the same for long, in war, business, communications, or the way that people provide services. All one has to do is look at the dismal history of certain big businesses in the United States to see how easy it is to fall into the trap of producing yesterday's product or service.

● **FOR EXAMPLE:** For forty years, General Motors made big, gas-guzzling cars for the American consumer. It made them poorly as well, because there was no real competition based on either quality or price. People bought a new car every three years like clockwork, and the cost of a car, even in constant dollars, was much less then than it is now. In the 1960's GM, Ford, and Chrysler all scoffed at the "silly little" German and Japanese cars, assured that no one would buy them. But Americans know a bargain, and they found that those silly little cars lasted longer, were easier to park, got better gas mileage, and had more amenities per dollar than the American models. In the late 60's, foreign imports became a real market threat to the American motor giants. How did they react? By building more of the same, opposing higher gasoline mileage standards, and fighting the requirements for seat belts, all the things that consumers said that they wanted and that the imports provided.

When gas prices rose to over $1 per gallon, the sale of high-mileage imports soared. What did American automakers do? They fought higher mileage standards, pressured Washington to limit imports, and continued to build more big, low-quality cars, and watched market share erode.

Finally, in the late 1970's, Ford and Chrysler did something. Ford designed and built the Taurus line, asking customers what they wanted, and putting in the car the best components and features of all the competition. Taurus was very successful, not only in sales, but in reliability as well—in part, because everyone in the assembly process, from engineers to factory workers, took part in the design process—a case study of inverted pyramid management.

Chrysler, for its part, introduced the minivan, the perfect car for the burgeoning families of the baby boom generation. By 1992, the Plymouth Voyager and Dodge Caravan made up *over 75%* of Chrysler's total domestic sales.

What did GM do? It continued building big, gas-hogging cars, fought the introduction of air bags, had, by all accounts, the least innovation of any auto company, fought for more import restrictions, and watched its market share go down the drain. Flexible GM was not. Auto makers in general were slow to learn to ask the customers what they wanted, were slow to realize that their markets could change, and were *product*-oriented rather than *market*-oriented. It was easier to just keep making what they knew rather than to change.

● **FOR EXAMPLE:** IBM is another example of inflexibility—even in a culture that worships the consumer. From the late 1950's through the early 1980's IBM's mainstay was mainframes, the large computers that made big business happy. Then Steven Jobs and Steve Wozniak invented the Apple computer and started the desktop computer revolution. IBM ignored it for 5 years, then jumped in in a big way with the PC, developing a new standard for the industry. In a sense, IBM was a victim of its own success. In the late 1980's and early 1990's PC's became a low-cost commodity with little brand loyalty and IBM lost PC market share. Its mainframe sales went into a spiral, due to the increasing speed and computing capacity of PC's. But IBM did not look ahead and see the results of its own technology, and when it did, it was not flexible enough to change. In 1992, for the first time, IBM announced involuntary layoffs, as well as the biggest losses in its history.

● **FOR EXAMPLE:** An example of the need for your organization to be able to accommodate to rapidly changing circumstances can be embodied in the story of my sister, Christie, who was born with severe mental retardation. In the mid-50's my parents lobbied hard for state funding for large institutions for the developmentally disabled, a situation that did not exist at the time (there were institutions, but parents had to pay the entire bill, and if they could not, the debt was passed on to their children and grandchildren!) With the passage of partial funding legislation (my parents had to co-pay) Christie went to the institution, which at the time was the "state of the art" for retarded children.

Times change, and so has our understanding of the developmentally disabled. In the mid-70's there was a controversial push to empty out such facilities, placing Christie and other developmentally disabled adults in small community residences. In fact, Christie was a "Class Action" client in a lawsuit that was brought in Federal court to deinstitutionalize persons with disabilities. She now resides in a small group home in Connecticut and works in a small assembly workshop each day.

The point? In twenty years, the focus of care for this single population has gone from centralized to decentralized, resulting in the need for thousands of community-based not-for-profit organizations who care for the developmentally disabled to develop entire new skill sets: renting, building, or purchasing real estate, financing their properties, running 24-hour-a-day residential settings, increasing staffing, cash flow, regulation, and life safety, all with stringent financial oversight and, in most cases, less-than-adequate funding. Organizations who have thrived on this rate of change have prospered, and have benefited the communities that they are in business to serve. Those that can't keep up have suffered, and so have their clientele.

There are dozens of other examples of the need to keep up-to-date in the not-for-profit sector: technology changes in health care, causing the capital investment just to keep open to quintuple in 15 years; the birth and growth of nearly the entire "environmental movement" and all of its not-for-profits since 1970; the whipsaw changes for almost every government-funded not-for-profit that accompanied the Reagan Revolution; the explosion of need in the areas of homelessness and AIDS—this list alone could take up the rest of this book. The point, of course, is that we in the not-for-profit sector are, like everyone else, subject to the increasingly rapid pace of change.

B. CHANGE—AND BEING A CHANGE AGENT

The Chinese language has a symbol meaning "change" that has two components, one meaning "opportunity" and one meaning "danger". This essentially sums up the issues involved in changing: there are both opportunities and pitfalls to change, and yet, as noted above, change is inevitable. You want to become an agent for *healthy, successful* change, change that makes the best of the opportunities, change that improves your ability to perform your mission.

We all know that nearly all of us resist change to some degree, often even when the change is to our benefit. We often prefer what we know (the status quo) to an unknown future (personified by change). In reality, all of our future is unknown, and we have a responsibility to attempt to meet the future in ways that most benefit our constituency. In other words, there is danger in inaction as well as in action. Whenever you think that inaction is the safer choice, remember GM and IBM!

In your work with your organization, you need to become a facilitator of change, someone who can both recognize the need for change in a particular part or program of your organization, see the barriers to meeting the challenges of that change, and then bring others along to implement the change. I want to give you two key points to remember as you adopt the role of change agent:

1. All Change is Ultimately Individual. This is the corollary of the maxim that "all politics is local". What it means is that, while you may engage in soaring rhetoric about how a particular change will benefit your clients, you need to marry the rhetoric with specifics about how the change in question will effect individuals. Your staff and board are naturally concerned about your mission and your service recipients, but they are also understandably curious about how the change will affect them, their job, their responsibility. They will ask questions such as: Will this change make me lose my job? Will I have to work different hours? Go back to school? Move my place of work (or residence)? Will I have to work for someone else? With a different type of service recipient? Will the change increase my personal risk on the job?

You need to acknowledge that these are legitimate questions, and ones that need to be answered quickly, thoroughly, and frankly. The sooner that you address these concerns the better: you will get ahead of the rumor and worry curve.

2. In Moving Your Organization to the Future, Don't Criticize the Past or the Present. One of the biggest mistakes we make in trying to institute change is to criticize, either implicitly or directly, the actions of our staff and board in the past. For example, when the movement to get persons with disabilities out of "sheltered workshops" and into competitive employment (known as supported employment) came into prominence in the mid-1980's it was championed as the good, best, and, in some cases, the *only* way to provide vocational services to those persons. The message many heard: you who have dedicated your careers to helping people the best way you knew how have done something less than good.

Other examples abound: in welfare administration (welfare or workfare?), in education (inclusion or specialization?), in child welfare (family preservation or the rights of the child?), in deaf education (ASL or Total Communications?), in low-income housing (tenant control or not?). In each of these areas, the reformers have had a valuable new idea, often supported with excellent research and evidence that their idea works—and works better than what has been done before. But all too often I have seen these bright peoples' bright ideas go aground when someone—usually a zealous convert who is intent on enlightening the world to this new idea (and sometimes on *enforcing* its adoption)—paints the new idea as the only way, and all that came before as antiquated, outmoded, useless, or negligent of the overall good of the persons receiving the service. How would you feel if told that your life's work was old, useless, or negligent? Would you get your hackles up, and defend yourself, your job, your dedication to your work? Of course you would. So would I. And it is just this schism, this unintentional polarization, that builds resistance to positive change.

There is, of course, a better way. Tell people, whether it be staff, board, or volunteers that the new policy, the change, will be another in the series of adaptations that your organization has made over the years to stay with the best in your field. "This continues our tradition of top quality service, of innovation on behalf of our clientele" is an excellent message, and much more readily received than an announcement that says, either directly or implicitly, "With this change, we'll finally get it right."

☞ **HANDS ON:** When initiating a change, *do* start with what you are doing right, and build on doing the "right" thing better. Use your mission and your organizational values to support the change. Evidence suggests that by doing things the "new" way, you will be able to ultimately help your clientele faster, better, more efficiently, or with greater effect. The more that you can use your mission as a vehicle to overcome inertia and resistance to change, the better.

Don't initiate the change by going through a laundry list of what is wrong, about how your current method of service is "old", "outmoded", or "out-of-date". I also suggest that you avoid using the term "state of the art". To a lot of people that either sounds technical or trendy, both things that you want to avoid.

Do try to look at things from the point of view of those the change will most affect. What will they think? How will they view this, as more work, another fad, a direct threat to their professionalism?

Remember, the key to being a good manager in a changing environment is to *facilitate* change, not to *force* it.

C. HOLDING ON TO YOUR VALUES

A key element of working with change is to decide how to evaluate the changes that are possible and adopt the ones that most improve your ability to deliver your services *without compromising your mission and values*. This is somewhat akin to going to an opulent Sunday brunch buffet at a fancy restaurant and trying to decide which items are the most interesting and tasty—but least fattening. If you adopt changing styles, patterns of service, or management models wholesale, you will abandon your moral high ground—the mission and values that have made you what you are today. People will stop associating you with your core beliefs, and won't really know who or what you are, or how to interact with you.

● **FOR EXAMPLE:** Recently the faculty of a public school in our community sought and was awarded a grant to develop a more interactive and technology-based curriculum for the elementary students at the school. The new philosophy was to let students work as teams—as they do when they get into the real world—to study issues and solve problems. It also focused all activities throughout the day around a single issue: if the children were studying floods, for example, the social studies class would look at the impact on communities of floods, while the math class might apply an arithmetic model to calculate the volumes of water passing through a levee, while the science class looked at the forces that would be required to break the levee, and the language arts class could read a first-person account of the great Johnstown flood. This was a great theory—state of the art. The problem was that this new method of teaching required enormous amounts of teacher coordination and planning that the teachers could not do at night. This need for planning time meant that the teachers were out of the classroom a significant amount of time during the day—thus the children had substitutes. As a result, the best of ideas—to teach children in a better way—went aground on the shoals of reality: the top-flight teachers were out of the room and thus couldn't teach!

What are your core values and how strongly do you hold to them? Here are some controversial situations to ponder:

SITUATION 1: Assume that you are a health care provider, a counselor, or someone who interacts with young women. Do you (and your agency) believe in offering a pregnant woman information about abortion as an option? Or is that absolutely forbidden? What if the government funding patterns change, and the $250,000 a year you traditionally get for counselling teenage women, now comes with the stipulation that you hand the women a brochure describing their choices (including abortion) if they became pregnant? Do you take the money?

SITUATION 2: You are a provider of day care services. A new model of services is proposed by a large employer in your town who wants you to run its day care center. The employer's data show that it is perfectly safe to run the center at much higher child-to-staff ratios than you have in the past if the physical design of the center is changed. The contract would provide you with enough profits to allow your other two day care centers, which are now financially marginal, to thrive. You have always put the children's well-being first, and you are unsure about the safety of the children at this new, lower staff-to-child ratio. What do you do?

SITUATION 3: You are a museum director who is offered the opportunity to host an important exhibition of avant garde (and quite graphic) photographs by nationally known artists. One of your core values has been to represent your community's tastes. This exhibit may be on the cutting edge. Are you violating your values here or not?

The issue that I want to highlight here is that change can often challenge your values. You need to adapt to change without changing the core of what you are. This requires vigilance about your mission and values, and regularly using your mission as a management tool as we discussed in Chapter 4.

D. KEEPING FLEXIBLE

When you do decide to change you need to do it in the quickest, least painful, least costly, and least disruptive manner. This requires flexibility at all levels of the organization. The keys here are simple, and very consistent with the model of management we discussed in Chapter 7.

First, push as many decisions as close to the point of service as possible. With change, this means setting overall policy ("We want to reduce the turnaround time to initiate services") and letting the staff closest to the point of service figure out how to do it, what resources they need, etc. Bottoms-up change will be the most empowered and will foster the most ownership, and the least resistance. These people thus become your change agents, the people that will actually do the changing for much of the organization, seeing it through, pushing from the point of service toward management, rather than the other way.

Second, you will need to check in regularly with your change agents, focusing particularly on their progress, and how you can help them, as well as on the results of the change in terms of your mission and values: have there been unexpected effects on your clientele, on your staff, or community? If so, are they consistent or inconsistent with your mission statement?

Third, as with any change, evaluate the process and the outcome. Did the change bring about the anticipated results? Was the change process optimal or can it be improved? If so, how? Most importantly, if the change has not turned out well, can you now turn back or go in another direction?

RECAP

I have been told that there are three stages of change: the Ending, the Confused Middle, and the New Beginning. I like the descriptions, and anyone who has been through organizational change will recognize each stage, usually associated with some pain. This is particularly true with the Ending. I hope that in this chapter you have seen how we as managers can avoid making the Ending too painful, easing the transition by complementing the past and building on it, rather than tearing it down wholesale to start again.

We've also reviewed the methods of getting through the Confused Middle, by empowering change agents and recognizing that all change is local: you must look at any new processes or policies through the eyes of the people that it affects.

We have covered the value of remaining flexible, and that staying in place means falling behind. We have reviewed the fact that change agents are best if they facilitate rather than dictate, something that is very much in line with our overall prescription for management: let the people who do the work make the decisions. Finally, you read about the importance of hanging on to your core values, even while you change with your market's wants and your field's techniques.

Change is with us all. A lot has occurred since you started reading this book, some of which will ultimately affect you, your staff, and your clientele. Remember, the only thing that is constant in life is change, and that part of being an effective manager is to be a change agent, bringing your organization along so that it can change in ways that make your ability to perform your mission a win-win situation for everyone involved.

15. A National Agenda: Empowering Our Not-for-Profits

OVERVIEW

In this book we have covered the key components of how to achieve success at your not-for-profit. You have read suggestions and applications of how to deal with you mission, your board, your staff, your markets, your money, and your long-range goals. Hopefully, by applying the ideas encompassed in the previous pages, you can change your organization for the better, become more mission-oriented, more market-sensitive, and a better financial manager. But one key component remains: how your funders and the community-at-large view and treat your organization.

This chapter will address three outdated theories of how funders look at you, look at three new ways that our nation needs to view its not-for-profits, and provide a specific list of action items for government, United Ways, and foundations to use as they consider how to assist (or at least not impede) not-for-profits as we move into the 21st century.

A. THREE OUTDATED THEORIES

In the second chapter of this book, I recounted how not-for-profits came to the state that confronts us today. I related to you the three big driving principles of most funders' views of how not-for-profits really run. To review briefly, these principles (from the funders' point of view) are:

1. WHAT WE SAY GOES. Whether or not it makes any sense in your community, or with your mission, since we are paying the piper we call the tune—much more invasively and comprehensively than any for-profit customer would ever dream of doing.

2. YOU CAN'T DO WELL DOING GOOD. You are suspected of stealing if you are not threadbare, scrutinized well beyond the cost-benefit curve, and, in general, must take a vow of poverty to get our (the funders') money.

3. WHAT IS YOURS IS OURS. If you take our money (even if it is just a portion of your overall income), we have the right to come and strip you naked and judge you at our whim. Additionally, anything that you buy with "our" money, is ours, not yours.

As I said earlier, it is my belief from being part of and working for and around not-for-profits for nearly 20 years, that these policies are not only outdated, but are counterproductive social policy, short-sighted fiscal policy, and just plain egocentric at their core. They assume that the funder knows best, that the not-for-profit is an inept, if not felonious, manager of public funds, and that the not-for-profit should be poor to prove its honesty. They also forget that at the center, the relationship between government and funder and agency is really one of purchasing services. It is not parenthood. Neither is it indentured servitude.

These policies and views must change and there are five groups of people who must change them: the governments, the foundations, the United Ways, the public, and you, the staff members of the nation's not-for-profits. Without fundamental change in the ways that these five groups view your not-for-profit and the 950,000 others in the United States, there are limits to what you can achieve. For example, if your funders demand that you have no fund balance, and go to extraordinary lengths to recover funds from you, you can never be financially empowered and you can never help the community without running back to the funder for more funds—funds that come with all strings attached.

This concern with the way government contracts with and treats its providers of service is not, of course, unique to me. Not only have the trade associations been harping on the issue for years, our centers of academic research have been looking at the issue as well. Such notables as Brian O'Connell at the *Independent Sector* in a series of publications, and David Osborne, in his excellent book *Reinventing Government*, have both called for a reexamination of the ways that government funds and supervises its contractual obligations. Osborne, in particular, has developed a large number of examples of ways to make government more efficient and effective. Many, including the call for an end to "use it or lose it" and competitive bidding, parallel the ideas that I lay out below.

But, having criticized just about everyone in power positions, what can each group do to fix the problem? It would be unfair just to take potshots without offering solutions, so here are mine. These are not, as you will see, minor adjustments. They are radical realignments of our national view of the not-for-profit sector. They will, at some level, threaten just about everyone, as they are not designed to be slow and cautious in their approach. I don't think we have the time to be slow and cautious. America's social, educational, arts, scientific, and religious needs are obvious to all but the most callous or out-of-touch observer. Let's start now.

B. OVERALL PHILOSOPHY CHANGES THAT ARE NECESSARY

In the introductory chapter of this book, I started the discussion of my three umbrella theories of not-for-profits. Those three philosophies have appeared in many forms throughout the book. But do they apply to funders? I think that they do, and they bear another examination here.

The general philosophies below need to be adopted and practiced at all levels. As I noted just above, they require a radical rethinking of the role of not-for-profits by many of us. But, those not-for-profit funders whose grantees and contractors are succeeding have already adopted many, if not all, of these tenets.

1. NOT-FOR-PROFITS ARE BUSINESSES

First and foremost, we have to stop thinking of not-for-profits as *charities*. They are businesses, albeit ones whose primary motivation is mission, and not profit. In pursuit of that mission, not-for-profits must act as much like a business as possible without sacrificing their mission. This means adopting many of the skills taught earlier in this book: a bias for marketing, watching the bottom line, building up equity and financial flexibility, growing and retaining a strong staff, having a long-range vision, and understanding that profit is *not* a dirty word.

We also have to realize that our not-for-profits contribute to our communities economically as well as in arts, human services, education, or theology. Not-for-profits contribute over 9% of our gross national product, and employ more people than the domestic auto industry and its immediate suppliers. In many rural communities, not-for-profits are major employers, and in every community they contribute to the local payroll in a significant way. Thus, a healthy, growing, and stable not-for-profit network can stimulate job growth just as much as our small businesses, which get so much good press on the issue of economic stimulus.

Now, I have not ever said, and never wish to be quoted as saying, that this business mentality should come at the expense of doing good mission. It does not mean that watching your cashflow equates with cutting all of your unprofitable programs. Doing some things that lose money is part-and-parcel of the service array that not-for-profits should continue to provide. But, using good, sound, businesslike practices at the staff and board level can make all the difference: *it means getting more mission for your money, not having more money and doing less mission.*

2. NO ONE GIVES A NOT-FOR-PROFIT A DIME

Whoa, say the governments, we *give* them billions. Hold on, say the United Ways, we *give* them millions. Wait a second, say the foundations, what about our millions? And don't forget us, say the millions of Americans who dip into their wallets and purses each year to contribute to the nation's not-for-profits.

To all of you who fund America's not-for-profits, I say this: You're still focusing on not-for-profits as *charities*, not as the mission-oriented businesses that they are. Let's look at the transactions that *really* take place when you make a donation:

● **FOR EXAMPLE:**

▶ The local Art Museum comes to you for a $100 donation. They describe their programs, explain their funding patterns, and ask for your help in meeting their program goals. You write them a check for $100.

▶ The statewide drug prevention hotline calls you for a $50 monthly donation to allow them to keep taking 800 calls from people who need drug rehabilitation services and are in crisis. You sign up for a monthly contribution.

▶ The county shelter for the homeless is taking contributions to pay for a holiday dinner for the residents. You chip in $20.

Now, here is the crux of the issue. In each of these cases what did you do? Did you *give* the museum, hotline, or shelter anything? Most people would say "Yes, I *gave* them money". No. What you did was *buy services on behalf of someone else.* For the museum, that money might go to a new display of impressionist paintings that all can see; for the hotline, it might help pay for the 800 service; for the shelter, it literally will put food in someone's mouth. Thus you purchased something, perhaps not as precisely as you would purchase food from the grocery or a repair service from your plumber, but, at its core, the transaction is the same.

There is still the other side of the equation—the side that is even more important than realizing that you (and all of the other funders, the governments, foundations, and United Ways) are buying something, rather than just giving money away. It goes like this:

Not-for-profits earn every cent that they get.

Step back and think about it. The government doesn't give money away for nothing (although I will be the first to contend that they regularly don't get their money's worth). The government wants something for its money: it *buys* services, whether they be scientific research, outreach to teenage moms, public broadcasting, or breakfasts for poor children. If it buys something, then the relationship is one of purchaser (the government) and seller (the not-for-profit). Thus the not-for-profit has to do something to *earn* the money, which usually means providing a service or array of services. The same is true for other funders.

The understanding that not-for-profits are earning their money rather than accepting a handout is, obviously, a critical part of the philosophy change. If not-for-profits are businesses and have economic value beyond their social, educational, or religious worth, then they also can and should stand up and stop being treated like poor cousins.

3. NOT-FOR-PROFIT DOES NOT EQUAL NON-PROFIT

Here's the most important issue. Throughout this book, and all of my other writings, I always use the term not-for-profit, rather than the more commonly used "non-profit". I do this for two reasons. The first is that the term not-for-profit is technically the correct one: the corporation is established in the IRS code as a corporation "not for profit". The second reason, and the more important one for this discussion, is that the term non-profit sends the wrong message.

A non-profit is an entity that loses money. Unfortunately, most not-for-profits are also non-profits. What the 501(c)(3) is, however, is a corporation formed, under law passed by Congress, to serve a variety of areas such as education, religion, social services, the arts, etc. Here is the key:

Nowhere, in any state or federal law or regulation, does it say that a not-for-profit must lose money or break even financially. In fact, *in the IRS code, it says that "the <u>profits</u> of the corporation shall not inure to the benefit of (various people)".* (Emphasis added)

Thus, having profits is fine with the law, and with IRS regulations. However, it has not traditionally been OK with funders. Thus, the less they can pay, the better, and if a not-for-profit is "making money" or has a reserve, that is immediately suspect and cause for a reduction in funding for the next funding cycle, a special audit, or both. This is absurd. It is amazing that all of us in the not-for-profit community have allowed it to continue this long.

Not only is it OK for not-for-profits to make money, I contend that not-for-profits *must* make money in most, if not every year, if they are to do their job right. Only financially stable organizations will be able to react quickly to changing needs in their communities. Only financially stable organizations will be able to recruit and retain excellent staffs, take risks on behalf of their clientele, and do their job as it needs to be done. Finally, only financially stable not-for-profits will be able to stop the cycle of dependence on government for hand-to-mouth funding (for more on this see Chapters 12 and 13 on Financial Empowerment).

Profit is accepted in every other sector of our economy—even in some sectors of the not-for-profit economy—hospitals being the primary example. Why then should profit, and the stability, flexibility, and quality that it produces be such a pejorative when it is applied to not-for-profits in general?

Again, I fear misinterpretation and misquoting here. I am not contending that not-for-profits should make money just to make money, or to buy nice offices, or pay high salaries. The profits should be reinvested in a way that each organization's board and staff feel best maximizes the use of those funds to accomplish the mission.

4. COMPETITION IS OK

Imagine that the owner of a new fast food franchise came to a zoning hearing in your town and asked the zoning commission to rezone a parcel of land so that she could build a burger stand at the same intersection where another fast food restaurant already operated. Now, imagine the zoning commission turning the zoning request down because it "duplicates an existing service". The franchise owner would scream bloody murder and sue, and win, with a great deal of popular support in the community, because we have a long and successful tradition of free enterprise and competition. Now, and this is not so hard to envision, imagine that same franchise owner sitting on a funding panel at your United Way, and voting to turn down a funding request for a new program because it "duplicates an existing program already operating in the community".

It happens all the time. Agencies, particularly in social services, are regularly given geographic monopolies by their government funders. This is done to avoid duplication and in the spirit of efficiency and economy. It's amazing to me that we (a): let this start, and (b): let it continue, when all of the evidence from every corner of the globe shows that competition (if profits are allowed and retained) will encourage better service, at more economical prices, than monopolies.

In short, competition for customers is OK, and should be encouraged. I am not naive enough to say that this should be done wholesale next fiscal year. The staffs and boards of not-for-profits are well trained as monopolies, and a transition time is needed and will be rocky for some. Much of the advice in this book is designed to get them ready for just such competition.

C. A SPECIFIC LIST OF ACTION ITEMS

This list of action items is offered as an agenda for change for the five major groups that need to act now: the government, the foundations, the United Ways, the community-at-large, and the staffs and boards of our not-for-profits. All of them are designed to mesh with the four overall philosophical changes discussed above.

To be fair, I also must note here that some governments, some foundations, and some United Ways are already doing many, if not all, of the things I suggest below. In fact, with the exception of the idea of national management certification for not-for-profits, there is little here that has not already been tested and found to work. Thus, as you read these suggestions, don't put them aside saying "Never happen" or "Never work". They already are happening, and already do work in other communities. What you need to do is to make them work in yours.

▶ **GOVERNMENT** (Federal, State, County, Local)

1. End the policy of "use it or lose it". Let not-for-profits bid on work that you want done, and then, if they do what you contracted for, and have money left over afterwards, fine, let them keep it. If you bid the contract fairly, and the contractor did what you asked, why should they have to return what they didn't spend? All this encourages is waste, fraud, or both. (Note: the Feds are making major strides here, while the states in general are lagging far, far behind.)

2. End monopolies. Let the not-for-profits you fund bid against each other, and against for-profits. Open the markets up. To do this well, you will need to learn how to write contracts and Requests for Proposals in new ways, and you will have to link the end of monopolies to the end of "use it or lose it", but it will work. You will, in the end, get better services, better quality, and more productivity.

3. Encourage productivity and quality. Compensate contractors if they meet high quality and productivity standards: ones that are set forth in the contract. Even small financial incentives can bring up standards rapidly. Again, this has to be linked with the end of "use it or lose it", or you will lose any beneficial effect.

4. Pay on time, and pay fair scale. In an era of tight government budgets and a popular prohibition on new taxes, there is, of course, a great temptation to cut across the board, as well as to pay later. This is a short-term solution that creates (and has created) a long-term problem: chronically underfunded agencies that are perpetually dependent on the government.

5. Reduce or end the use of matching fund requirements. The theory of the match is that it shows agency or community commitment, and the likelihood of program continuity later on if funding ceases. In reality, this requirement both impoverishes not-for-profits and/or encourages them to cheat by allowing "in-kind" contributions—those of time or overhead that are already paid for—often by another government agency. Can you imagine the same government asking IBM to sell a PC at 25% *below* cost? That's exactly what a 25% match does. Stop it.

6. Develop a universal accounting and audit format. For every type of funding, a not-for-profit often has to go through a different set of bookkeeping and year-end audit and accounting forms. Sometimes this means one agency has to do ten separate types of forms. As you can imagine, this does not result in administrative efficiencies. I refuse to believe that with all the expertise in this country, governments and CPA's cannot come up with a universal set of accounting and year-end program audit protocols that would save millions of dollars in oversight costs each year.

▶ **FOUNDATIONS**

1. Require management certification for funding. I put this on the foundation's agenda because they could commission such a certification effort more easily than the government. My vision here is of a management certification, such as Commission on the Accreditation of Rehabilitation Facilities, for not-for-profits. All agencies that could meet the certification would be certified for three years, and that would make them eligible (or more competitive) for foundation funds, and could even be a prerequisite for funding continuation. Certification could also be made a competitive edge for government and/or United Way funding. I suggest that the foundations link up with the graduate programs in not-for-profit management, such as Case Western Reserve and Yale, to develop the certification.

2. Encourage and fund seed projects with business outcomes. Program Related Investments (PRI's) do this to some extent, and are the most laudable development from the foundations of the past decade, in my view. But I feel that foundations can go further to encourage financial empowerment, and seeding outside business ventures is one way to do that.

3. Stop the practice of "use it or lose it". See # 1 under "Government".

4. Stop or reduce match requirements. See #5 under "Government".

▶ **UNITED WAYS**

1. Stop funding deficits. So many United Ways have policies of only funding deficits. All this does is encourage future deficits. If you accept my theory of not-for-profit transactions—that donors are buying services—then United Ways should purchase the most needed services, whether or not the agency is making money.

2. Demand Management Certification. See #1 under "Foundations".

3. Encourage Competition. Don't refuse funding just because a service is duplicated: let agencies compete to provide the best service. Demand quality, but even with higher quality, competition will ultimately lower your cost, and will probably weed out the weak and inflexible agencies. This *will* be painful. People *will* scream, but the community *will* be better off for it.

▶ **THE AMERICAN PUBLIC (and the press)**

1. Stop assuming that all not-for-profits are welfare recipients. They aren't. There are efficient, effective, and productive not-for-profits and, inefficient, underproductive ones, just like in the for-profit sector, and the ratio is probably about the same.

2. Corollary assumption: That all not-for-profits steal. They don't. I've never seen a study done, but I wouldn't be surprised if the rate of theft and corruption in the not-for-profit sector is less than in the proprietary or governmental sectors. But when a not-for-profit staff or board member steals and it makes the papers it is big news. At any rate, the public's and press's demands for incredibly expensive scrutiny of every dollar spent—spending millions to prevent the theft of thousands—is not only counterproductive, it is insulting to the hundreds of thousands of dedicated and honest not-for-profit staff and board that are serving us well. Reasonable accounting, and checks and balances, both within and outside not-for-profits are important, but we've got things way out of proportion, and our tax dollars are not well spent in this area.

3. When you serve on a board, don't check your common sense or business expertise at the door. I've lost count of how many times I've watched good solid businesspeople make incredibly dumb decisions for a not-for-profit "because we aren't really a business". Just because the organization is not in it for the money doesn't mean you suspend common sense in making policy decisions. You are on the board to contribute your wisdom, expertise, experience, and perspective to the discussion: don't leave home without them.

4. Demand productivity, flexibility, and quality from your not-for-profits. Just because it has "always been that way" is no excuse for stodgy management and outdated programming. Be as demanding of your not-for-profits as you are of stores and businesses you patronize. If you donate money, you are a customer: demand quality.

D. WHAT YOU CAN DO

If the items above are to become reality, you need to help. As a not-for-profit staff member, there are things you need to be doing to reinforce these new ideas and make them work in your community. While everything that I have tried to convey in this book moves you and your organization toward that end, I can distill it into two short phrases:

1. Be businesslike. Not cold, or profit-driven, but businesslike. The more you act like a business, the more you will be treated like one.

This includes dressing appropriately, using business language (markets, cash flow, quality management), and the like. Join the Chamber of Commerce, and get active. Not-for-profit staffs regularly complain that they "don't get any respect". Part of this wound is self-inflicted. Remember, you earn your money, you are not a charity. Go out and act like it and you will start to be treated accordingly.

2. Be competitive—accept the marketplace and try to adapt. This is, I know, a big change, but if the governments and foundations end *use it or lose it*, and end monopolies, you'll have to get with it sooner or later—I suggest sooner.

E. AN EXHORTATION

These agenda items are a start—and only a start. Until all parties involved buy into the major philosophies, we won't make significant progress. Until not-for-profits learn and practice the skills and policies outlined in this book, they won't become the lean, creative, and productive social entrepreneurs that would so benefit the social fabric of our society. Until the public sees our not-for-profits as more than charities, they will delay realizing the full potential that this vital sector of our economy has to assist and contribute to the nation as a whole.

However, none of us has to wait for the others to get on board before starting the change. Each board member can demand better policies, a strategic plan, better financial oversight, and quality control. Each mission-based manager can value the line staff, act as if every action impacts on the organization's marketing, and not recoil from the thought of competition. Each government agency can end the policy of "use it or lose it", even if another program does not. Each United Way can demand management training and excellence—even if there is not yet a national certification. Each citizen can trust the boards and staff to do good works—and provide reasonable oversight. If each of us did, we would be well on our way.

The sooner each of us start, the better for all of us.

16. Final Words

I hope that you feel that you are on your way to becoming an even better mission-based manager than you were at the beginning of this book. I've tried to give you the benefit of my experiences and observations about what not-for-profits nationwide are doing to get more mission for their money, to be more businesslike in pursuit of their mission.

We are at an important crossroads for America's not-for-profits, and thus for your organization as well. We can't go back to the federal largess of the 1970's: there isn't enough money. We can't stay as we are: often behind in technology, assuming that the money we need will magically show up. Too many people in our communities are depending on us to provide more and better services. We must go forward, but how? Will we as an industry, will your organization choose the path of becoming a mission-based business? Or will you continue to think of yourself and your organization as a charity? Will you aggressively pursue the use of all of the resources available to you, including lessons from the for-profit sector? Or will you continue to do business as usual?

The answer is, of course, up to you, your staff, and your board. But if you choose the path of being a mission-based manager, and want to manage a mission-oriented business, you have already been exposed to the keys in this book. One last time, let's review the characteristics that your organization needs to have to be successful and thrive in the coming years. In parentheses after each characteristic you will find the number of the chapter(s) where that characteristic is discussed in detail:

▶ *A VIABLE MISSION (Chapter 4)*

▶ *A BUSINESSLIKE BOARD (Chapters 5, 6)*

▶ *A STRONG, WELL-EDUCATED STAFF (Chapter 7)*

244

▶ *STRONG CONTROLS, CONSISTENTLY ENFORCED (Chapter 8)*

▶ *A BIAS FOR MARKETING (Chapter 9)*

▶ *A VISION FOR THE FUTURE (Chapter 10)*

▶ *FINANCIAL EMPOWERMENT (Chapter 11, 12)*

▶ *SOCIAL ENTREPRENEURSHIP (Chapter 13)*

▶ *FLEXIBILITY IN ADAPTING TO CHANGE (Chapter 14)*

You may have found that many or even all of the characteristics I advocate as necessary to your vitality are already present in your organization. If so, congratulations: your organization will probably continue to provide services well into the next century. But wait. Is it *your* opinion only that says that you are already doing all of these things? Or did you get the perspective of the staff and board? If it was just *your* opinion, remember that you do not always see things with total objectivity. Check with others, including some funders. See if they see your organization evidencing the same characteristics in the same way.

In the first chapter I suggested that you read this book as a team: have all the senior managers read the same one or two chapters and then discuss what ideas you can or should adopt in your organization. If you didn't do that, now that you are through the entire book, try team reading. Get a group of your senior staff together and have them read a chapter or two a week, discussing the content at a regular staff meeting. Going over any management text in this fashion is the best way to get the most good out of the book.

To me, the fact that you have been willing to read an entire book on managing your organization is clear evidence that you want to become a mission-based manager. But will you turn the investment of hours you took out of your busy schedule to read this text to good use? Will you continue to put in the effort to become a mission-based manager who runs a mission-based organization? Many of the changes needed are behavioral: developing a bottoms-up management style takes serious change for some people. Communicating with the attitude that the key is what people hear, and not what you say, takes some adjusting to. Developing a culture of new ideas, where all are encouraged; changing methods of thinking to ask all the markets what they want instead of "knowing what they need"; these are disciplines that are difficult to stick to.

Psychologists that I have talked to say that a behavioral change requires two years to "take". That is, if someone adopts a lifestyle of exercise and healthy eating after years of being a couch potato full of junk food, it takes two full years before that new lifestyle becomes the habit rather than a major effort.

I suspect that it is longer for an organization. All the changes that you want to facilitate will need to be adopted by *all* (or at least a sizable majority of) your staff and board, and that, in itself, will take a while. And only when they do make the change, the two-year clock starts ticking. You need to be there leading by example, encouraging, cajoling, showing, evaluating. You are the key to the success or failure.

I sincerely hope that you succeed. Our nation and your community need every one of the not-for-profits to make the transition from charity to mission-based business. Our national needs and wants in education, the arts, social services, research, and religion are growing, not waning, and it will take a full roster of mission-based managers to bring organizations serving these needs to their fullest potential.

Mission-based managers are different. They see the mission first, the outcome of their organization's services in very human terms. As a mission-based manager, don't ever lose that perspective. It's what sets you apart from your for-profit peers. Yes, it makes your job that much tougher, but it makes the satisfaction of your job that much greater. It's what makes all the work worth it.

Remember that the services you provide are all provided *by* a person, and they all are provided *to* a person. In between those two people is your mission: the what and why of your organization. The mission is what brings those two people together.

You are the champion of that mission both in your organization and in your community. With the skills you have learned here, you should find great success. **Good luck!**

Resources

BOOKS:

Brown, Peter C. *The Complete Guide to Money Making Ventures for Non-profit Organizations.* 1989: The Taft Group.

Connors, Tracy Daniel, ed. *The Nonprofit Management Handbook: Operating Policies and Procedures.* 1993: John Wiley and Sons.

Hopkins, Bruce R. *The Law of Tax-Exempt Organizations.* 1992: John Wiley and Sons.

Krueger, Richard A. *Focus Groups: A Practical Guide for Applied Research.* 1988: Sage Publications.

PERIODICALS:

INC. Published monthly by INC., 38 Commercial Wharf, Boston, MA 02110

Non Profit Counsel. Published monthly by John Wiley and Sons, 605 Third Ave., New York, NY 10158

NonProfit World. Published bimonthly by The Society for NonProfits, 6314 Odana Rd., Suite. 1, Madison, WI 53719

Index